The Adventures of Blanche™

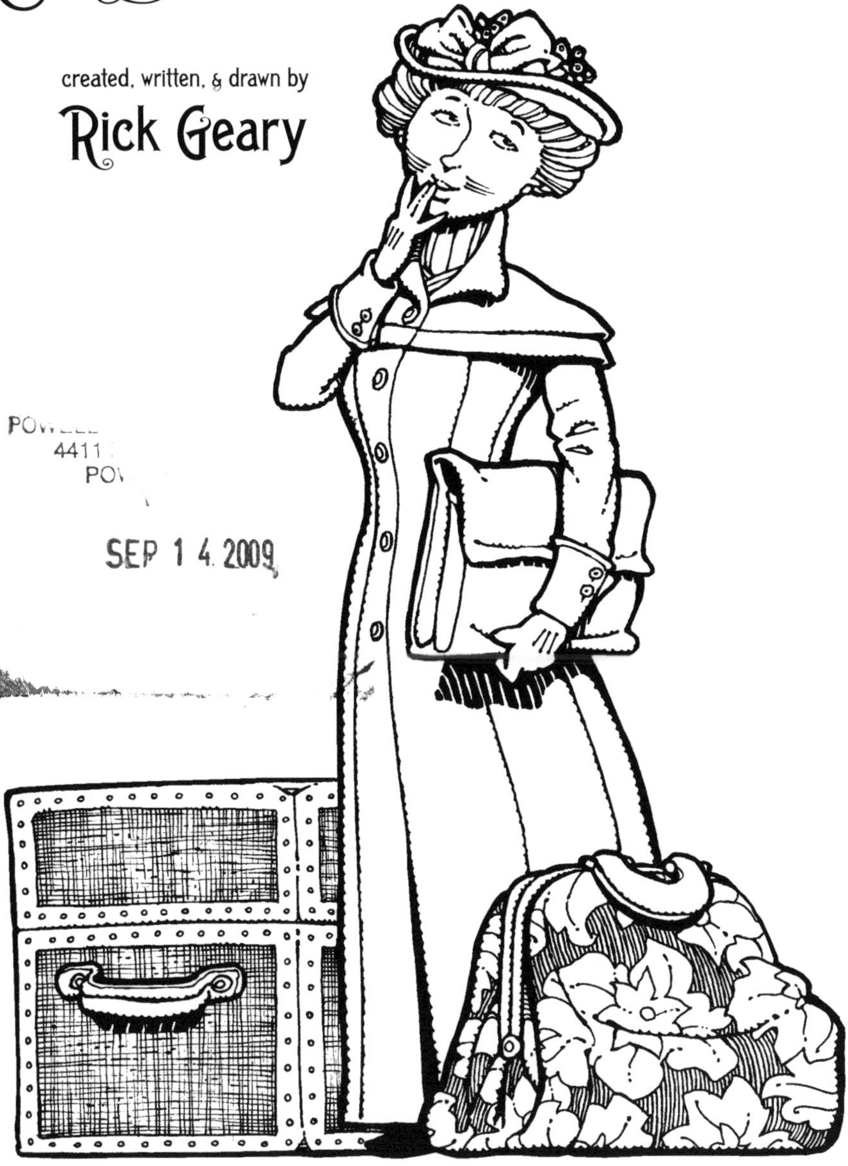

created, written, & drawn by

Rick Geary

Dark Horse Books®

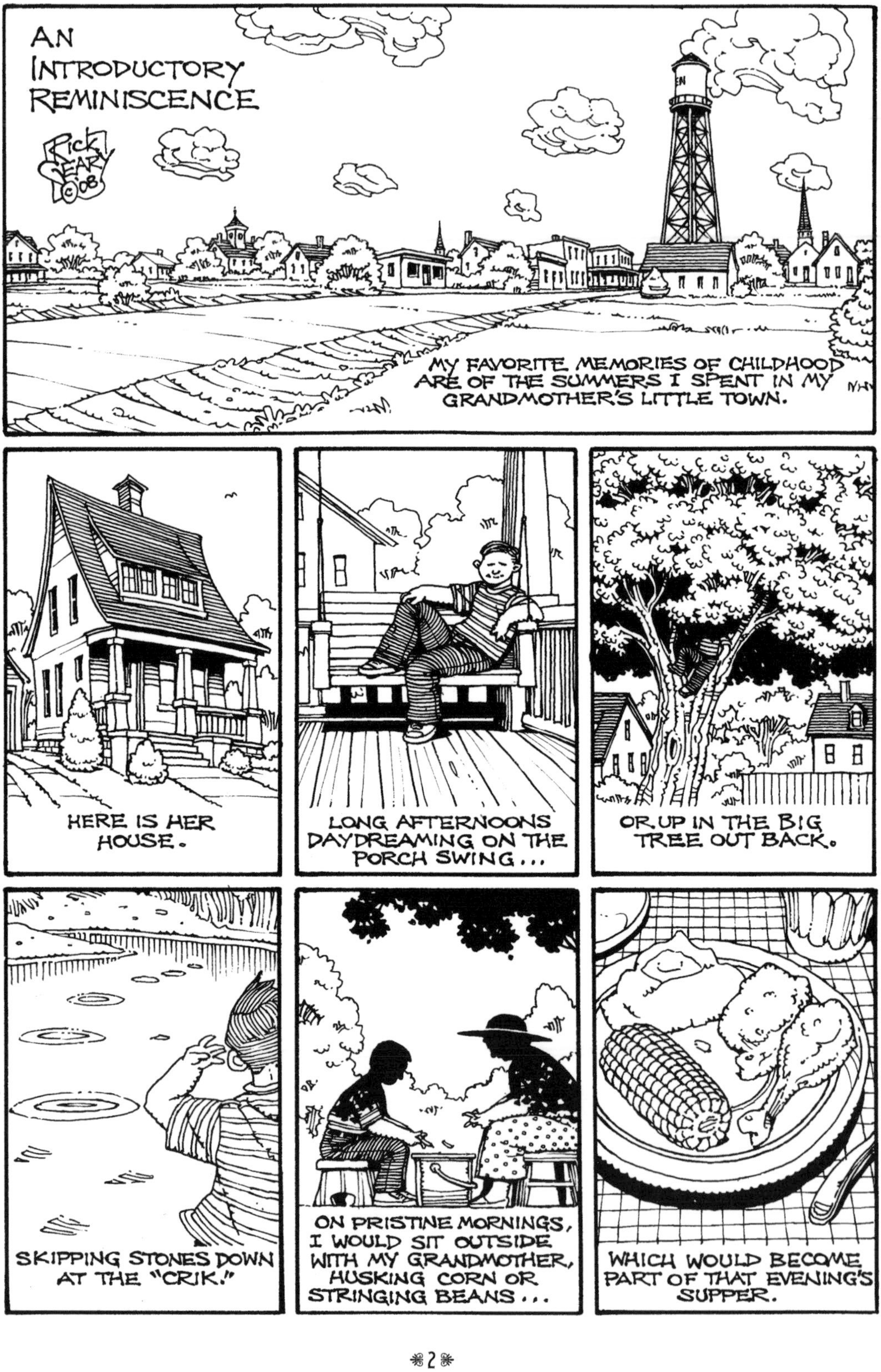
AN INTRODUCTORY REMINISCENCE
RICK GEARY ©08
MY FAVORITE MEMORIES OF CHILDHOOD ARE OF THE SUMMERS I SPENT IN MY GRANDMOTHER'S LITTLE TOWN.
HERE IS HER HOUSE.
LONG AFTERNOONS DAYDREAMING ON THE PORCH SWING...
OR UP IN THE BIG TREE OUT BACK.
SKIPPING STONES DOWN AT THE "CRIK."
ON PRISTINE MORNINGS, I WOULD SIT OUTSIDE WITH MY GRANDMOTHER, HUSKING CORN OR STRINGING BEANS...
WHICH WOULD BECOME PART OF THAT EVENING'S SUPPER.

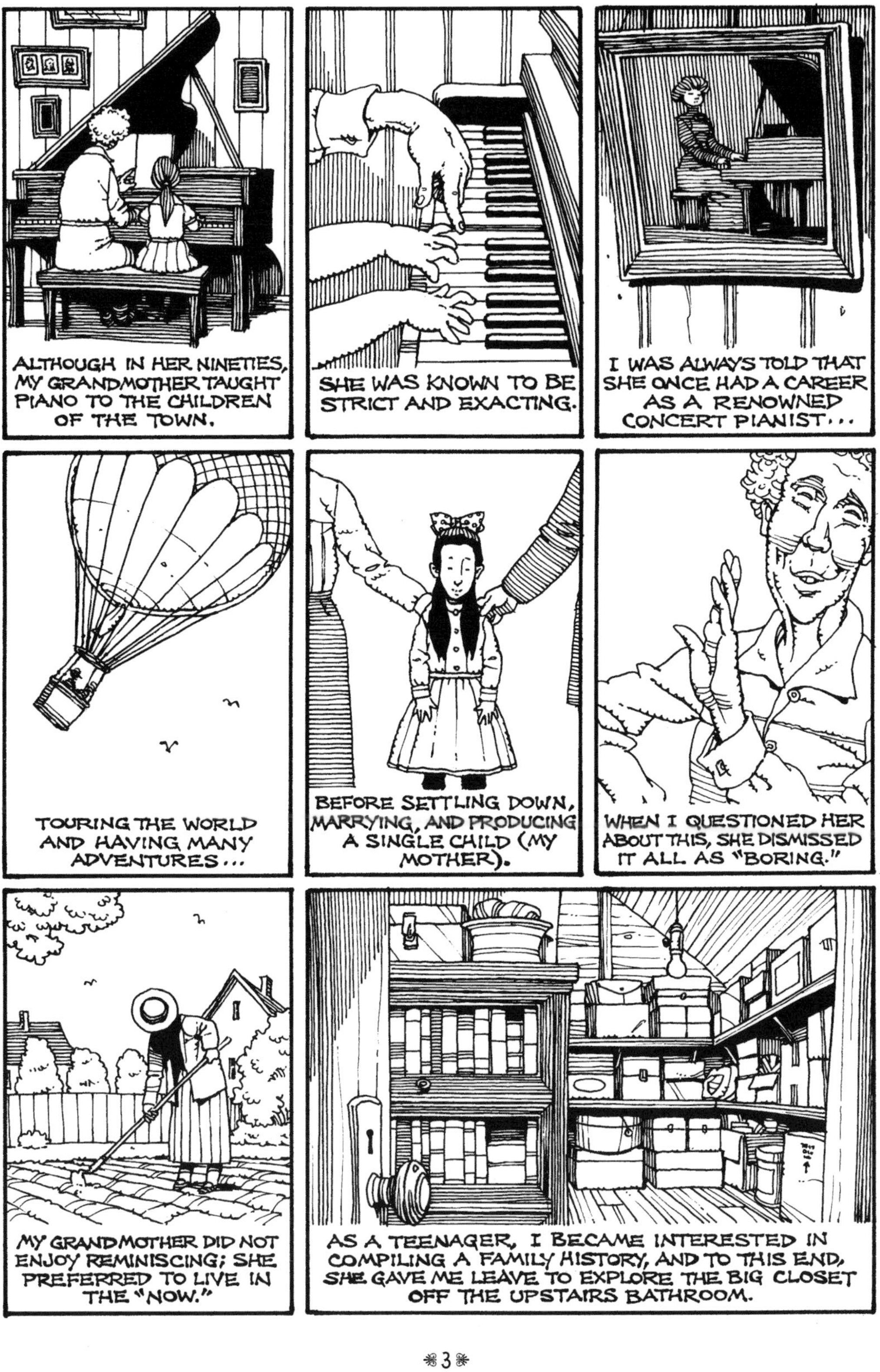
ALTHOUGH IN HER NINETIES, MY GRANDMOTHER TAUGHT PIANO TO THE CHILDREN OF THE TOWN.
SHE WAS KNOWN TO BE STRICT AND EXACTING.
I WAS ALWAYS TOLD THAT SHE ONCE HAD A CAREER AS A RENOWNED CONCERT PIANIST...
TOURING THE WORLD AND HAVING MANY ADVENTURES...
BEFORE SETTLING DOWN, MARRYING, AND PRODUCING A SINGLE CHILD (MY MOTHER).
WHEN I QUESTIONED HER ABOUT THIS, SHE DISMISSED IT ALL AS "BORING."
MY GRANDMOTHER DID NOT ENJOY REMINISCING; SHE PREFERRED TO LIVE IN THE "NOW."
AS A TEENAGER, I BECAME INTERESTED IN COMPILING A FAMILY HISTORY, AND TO THIS END, SHE GAVE ME LEAVE TO EXPLORE THE BIG CLOSET OFF THE UPSTAIRS BATHROOM.

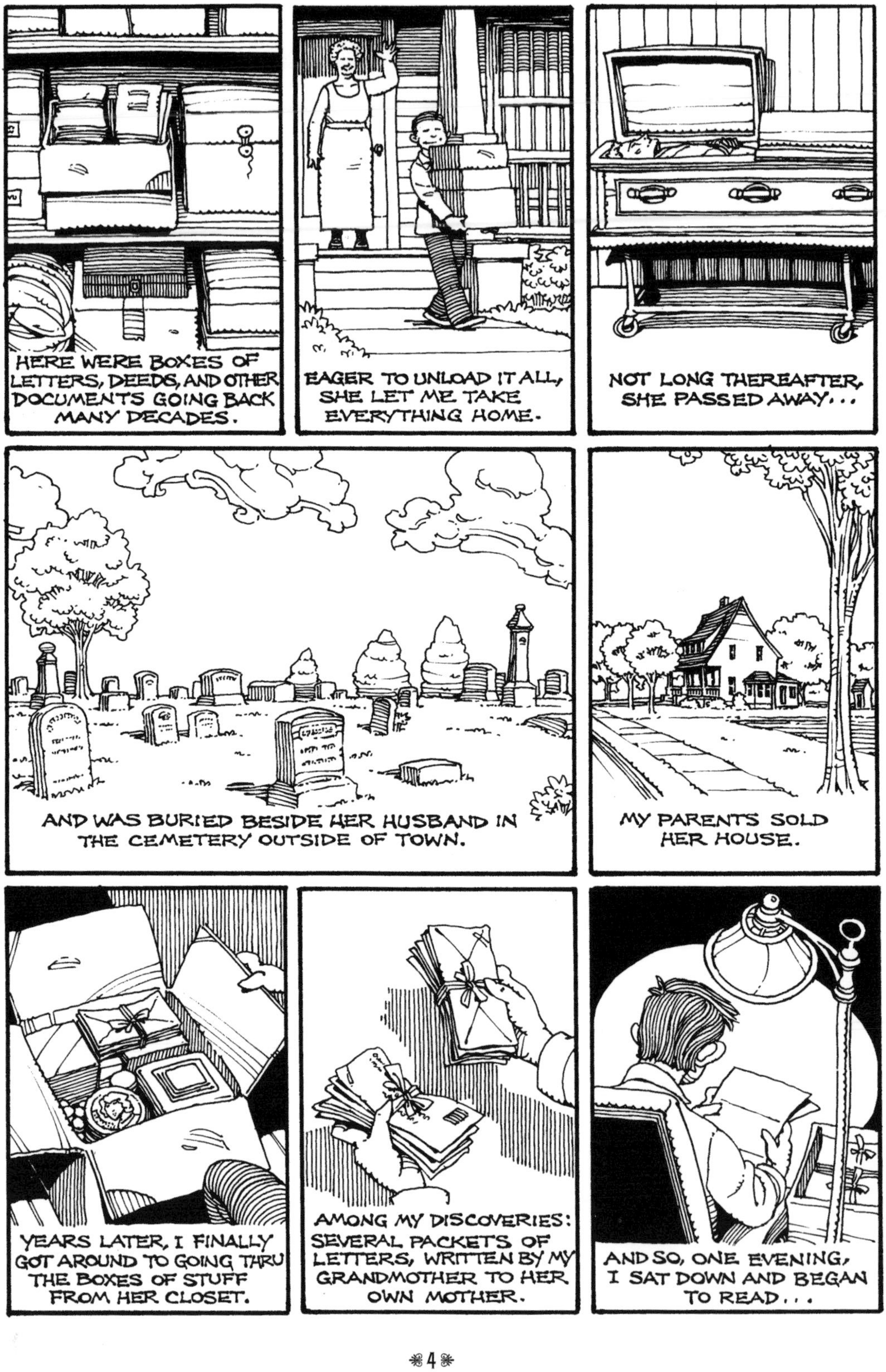
HERE WERE BOXES OF LETTERS, DEEDS, AND OTHER DOCUMENTS GOING BACK MANY DECADES.
EAGER TO UNLOAD IT ALL, SHE LET ME TAKE EVERYTHING HOME.
NOT LONG THEREAFTER, SHE PASSED AWAY...
AND WAS BURIED BESIDE HER HUSBAND IN THE CEMETERY OUTSIDE OF TOWN.
MY PARENTS SOLD HER HOUSE.
YEARS LATER, I FINALLY GOT AROUND TO GOING THRU THE BOXES OF STUFF FROM HER CLOSET.
AMONG MY DISCOVERIES: SEVERAL PACKETS OF LETTERS, WRITTEN BY MY GRANDMOTHER TO HER OWN MOTHER.
AND SO, ONE EVENING, I SAT DOWN AND BEGAN TO READ...

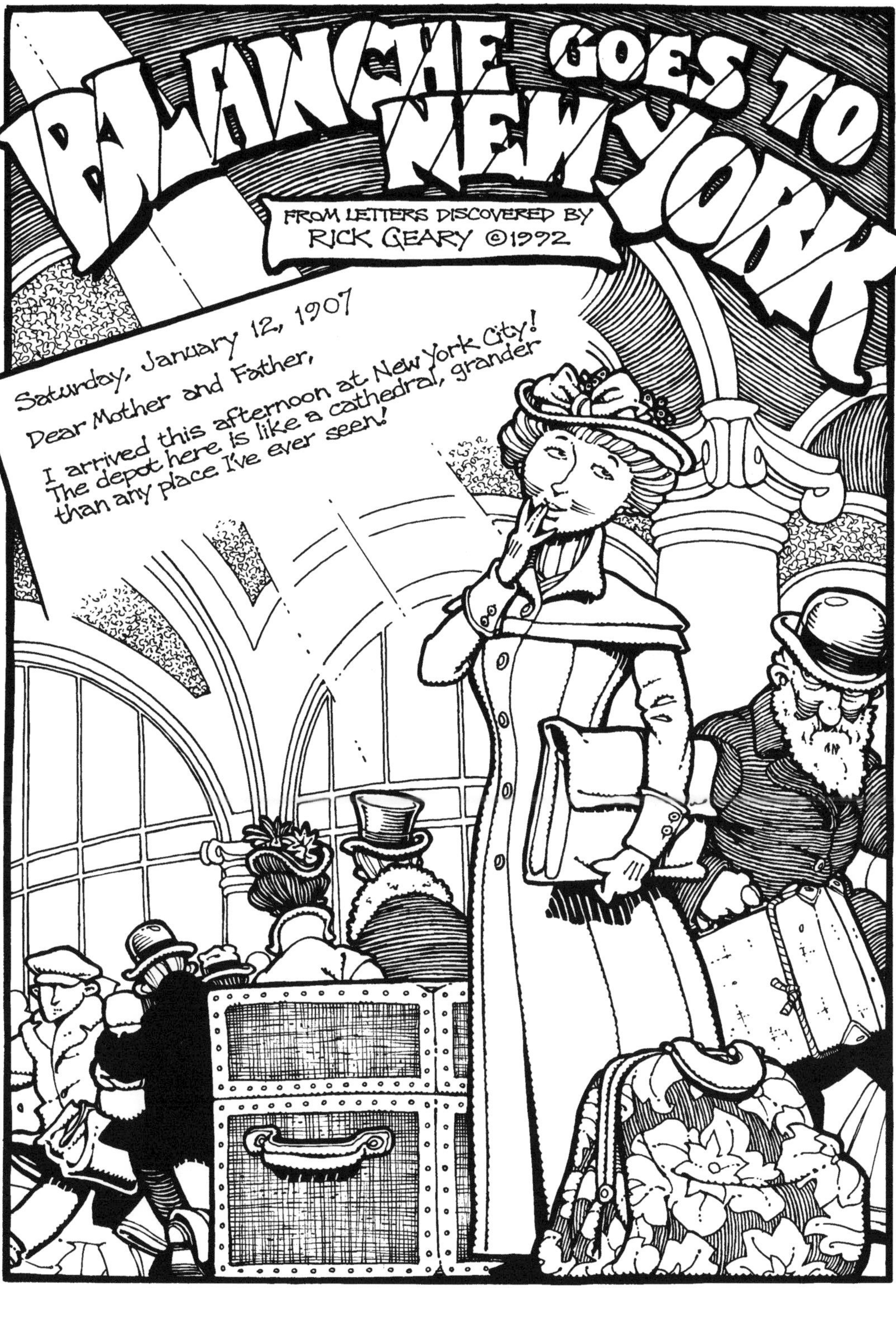
BLANCHE GOES TO NEW YORK
FROM LETTERS DISCOVERED BY
RICK GEARY ©1992
Saturday, January 12, 1907
Dear Mother and Father,
I arrived this afternoon at New York City! The depot here is like a cathedral, grander than any place I've ever seen!

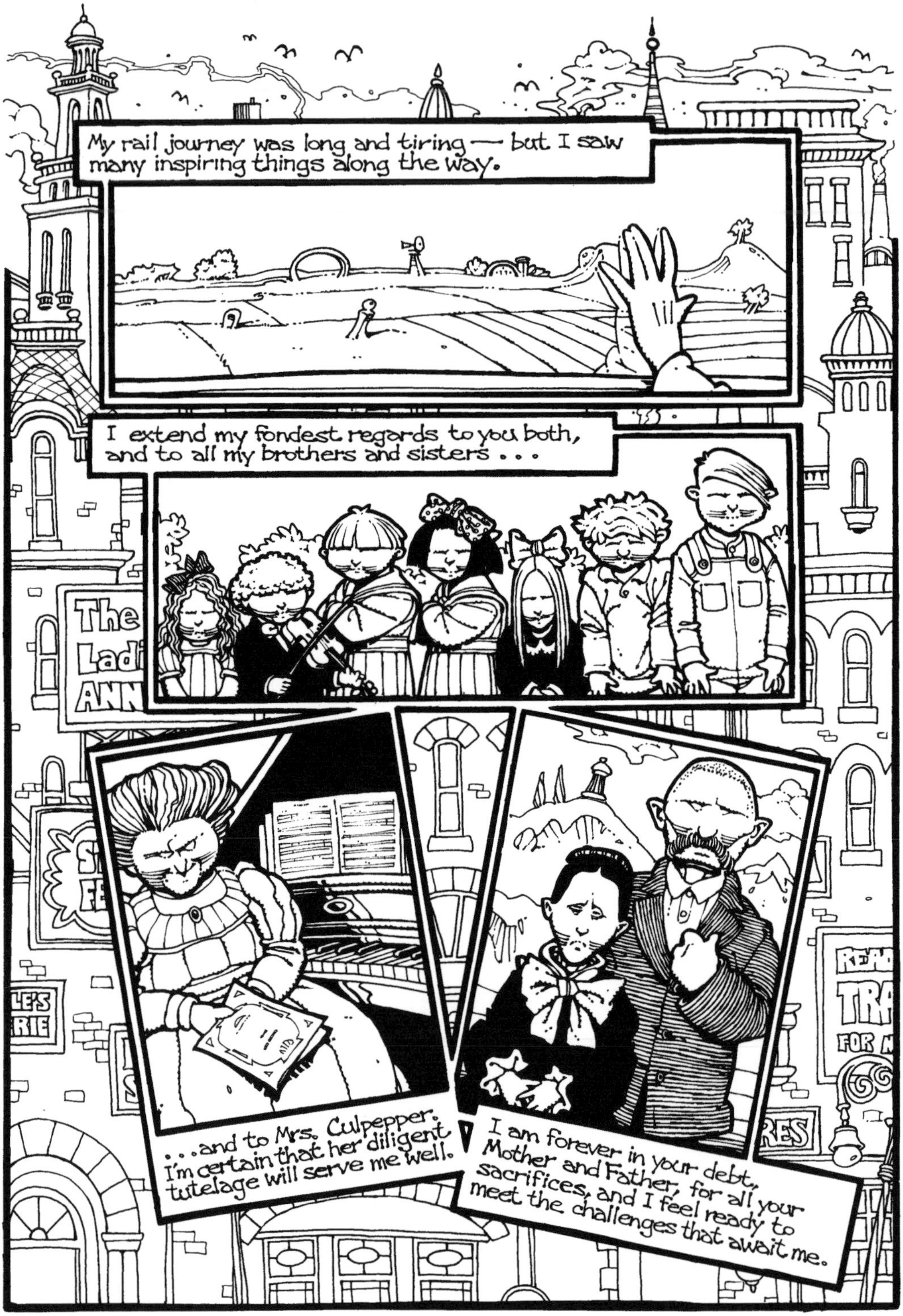
My rail journey was long and tiring — but I saw many inspiring things along the way.
I extend my fondest regards to you both, and to all my brothers and sisters . . .
. . . and to Mrs. Culpepper. I'm certain that her diligent tutelage will serve me well.
I am forever in your debt, Mother and Father, for all your sacrifices, and I feel ready to meet the challenges that await me.

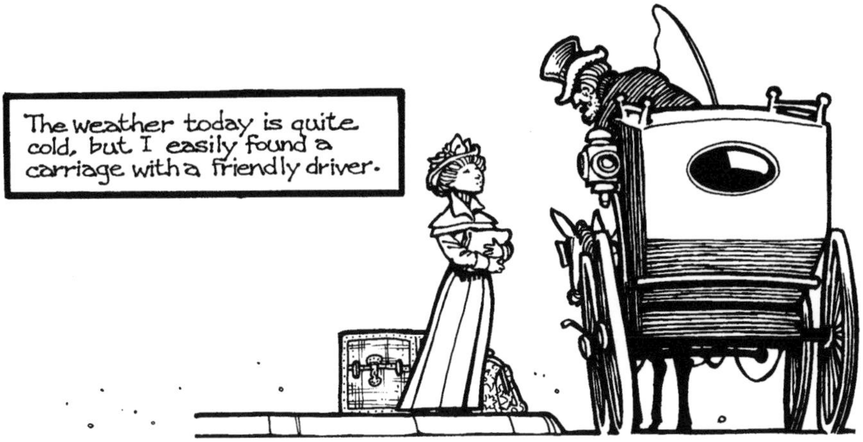
The weather today is quite cold, but I easily found a carriage with a friendly driver.

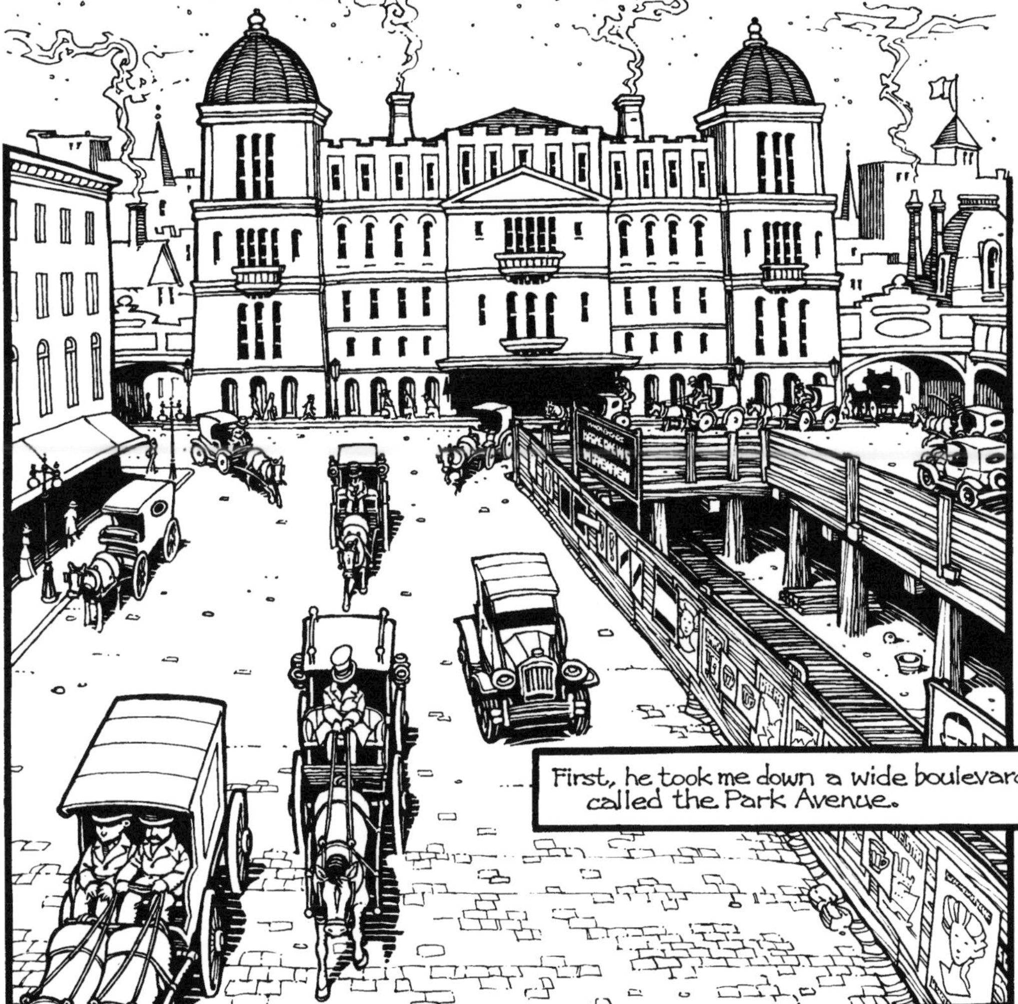
First, he took me down a wide boulevard called the Park Avenue.

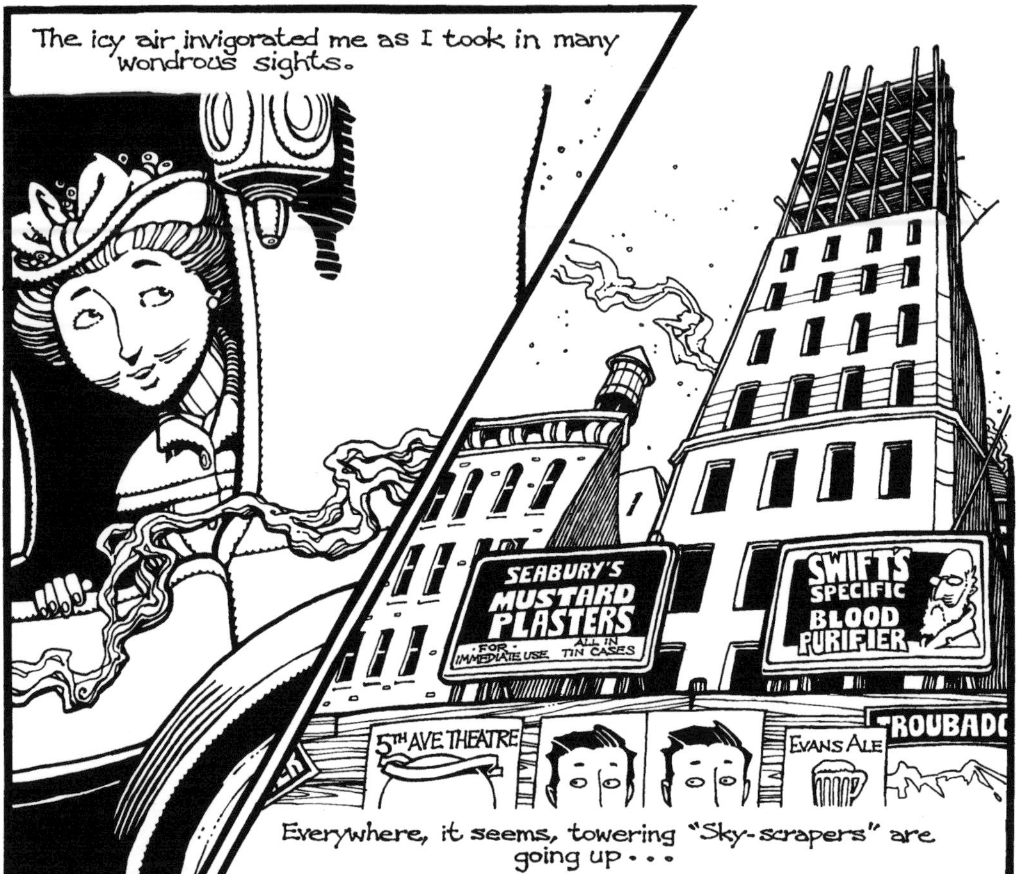
The icy air invigorated me as I took in many wondrous sights.
SEABURY'S MUSTARD PLASTERS
FOR IMMEDIATE USE
ALL IN TIN CASES
SWIFT'S SPECIFIC BLOOD PURIFIER
5TH AVE THEATRE
EVANS ALE
TROUBADO
Everywhere, it seems, towering "Sky-scrapers" are going up...

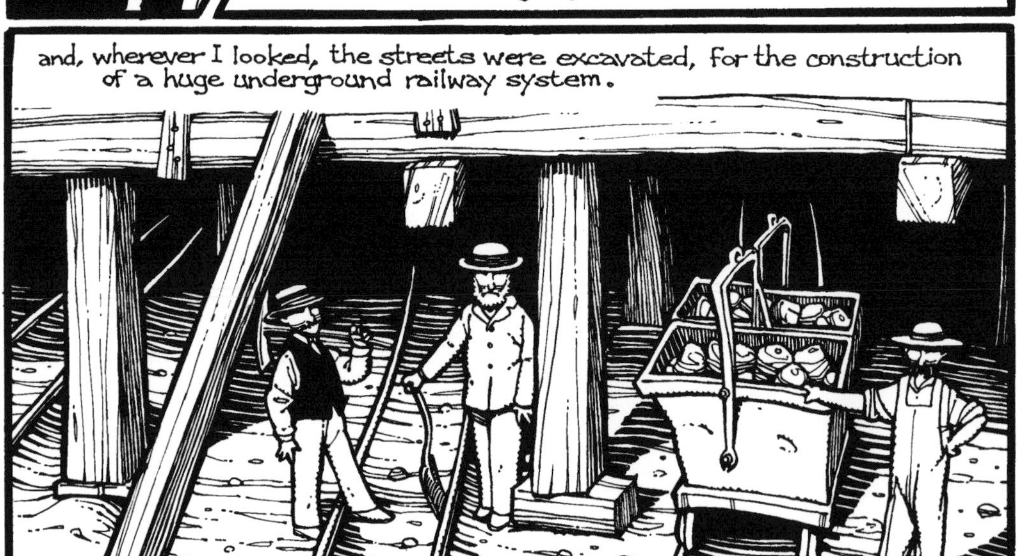
and, wherever I looked, the streets were excavated, for the construction of a huge underground railway system.

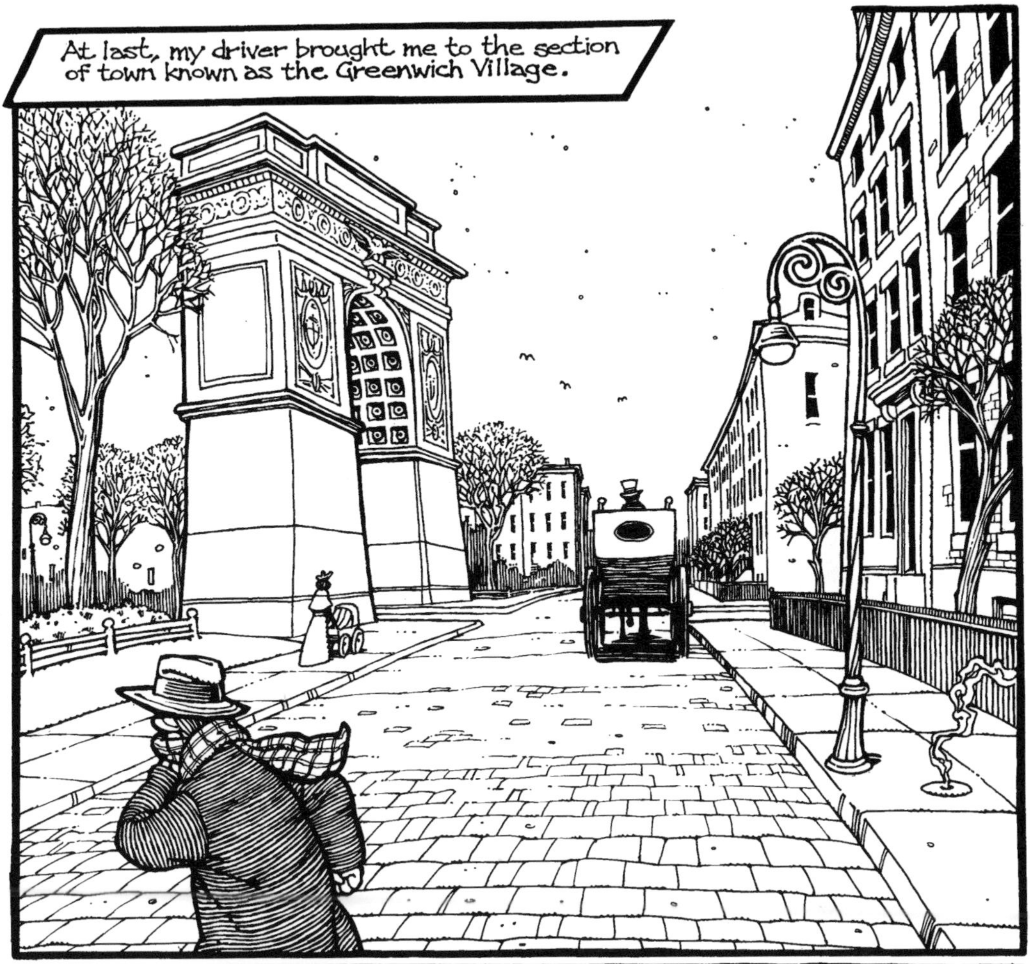
At last, my driver brought me to the section of town known as the Greenwich Village.

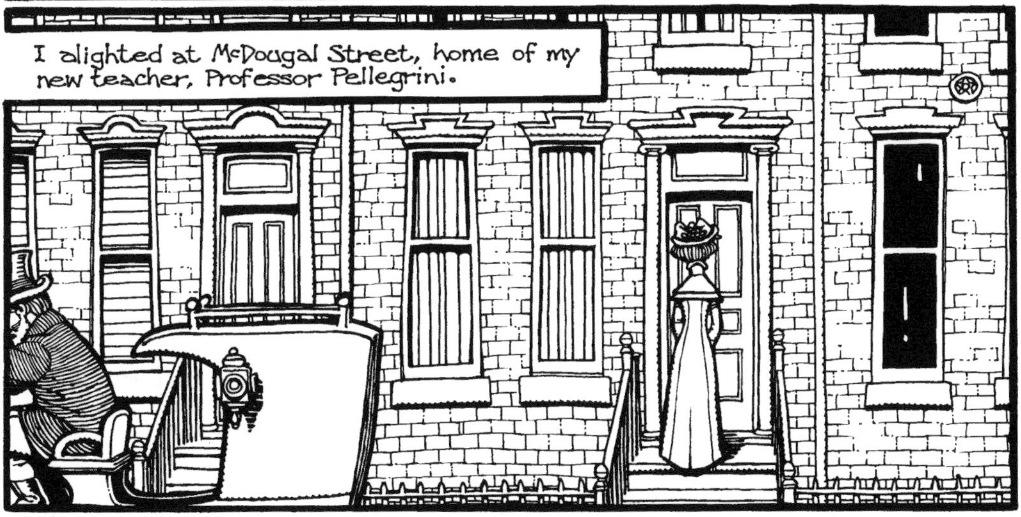
I alighted at McDougal Street, home of my new teacher, Professor Pellegrini.

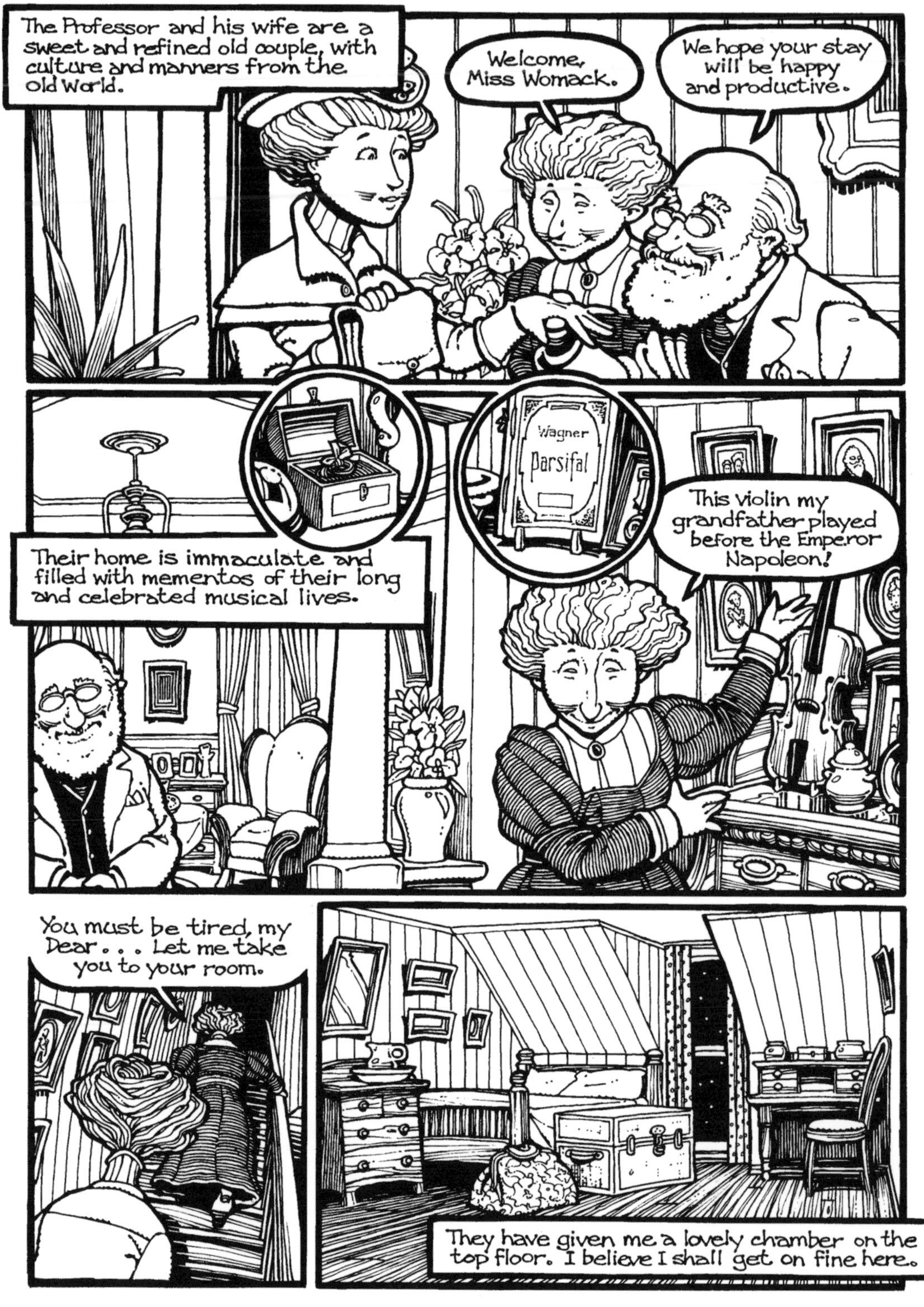
The Professor and his wife are a sweet and refined old couple, with culture and manners from the old World.
Welcome, Miss Womack.
We hope your stay will be happy and productive.
Wagner
Parsifal
Their home is immaculate and filled with mementos of their long and celebrated musical lives.
This violin my grandfather played before the Emperor Napoleon!
You must be tired, my Dear . . . Let me take you to your room.
They have given me a lovely chamber on the top floor. I believe I shall get on fine here.

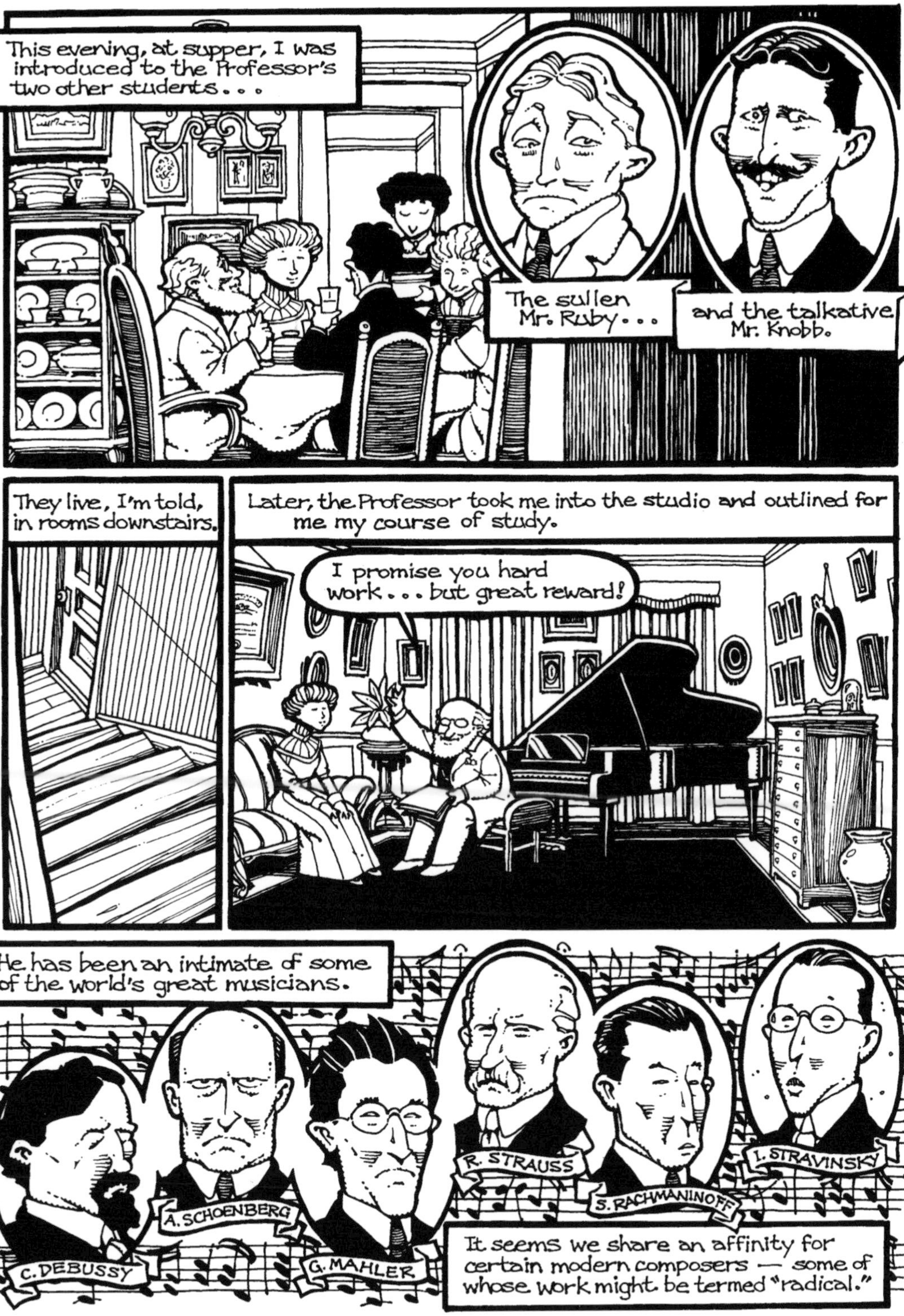
This evening, at supper, I was introduced to the Professor's two other students . . .
The sullen Mr. Ruby . . .
and the talkative Mr. Knobb.
They live, I'm told, in rooms downstairs.
Later, the Professor took me into the studio and outlined for me my course of study.
I promise you hard work . . . but great reward!
He has been an intimate of some of the world's great musicians.
C. DEBUSSY
A. SCHOENBERG
G. MAHLER
R. STRAUSS
S. RACHMANINOFF
I. STRAVINSKY
It seems we share an affinity for certain modern composers — some of whose work might be termed "radical."

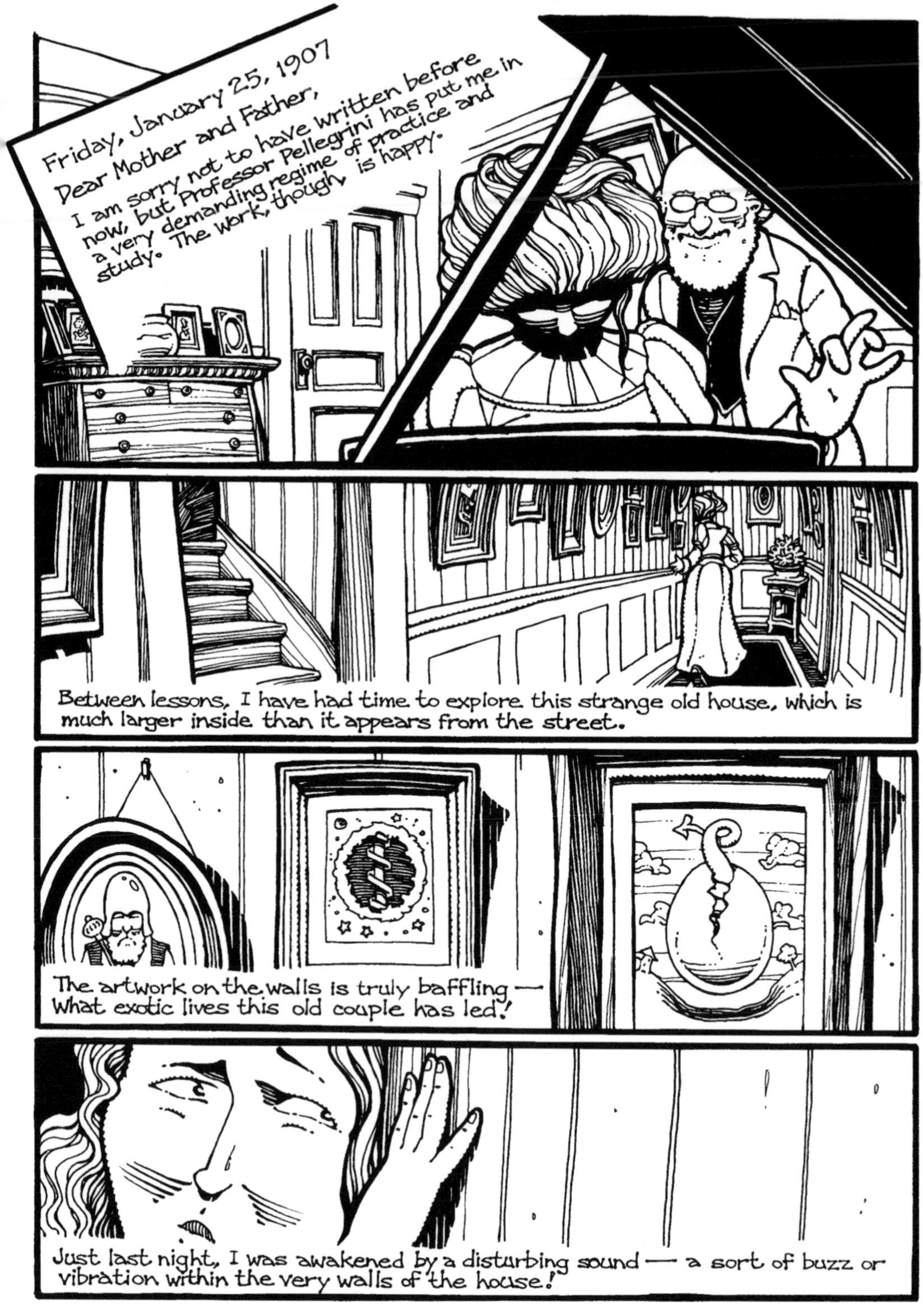
Friday, January 25, 1907
Dear Mother and Father,
I am sorry not to have written before now, but Professor Pellegrini has put me in a very demanding regime of practice and study. The work, though, is happy.
Between lessons, I have had time to explore this strange old house, which is much larger inside than it appears from the street.
The artwork on the walls is truly baffling — What exotic lives this old couple has led!
Just last night, I was awakened by a disturbing sound — a sort of buzz or vibration within the very walls of the house!

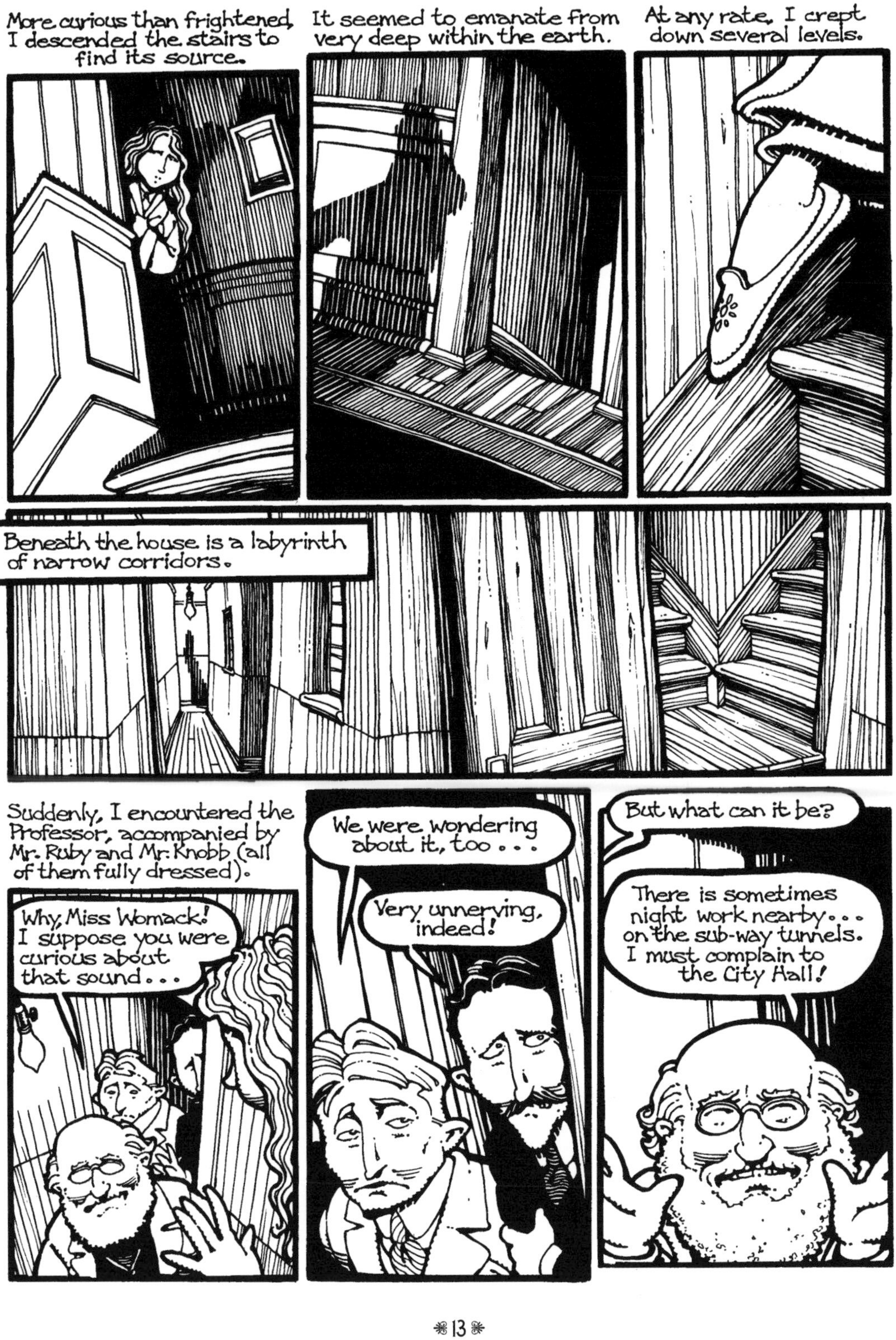
More curious than frightened, I descended the stairs to find its source.
It seemed to emanate from very deep within the earth.
At any rate, I crept down several levels.
Beneath the house is a labyrinth of narrow corridors.
Suddenly, I encountered the Professor, accompanied by Mr. Ruby and Mr. Knobb (all of them fully dressed).
Why, Miss Womack! I suppose you were curious about that sound...
We were wondering about it, too...
Very unnerving, indeed!
But what can it be?
There is sometimes night work nearby... on the sub-way tunnels. I must complain to the City Hall!

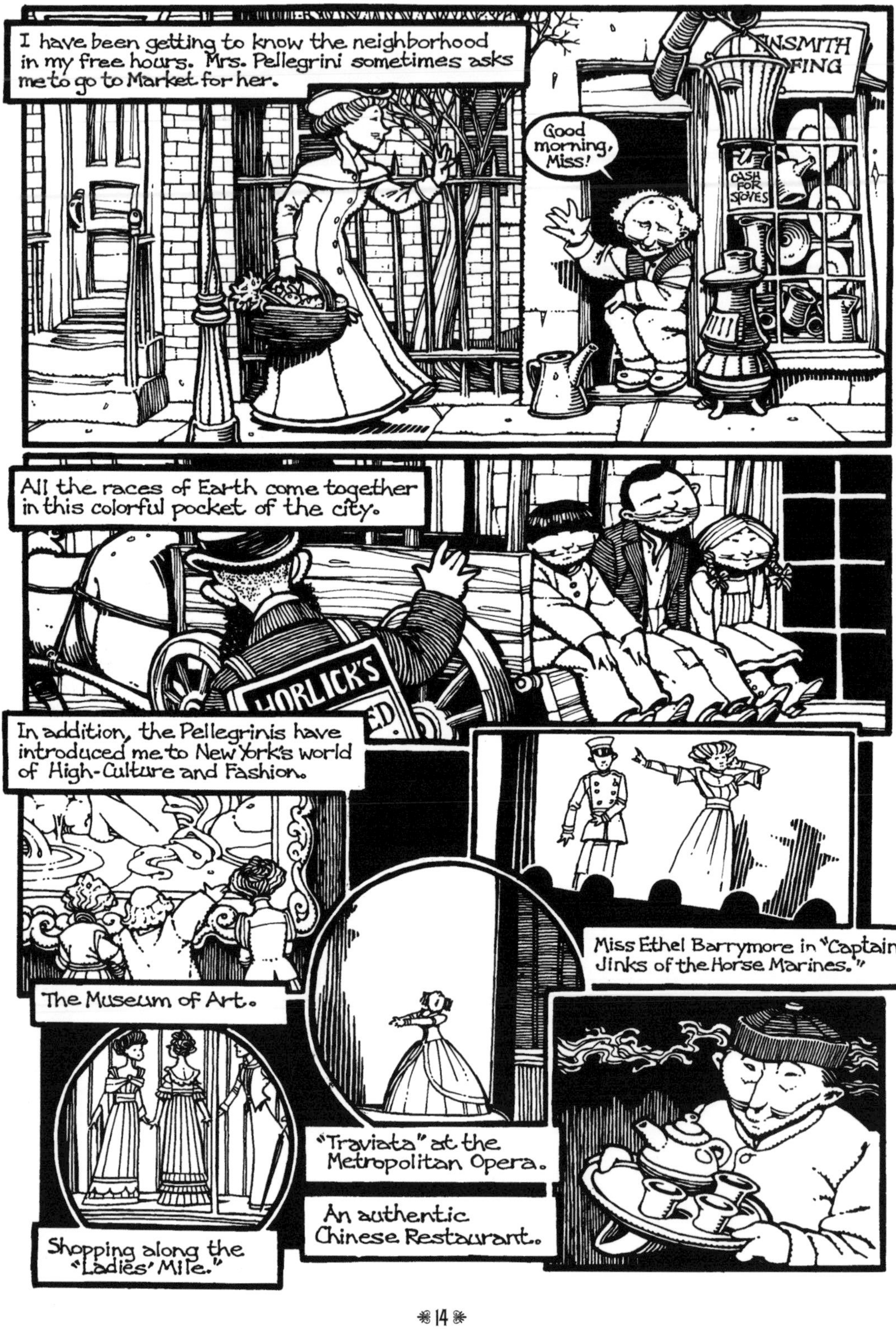
I have been getting to know the neighborhood in my free hours. Mrs. Pellegrini sometimes asks me to go to Market for her.
NSMITH
FING
Good morning, Miss!
CASH FOR STOVES
All the races of Earth come together in this colorful pocket of the city.
HORLICK'S
In addition, the Pellegrinis have introduced me to New York's world of High-Culture and Fashion.
Miss Ethel Barrymore in "Captain Jinks of the Horse Marines."
The Museum of Art.
"Traviata" at the Metropolitan Opera.
An authentic Chinese Restaurant.
Shopping along the "Ladies' Mile."

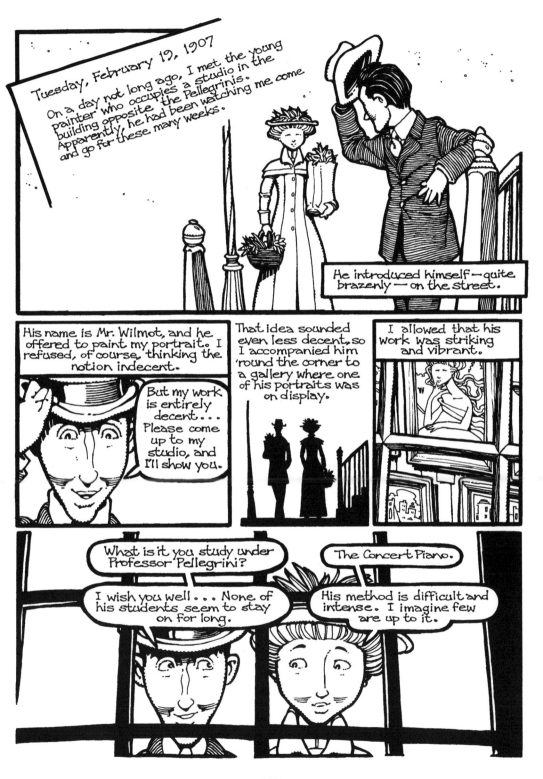

Tuesday, February 19, 1907

On a day not long ago, I met the young painter who occupies a studio in the building opposite the Pellegrinis. Apparently, he had been watching me come and go for these many weeks.

He introduced himself — quite brazenly — on the street.

His name is Mr. Wilmot, and he offered to paint my portrait. I refused, of course, thinking the notion indecent.

But my work is entirely decent... Please come up to my studio, and I'll show you.

That idea sounded even less decent, so I accompanied him 'round the corner to a gallery where one of his portraits was on display.

I allowed that his work was striking and vibrant.

What is it you study under Professor Pellegrini?

The Concert Piano.

I wish you well... None of his students seem to stay on for long.

His method is difficult and intense. I imagine few are up to it.

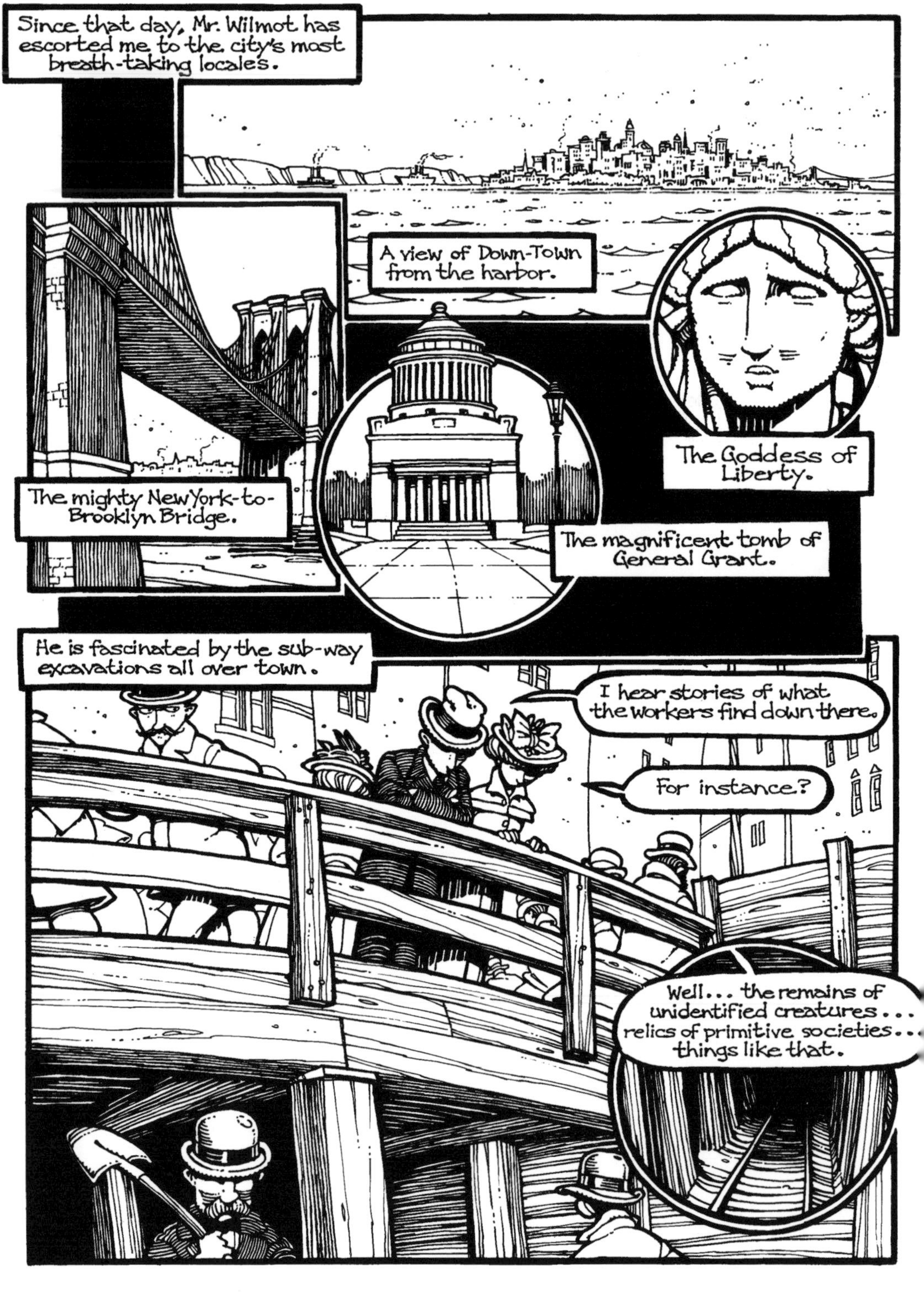

Since that day, Mr. Wilmot has escorted me to the city's most breath-taking locales.
A view of Down-Town from the harbor.
The mighty New York-to-Brooklyn Bridge.
The magnificent tomb of General Grant.
The Goddess of Liberty.
He is fascinated by the sub-way excavations all over town.
I hear stories of what the workers find down there.
For instance?
Well... the remains of unidentified creatures... relics of primitive societies... things like that.

We spent a day in the great Central Park, where the citizens of New York migrate for fresh air and relaxation.

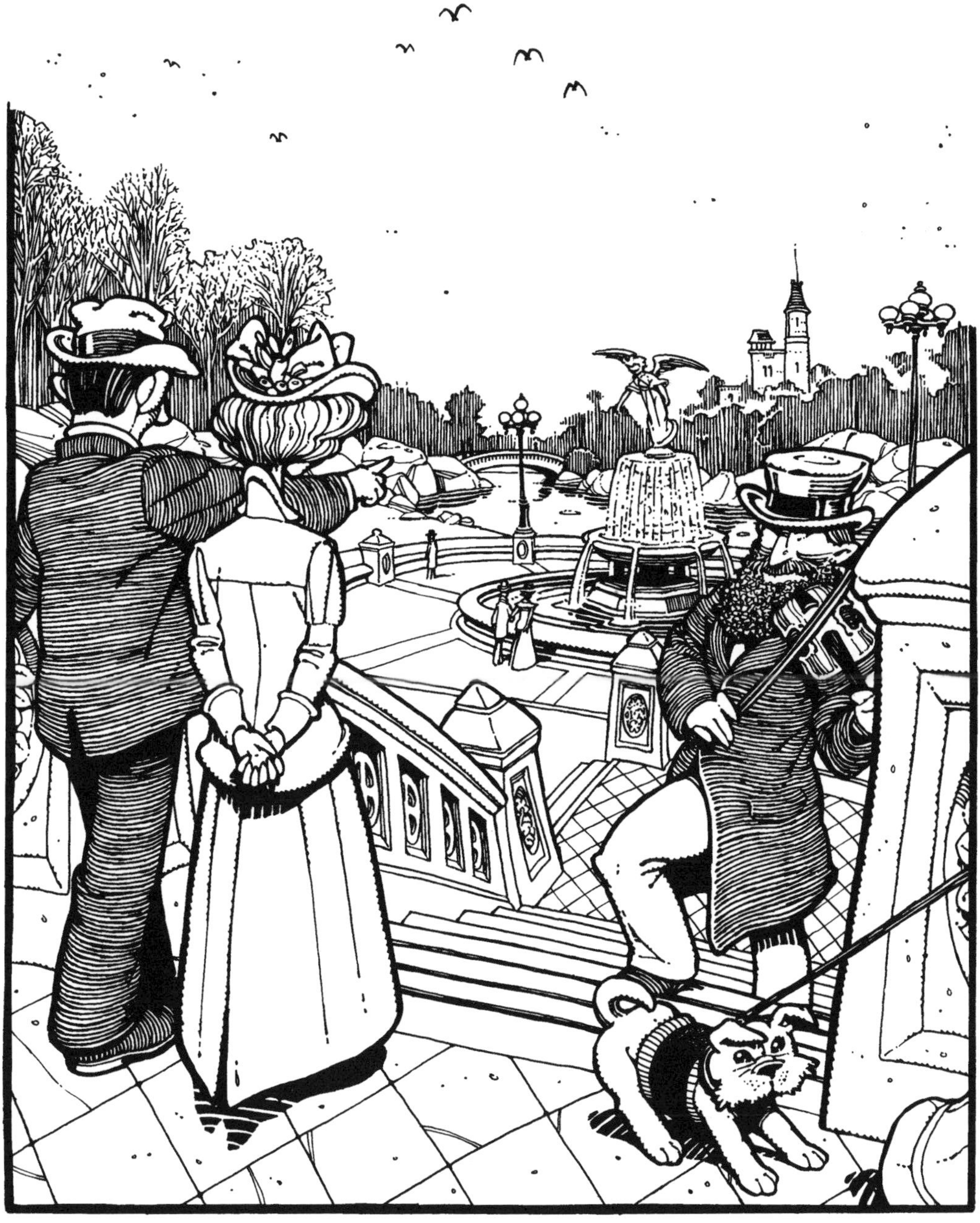

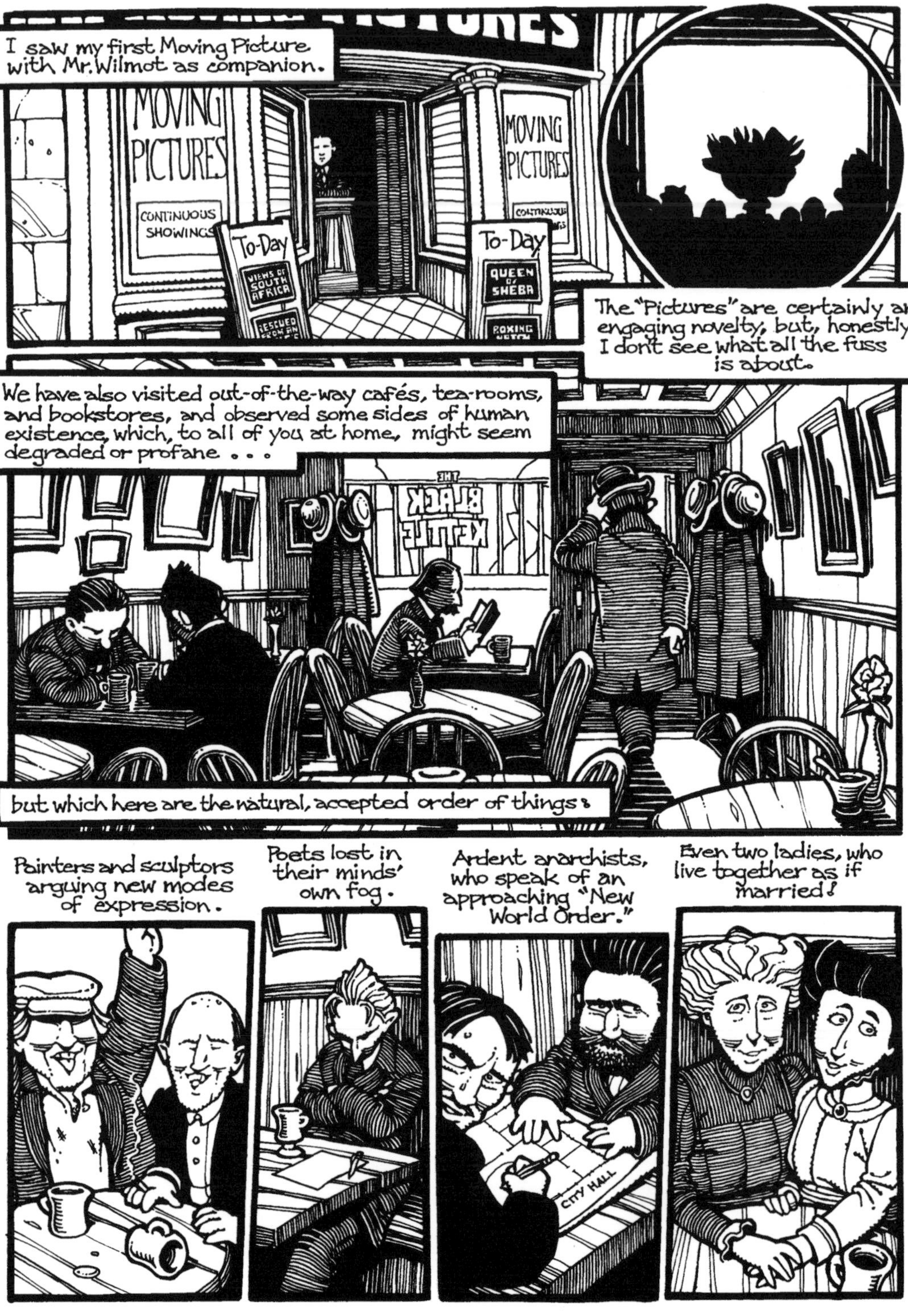
I saw my first Moving Picture with Mr. Wilmot as companion.
MOVING PICTURES
CONTINUOUS SHOWINGS
To-Day
VIEWS OF SOUTH AFRICA
RESCUED FROM AN
MOVING PICTURES
To-Day
QUEEN OF SHEBA
The "Pictures" are certainly an engaging novelty, but, honestly, I don't see what all the fuss is about.
We have also visited out-of-the-way cafés, tea-rooms, and bookstores, and observed some sides of human existence which, to all of you at home, might seem degraded or profane . . .
THE BLACK KETTLE
but which here are the natural, accepted order of things:
Painters and sculptors arguing new modes of expression.
Poets lost in their minds' own fog.
Ardent anarchists, who speak of an approaching "New World Order."
CITY HALL
Even two ladies, who live together as if married!

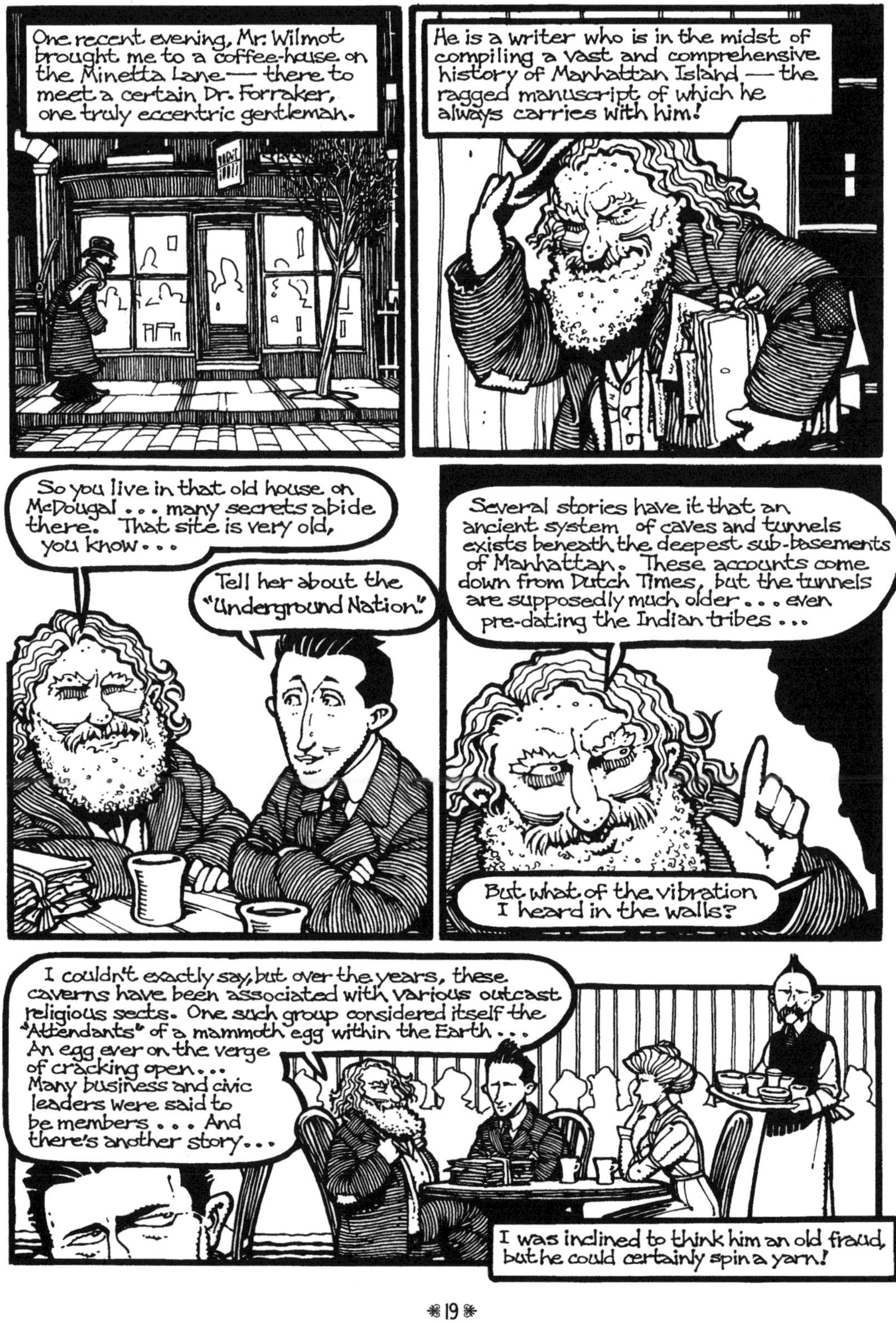
One recent evening, Mr. Wilmot brought me to a coffee-house on the Minetta Lane — there to meet a certain Dr. Forraker, one truly eccentric gentleman.
He is a writer who is in the midst of compiling a vast and comprehensive history of Manhattan Island — the ragged manuscript of which he always carries with him!
So you live in that old house on McDougal . . . many secrets abide there. That site is very old, you know . . .
Tell her about the "Underground Nation."
Several stories have it that an ancient system of caves and tunnels exists beneath the deepest sub-basements of Manhattan. These accounts come down from Dutch Times, but the tunnels are supposedly much older . . . even pre-dating the Indian tribes . . .
But what of the vibration I heard in the walls?
I couldn't exactly say, but over the years, these caverns have been associated with various outcast religious sects. One such group considered itself the "Attendants" of a mammoth egg within the Earth . . . An egg ever on the verge of cracking open . . . Many business and civic leaders were said to be members . . . And there's another story . . .
I was inclined to think him an old fraud, but he could certainly spin a yarn!

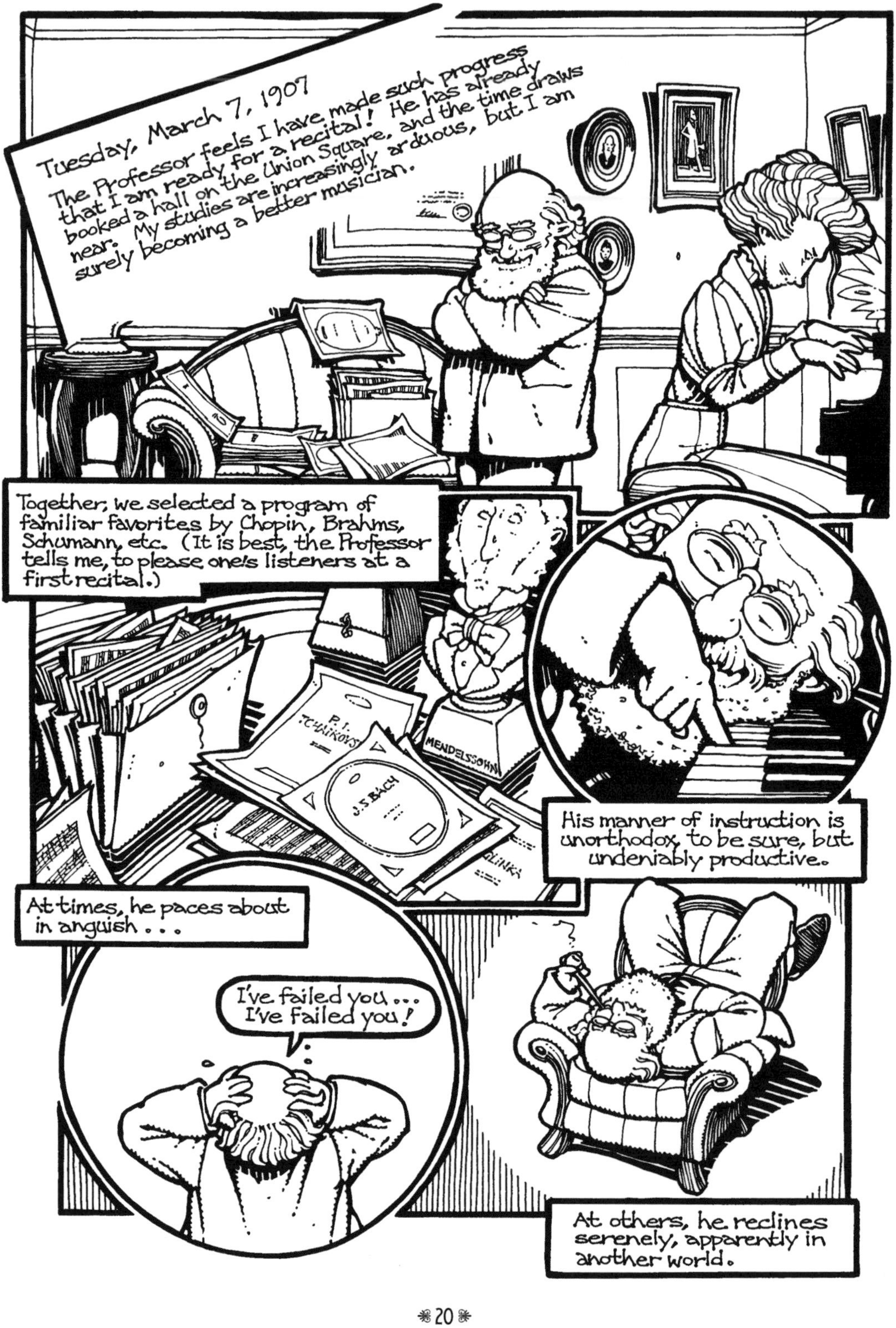
Tuesday, March 7, 1907
The Professor feels I have made such progress that I am ready for a recital! He has already booked a hall on the Union Square, and the time draws near. My studies are increasingly arduous, but I am surely becoming a better musician.
Together, we selected a program of familiar favorites by Chopin, Brahms, Schumann, etc. (It is best, the Professor tells me, to please one's listeners at a first recital.)
P. I. TCHAIKOVSKY
MENDELSSOHN
J. S. BACH
GLINKA
His manner of instruction is unorthodox, to be sure, but undeniably productive.
At times, he paces about in anguish . . .
I've failed you . . . I've failed you!
At others, he reclines serenely, apparently in another world.

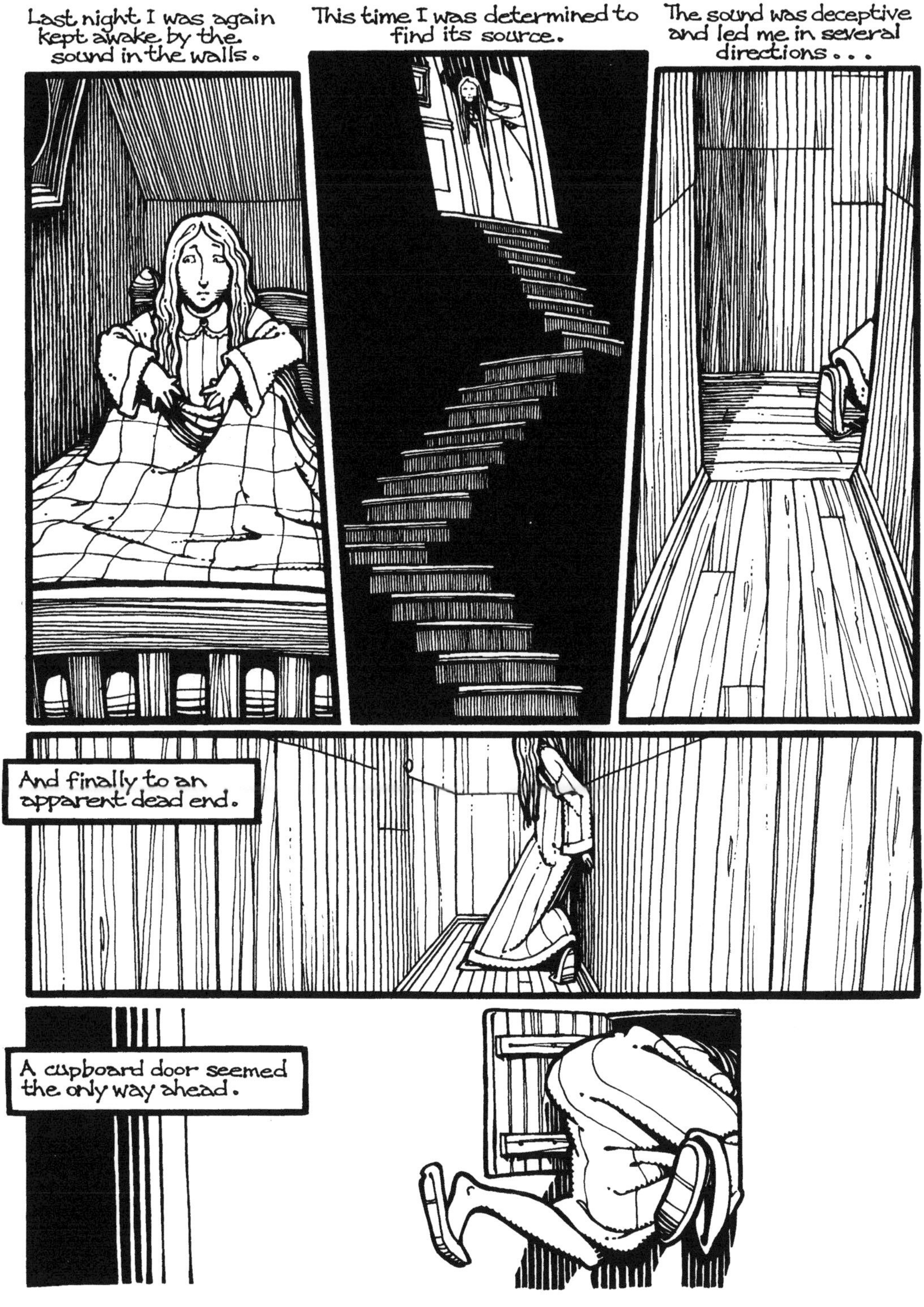
Last night I was again kept awake by the sound in the walls.
This time I was determined to find its source.
The sound was deceptive and led me in several directions . . .
And finally to an apparent dead end.
A cupboard door seemed the only way ahead.

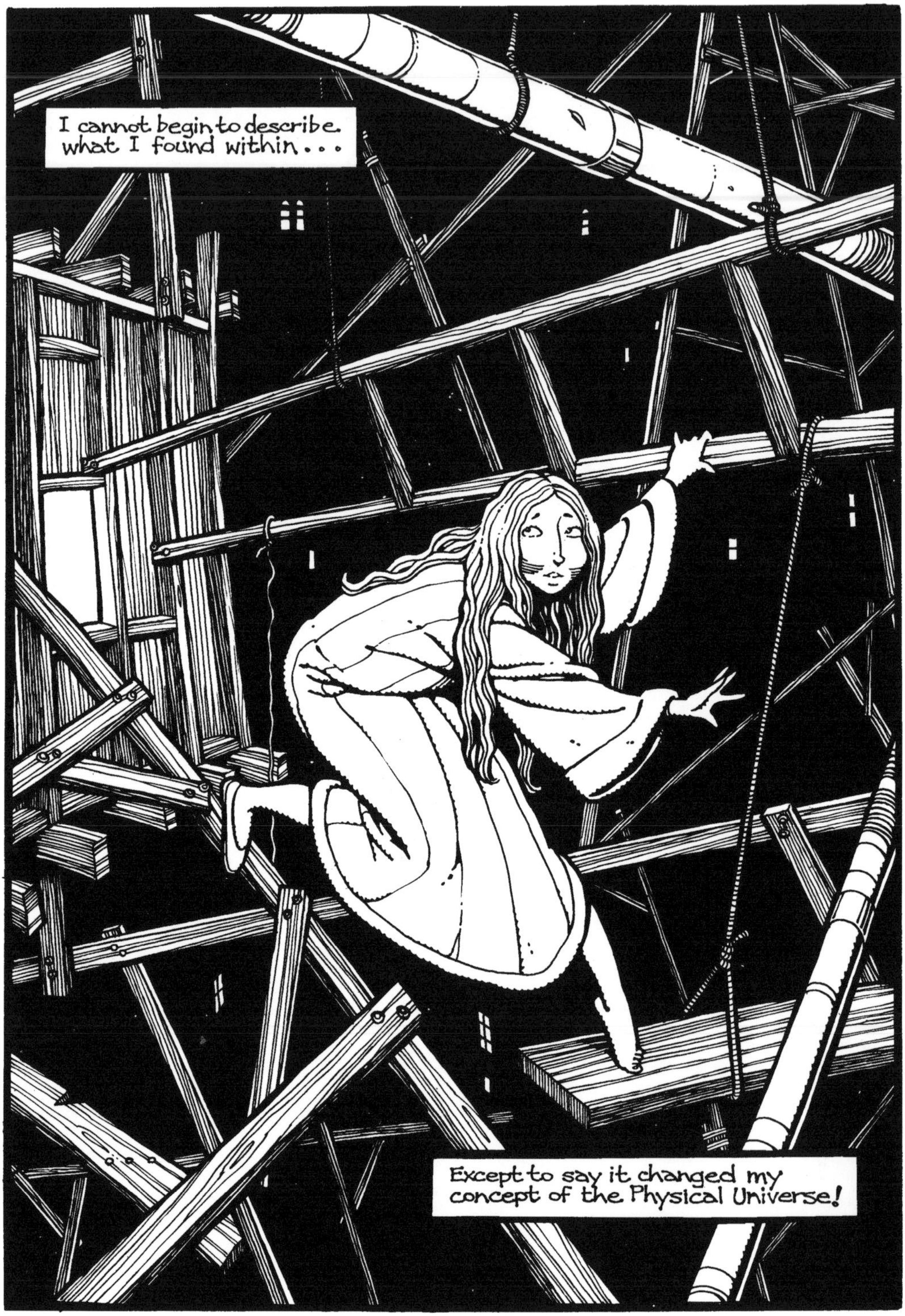
I cannot begin to describe what I found within . . .
Except to say it changed my concept of the Physical Universe!

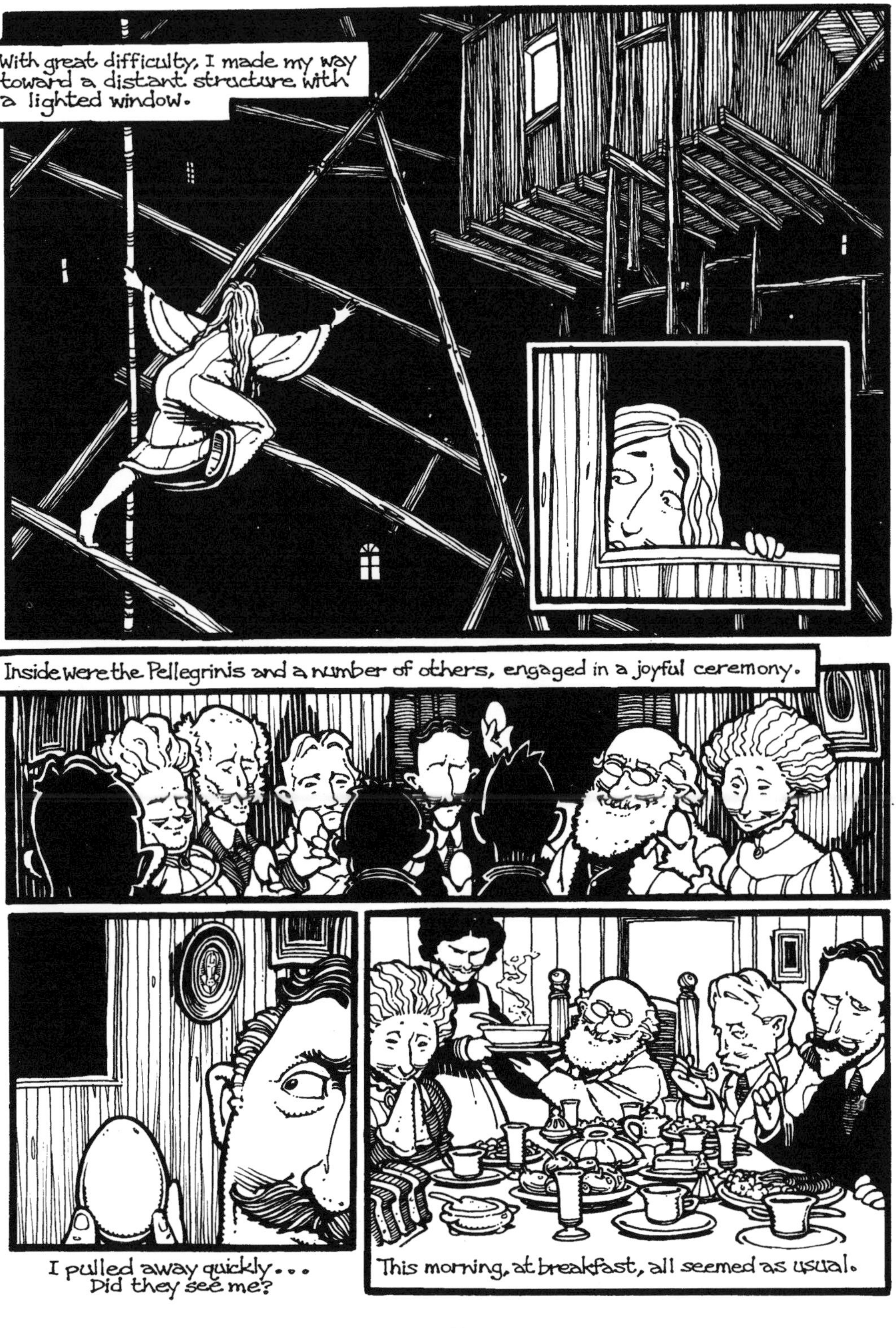

With great difficulty, I made my way toward a distant structure with a lighted window.
Inside were the Pellegrinis and a number of others, engaged in a joyful ceremony.
I pulled away quickly... Did they see me?
This morning, at breakfast, all seemed as usual.

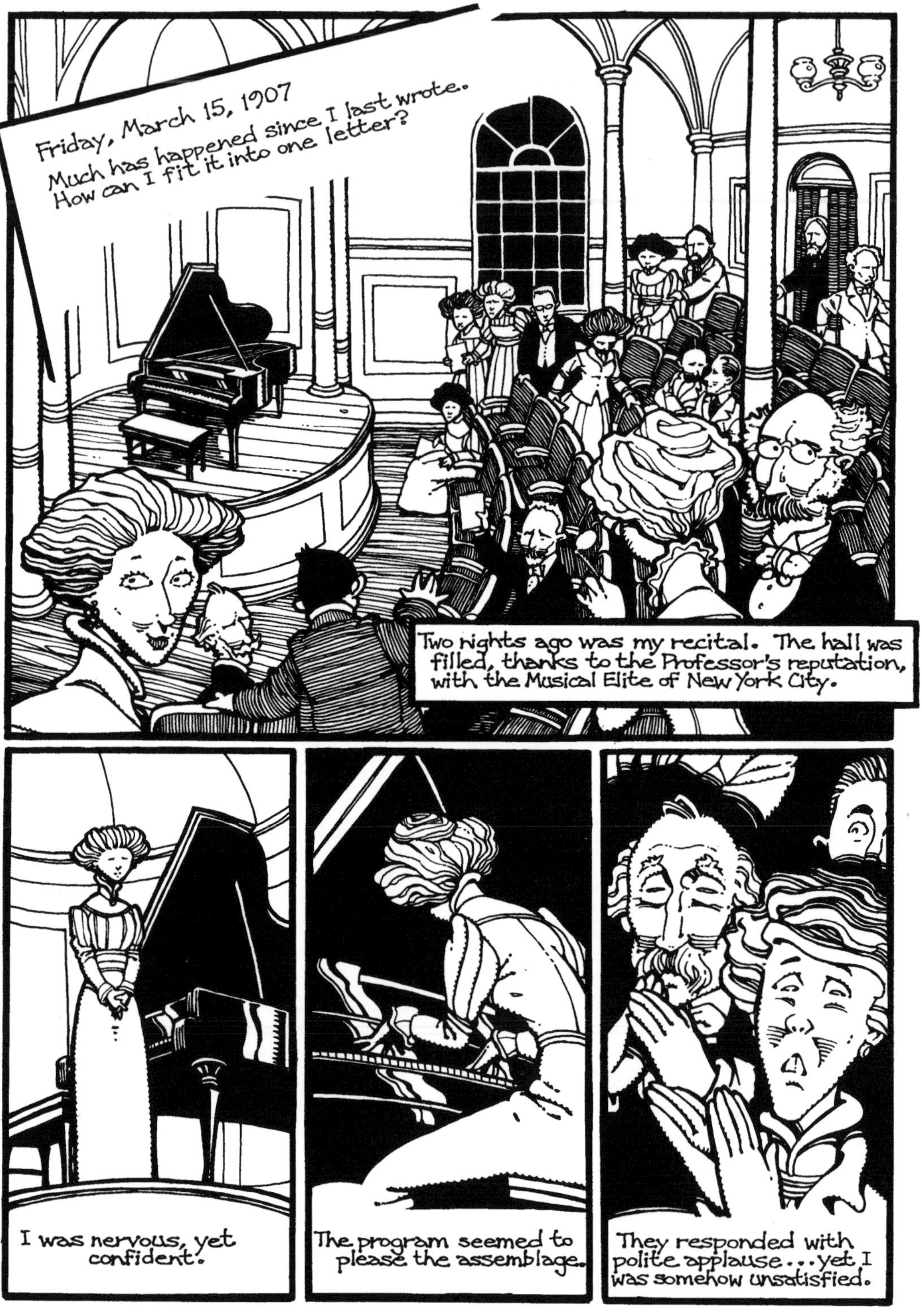

Friday, March 15, 1907
Much has happened since I last wrote. How can I fit it into one letter?
Two nights ago was my recital. The hall was filled, thanks to the Professor's reputation, with the Musical Elite of New York City.
I was nervous, yet confident.
The program seemed to please the assemblage.
They responded with polite applause...yet I was somehow unsatisfied.

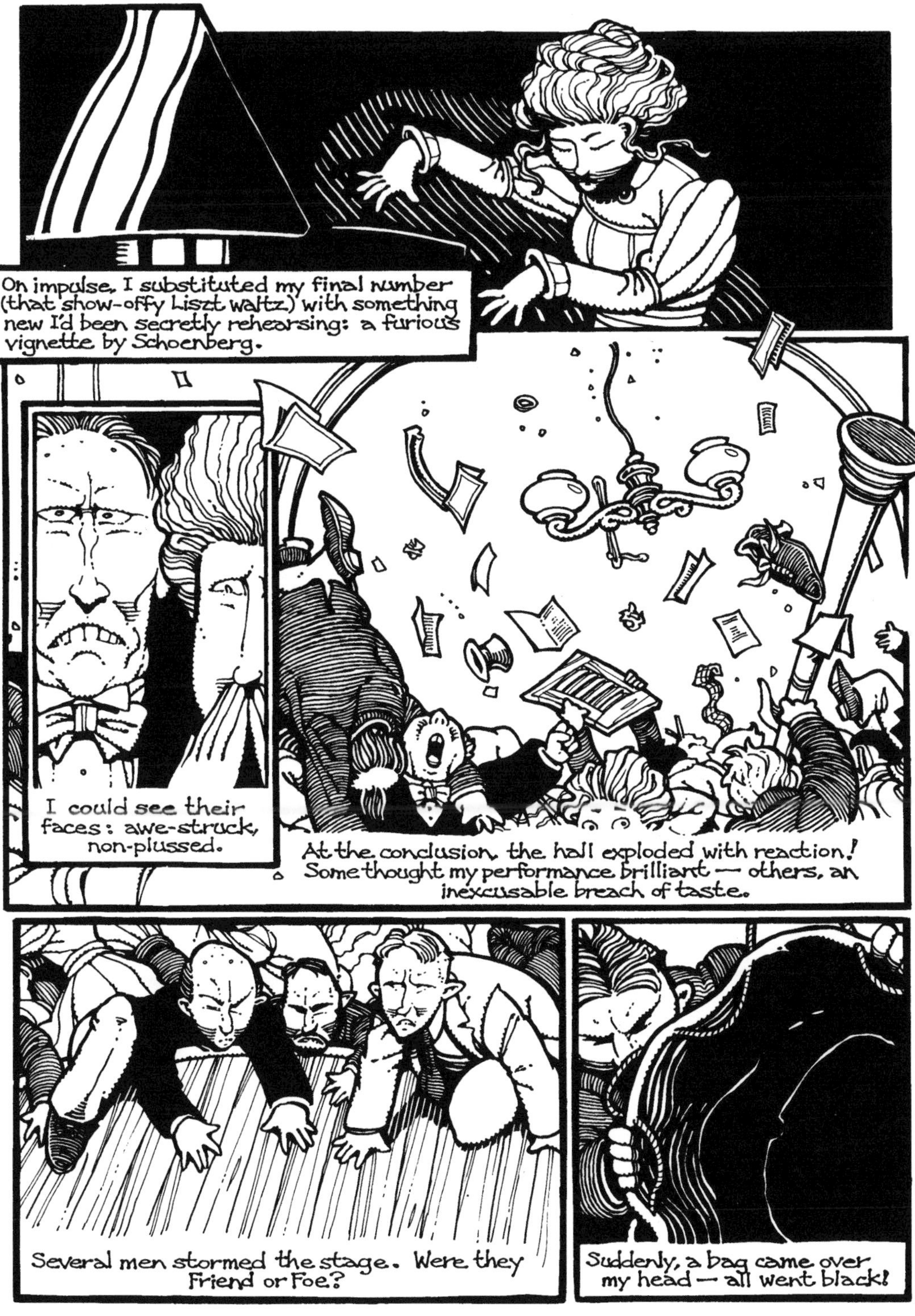
On impulse, I substituted my final number (that show-offy Liszt waltz) with something new I'd been secretly rehearsing: a furious vignette by Schoenberg.
I could see their faces: awe-struck, non-plussed.
At the conclusion, the hall exploded with reaction! Some thought my performance brilliant — others, an inexcusable breach of taste.
Several men stormed the stage. Were they Friend or Foe?
Suddenly, a bag came over my head — all went black!

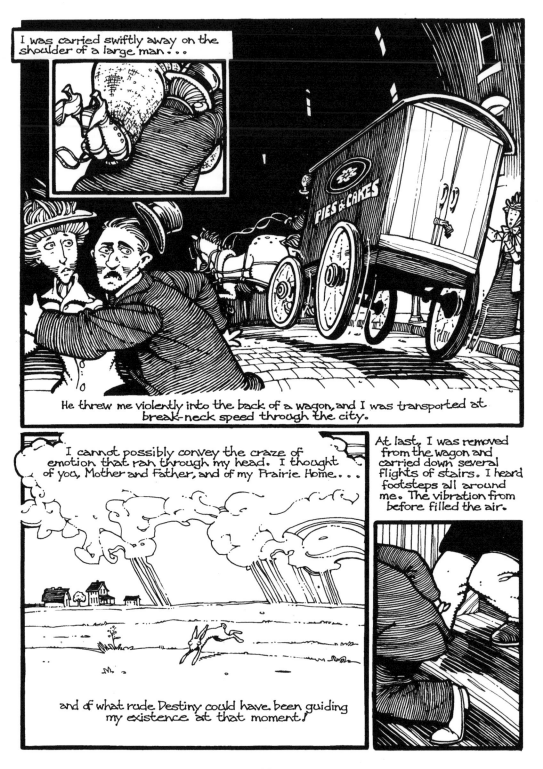

I was carried swiftly away on the shoulder of a large man...

He threw me violently into the back of a wagon, and I was transported at break-neck speed through the city.

I cannot possibly convey the craze of emotion that ran through my head. I thought of you, Mother and Father, and of my Prairie Home....

and of what rude Destiny could have been guiding my existence at that moment!

At last, I was removed from the wagon and carried down several flights of stairs. I heard footsteps all around me. The vibration from before filled the air.

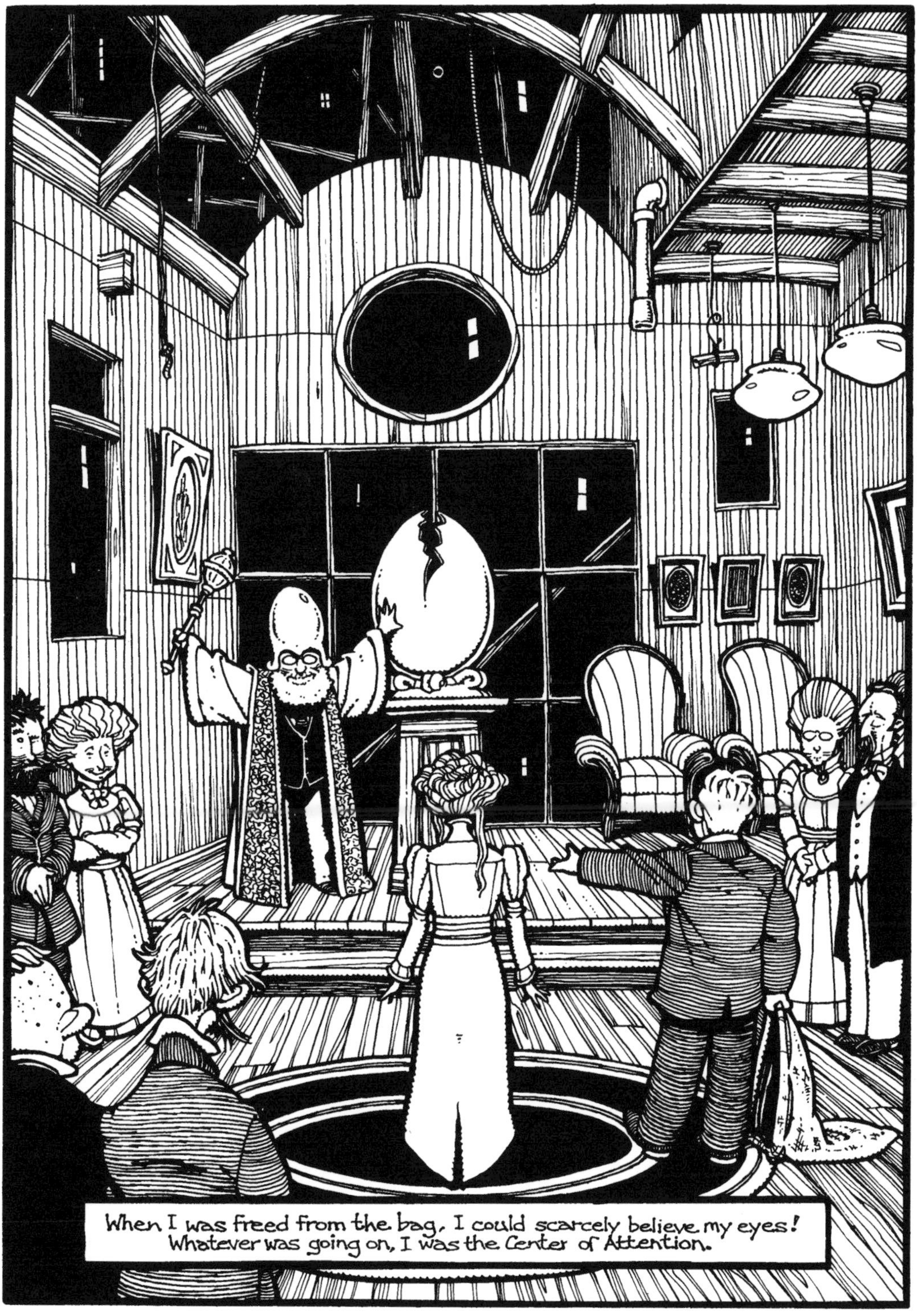
When I was freed from the bag, I could scarcely believe my eyes! Whatever was going on, I was the Center of Attention.

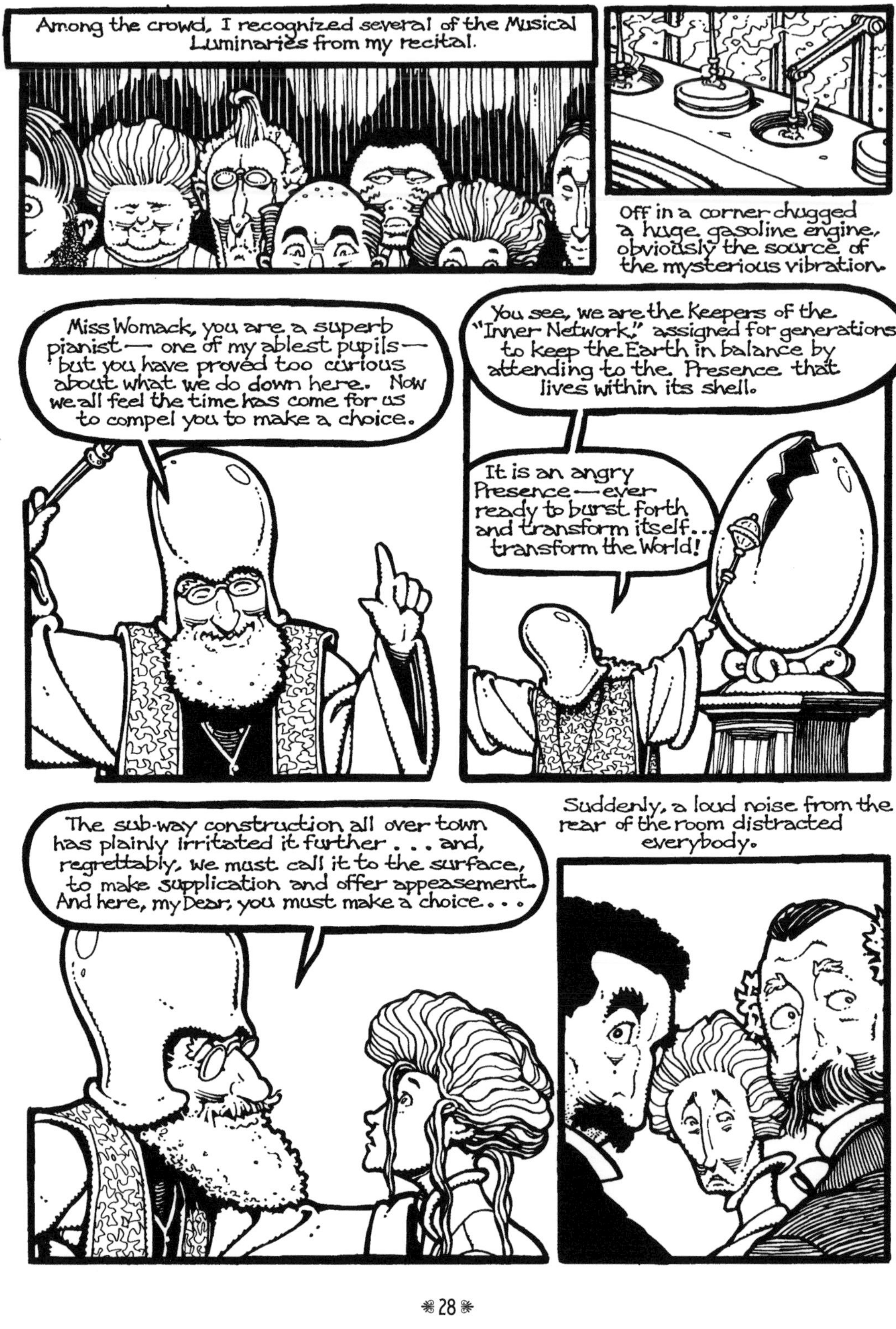
Among the crowd, I recognized several of the Musical Luminaries from my recital.
Off in a corner chugged a huge gasoline engine, obviously the source of the mysterious vibration.
Miss Womack, you are a superb pianist— one of my ablest pupils— but you have proved too curious about what we do down here. Now we all feel the time has come for us to compel you to make a choice.
You see, we are the Keepers of the "Inner Network," assigned for generations to keep the Earth in balance by attending to the Presence that lives within its shell.
It is an angry Presence—ever ready to burst forth and transform itself... transform the World!
The sub-way construction all over town has plainly irritated it further . . . and, regrettably, we must call it to the surface, to make supplication and offer appeasement. And here, my Dear, you must make a choice . . .
Suddenly, a loud noise from the rear of the room distracted everybody.

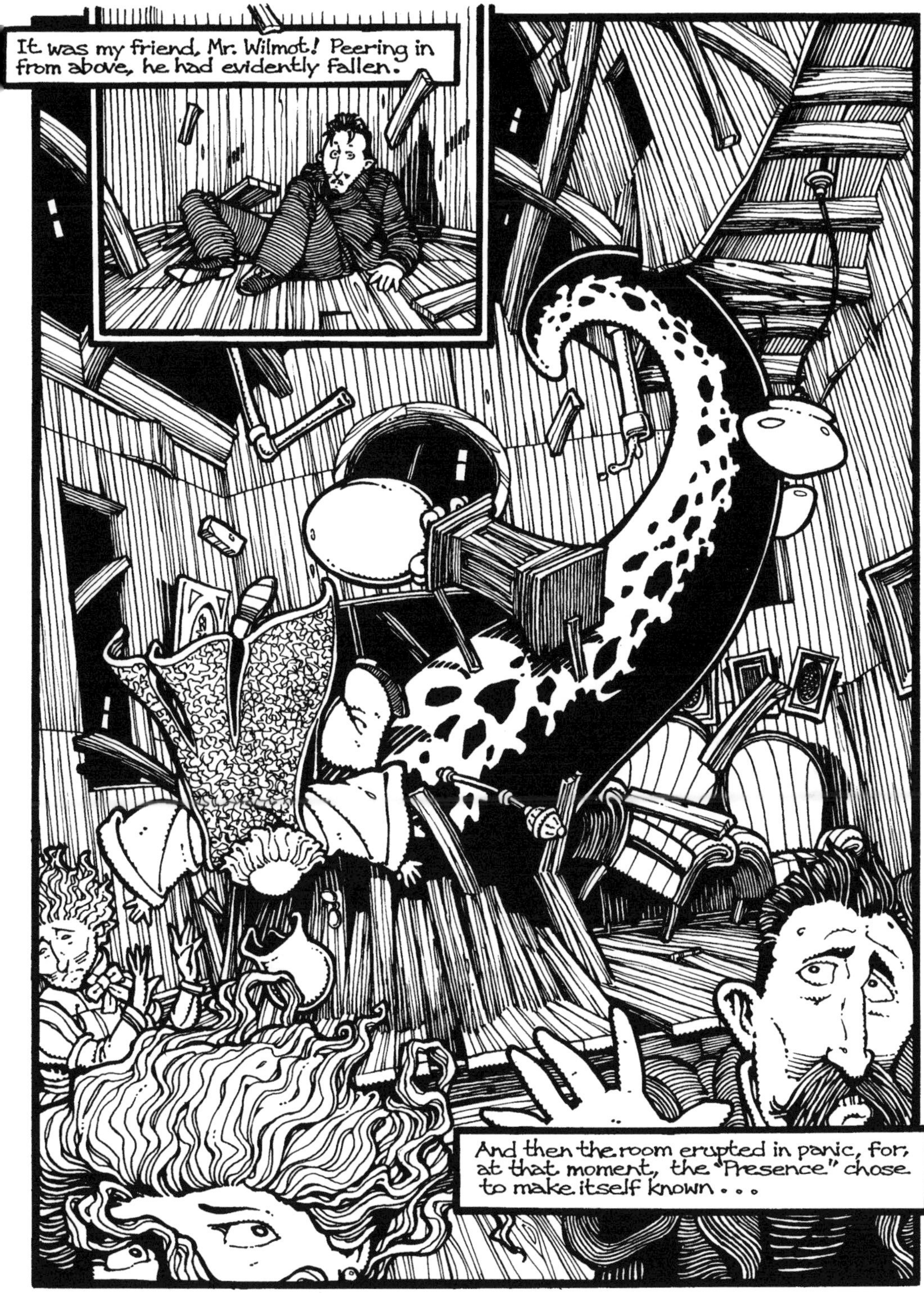
It was my friend, Mr. Wilmot! Peering in from above, he had evidently fallen.
And then the room erupted in panic, for, at that moment, the "Presence" chose to make itself known . . .

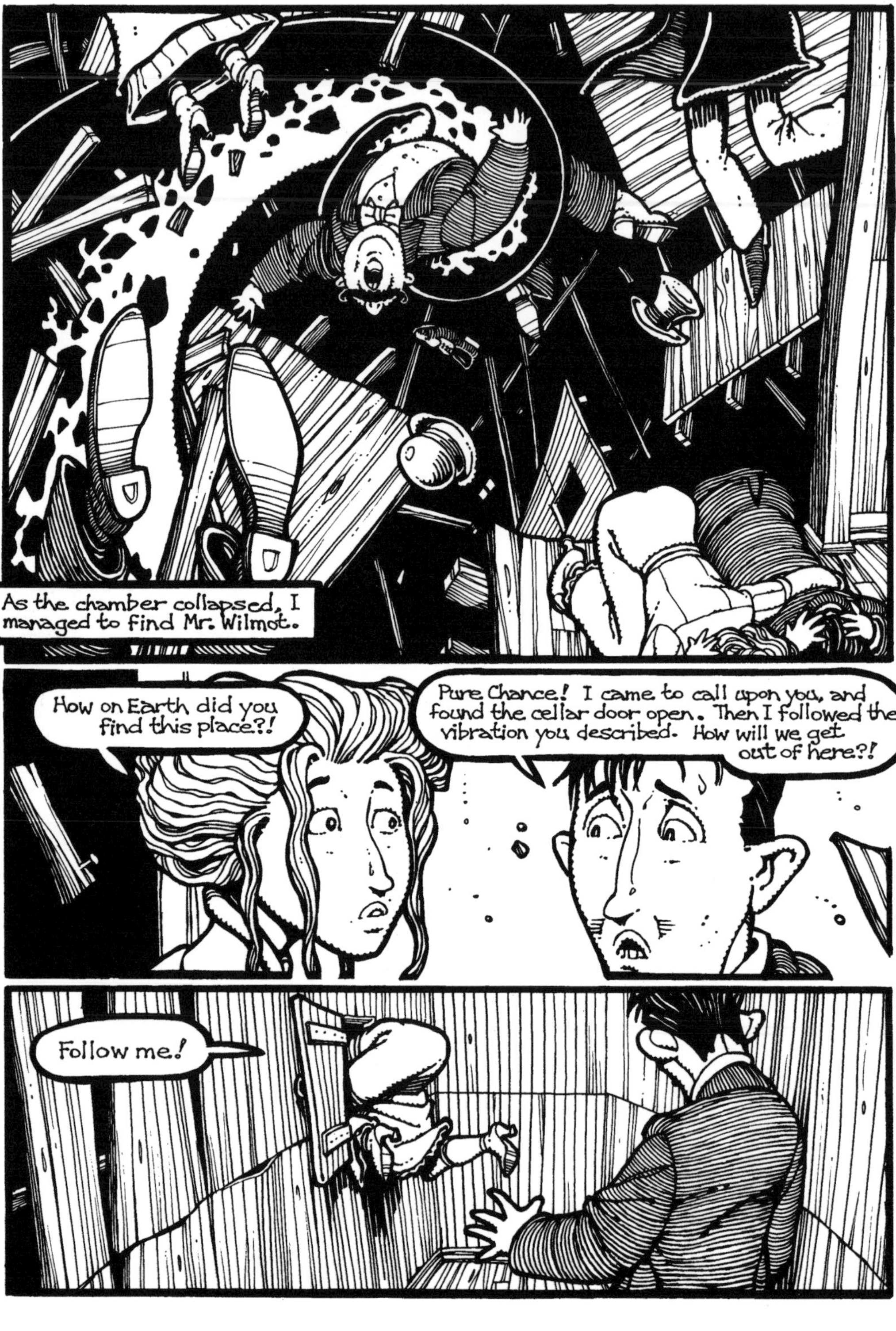
As the chamber collapsed, I managed to find Mr. Wilmot.
How on Earth did you find this place?!
Pure Chance! I came to call upon you, and found the cellar door open. Then I followed the vibration you described. How will we get out of here?!
Follow me!

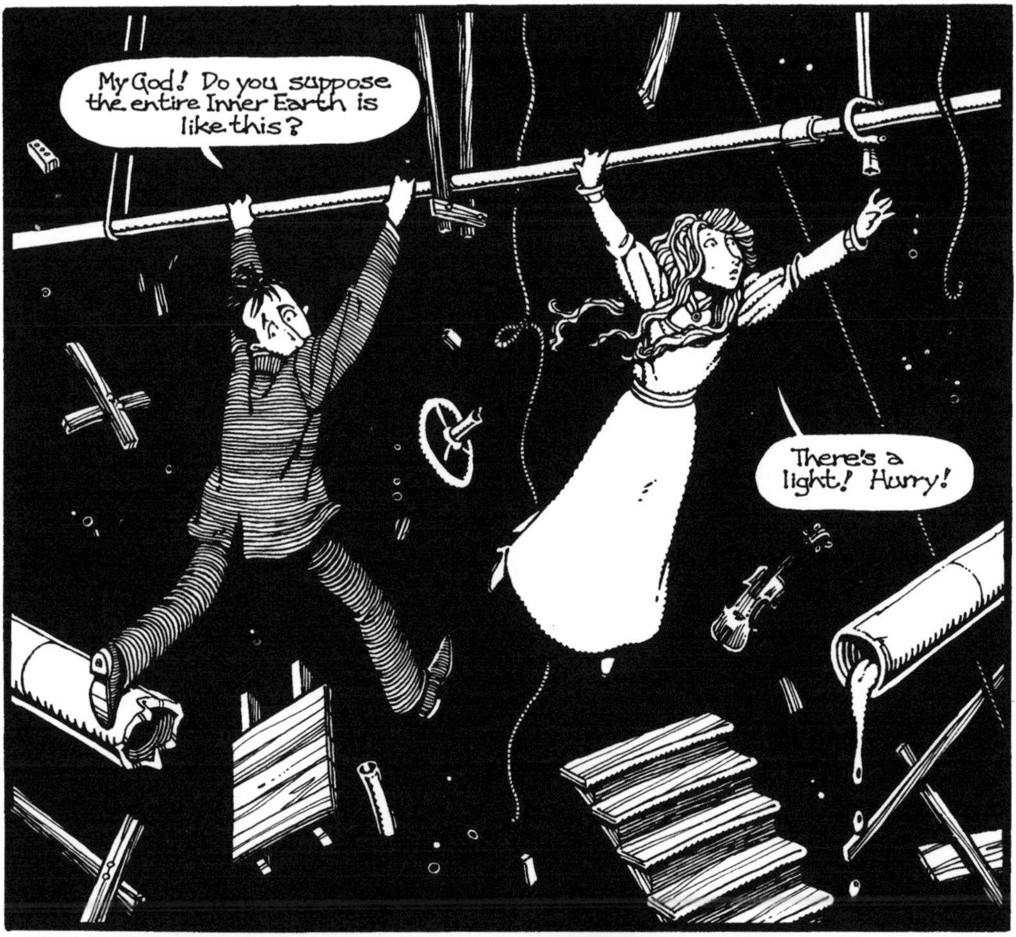
My God! Do you suppose the entire Inner Earth is like this?
There's a light! Hurry!

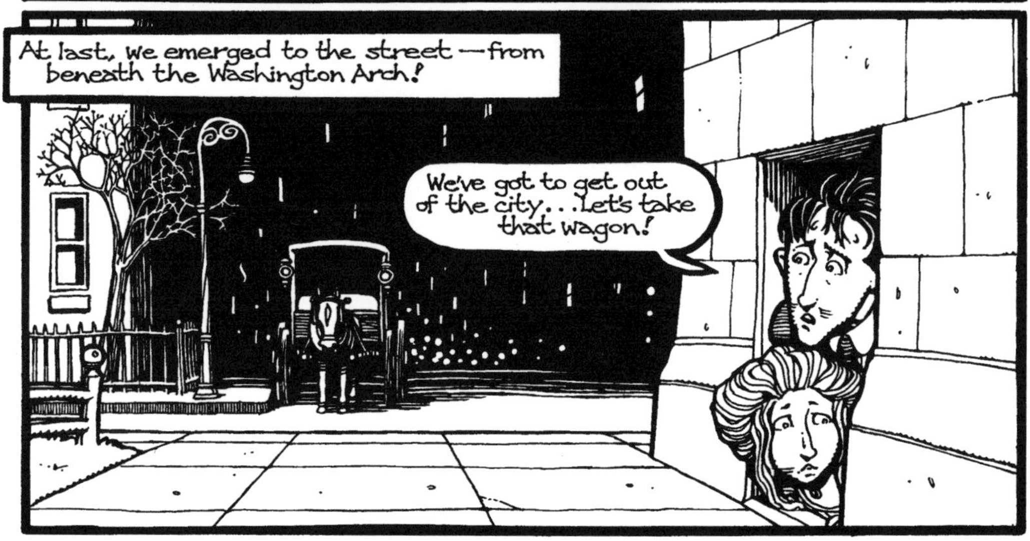
At last, we emerged to the street — from beneath the Washington Arch!
We've got to get out of the city. . . Let's take that wagon!

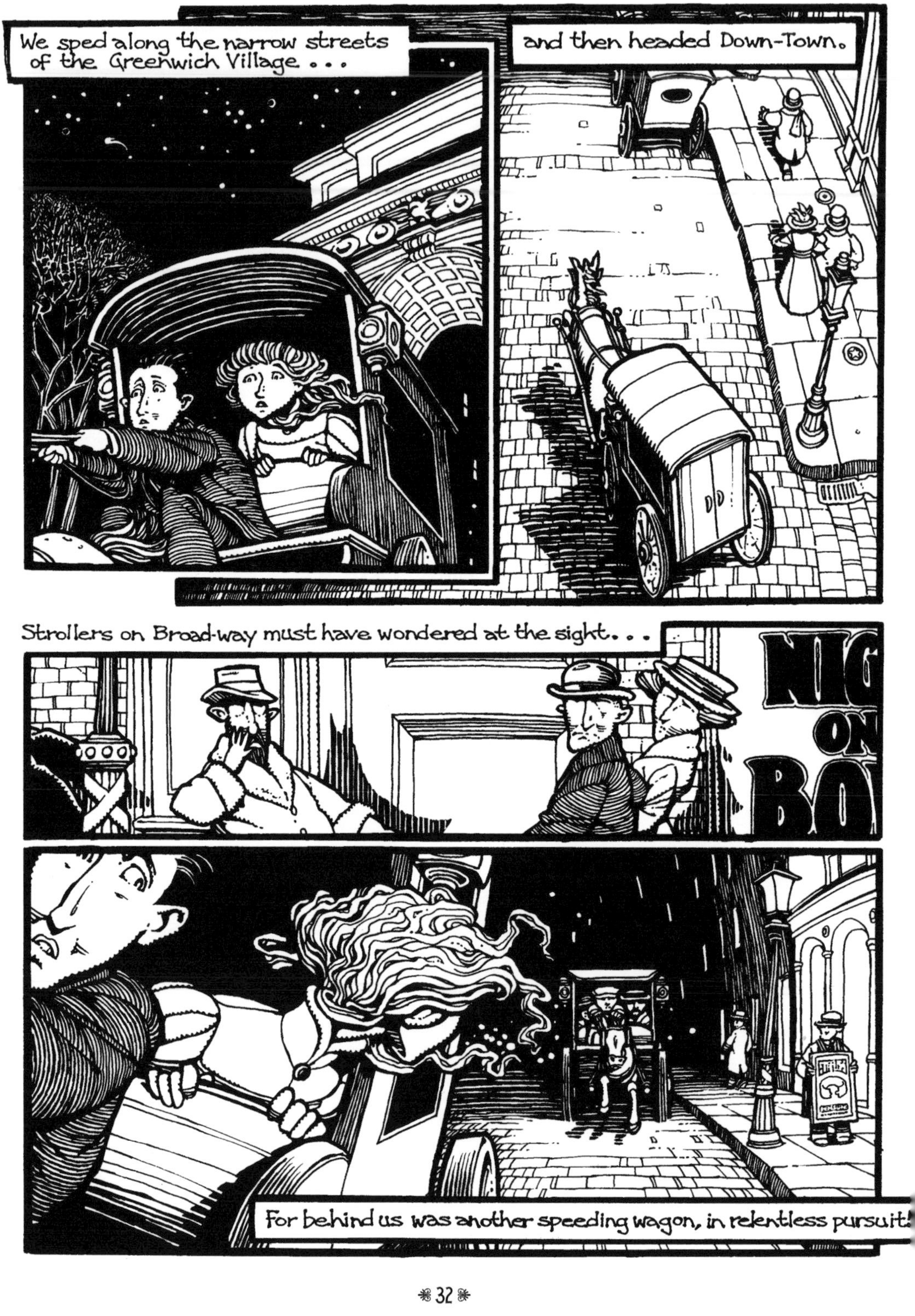
We sped along the narrow streets of the Greenwich Village . . .
and then headed Down-Town.
Strollers on Broad-way must have wondered at the sight. . .
NIG ON BO
For behind us was another speeding wagon, in relentless pursuit!

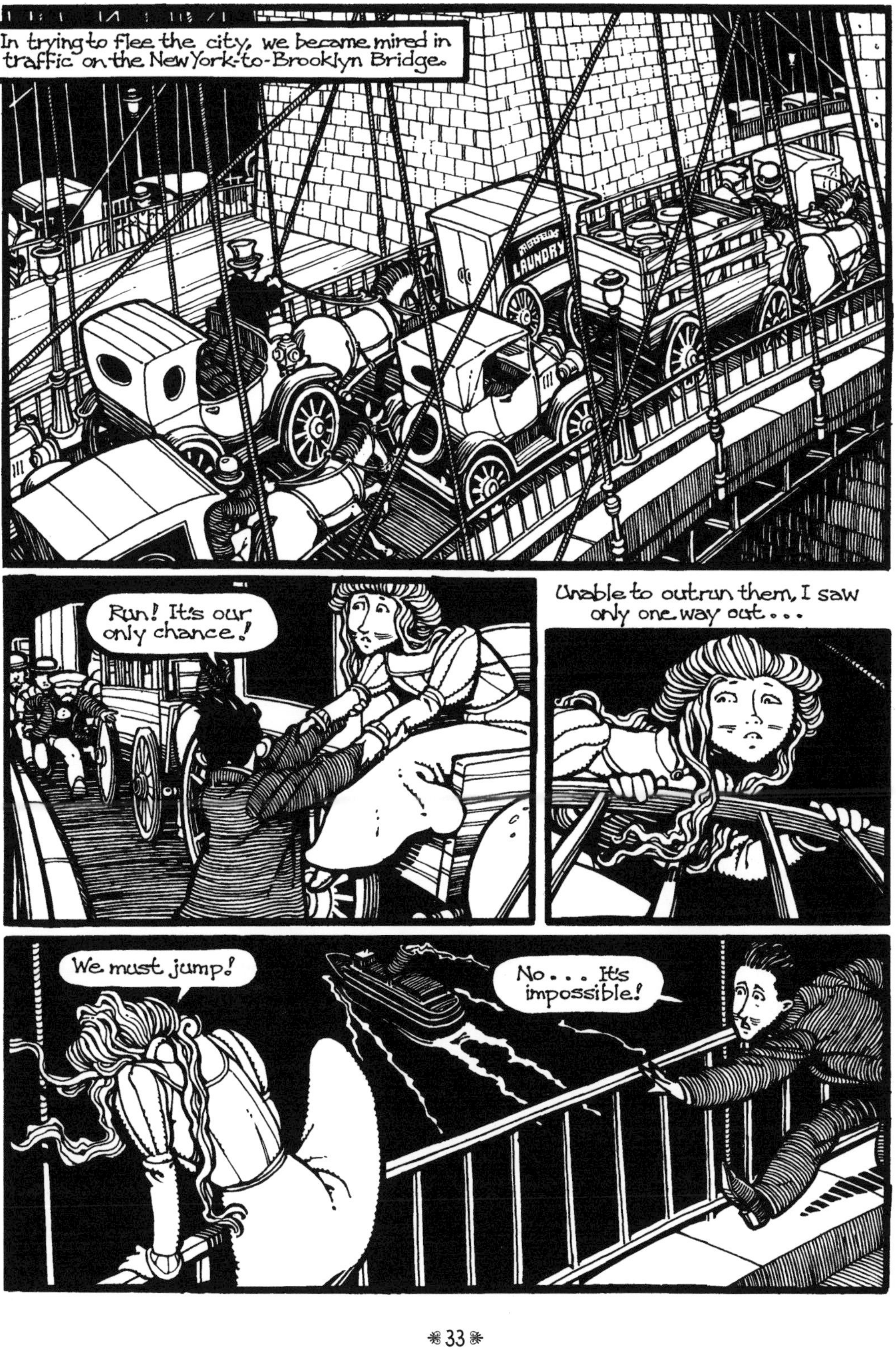
In trying to flee the city, we became mired in traffic on the New York-to-Brooklyn Bridge.
LAUNDRY
Run! It's our only chance!
Unable to outrun them, I saw only one way out...
We must jump!
No... It's impossible!

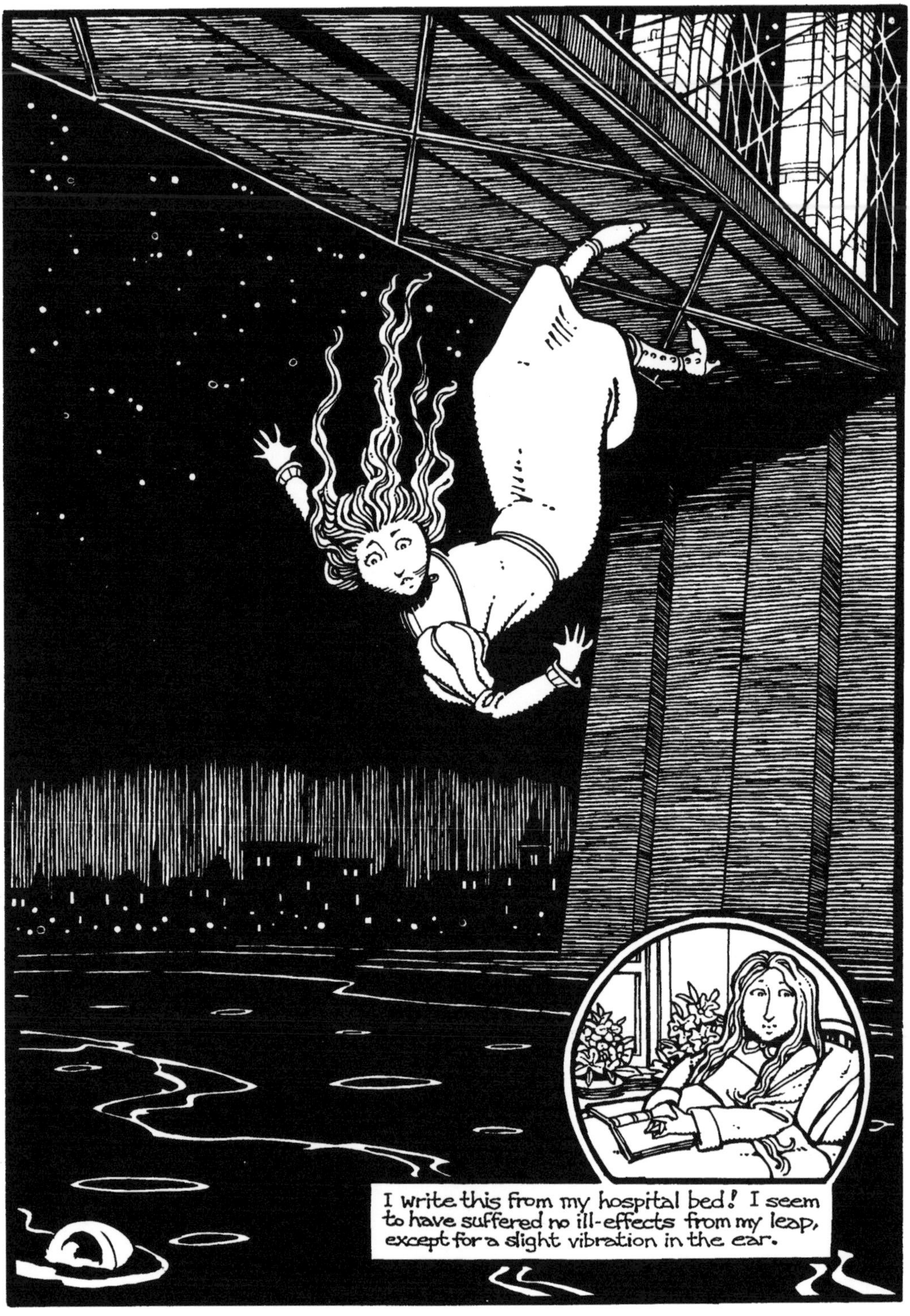
I write this from my hospital bed! I seem to have suffered no ill-effects from my leap, except for a slight vibration in the ear.

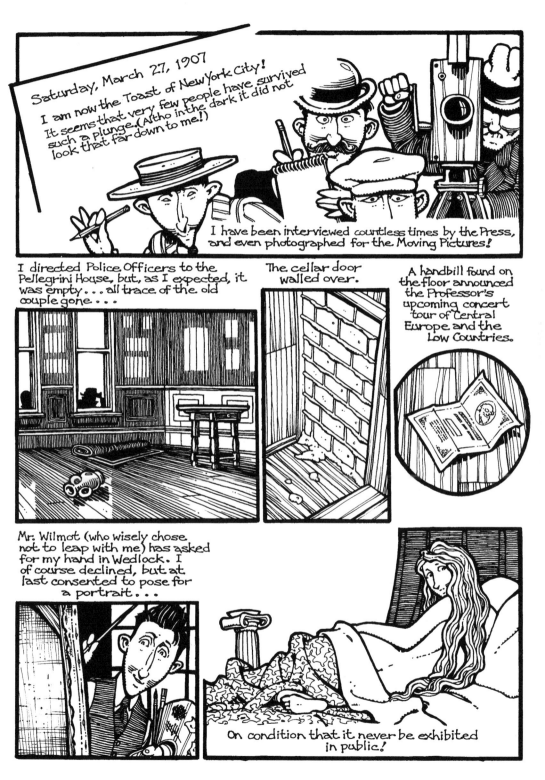

Saturday, March 27, 1907!
I am now the Toast of New York City!
It seems that very few people have survived
such a plunge.. (Altho in the dark it did not
look that far down to me!)

I have been interviewed countless times by the Press,
and even photographed for the Moving Pictures!

I directed Police Officers to the
Pellegrini House, but, as I expected, it
was empty.... all trace of the old
couple gone....

The cellar door
walled over.

A handbill found on
the floor announced
the Professor's
upcoming concert
tour of Central
Europe and the
Low Countries.

Mr. Wilmot (who wisely chose
not to leap with me) has asked
for my hand in Wedlock. I
of course declined, but at
last consented to pose for
a portrait...

On condition that it never be exhibited
in public!

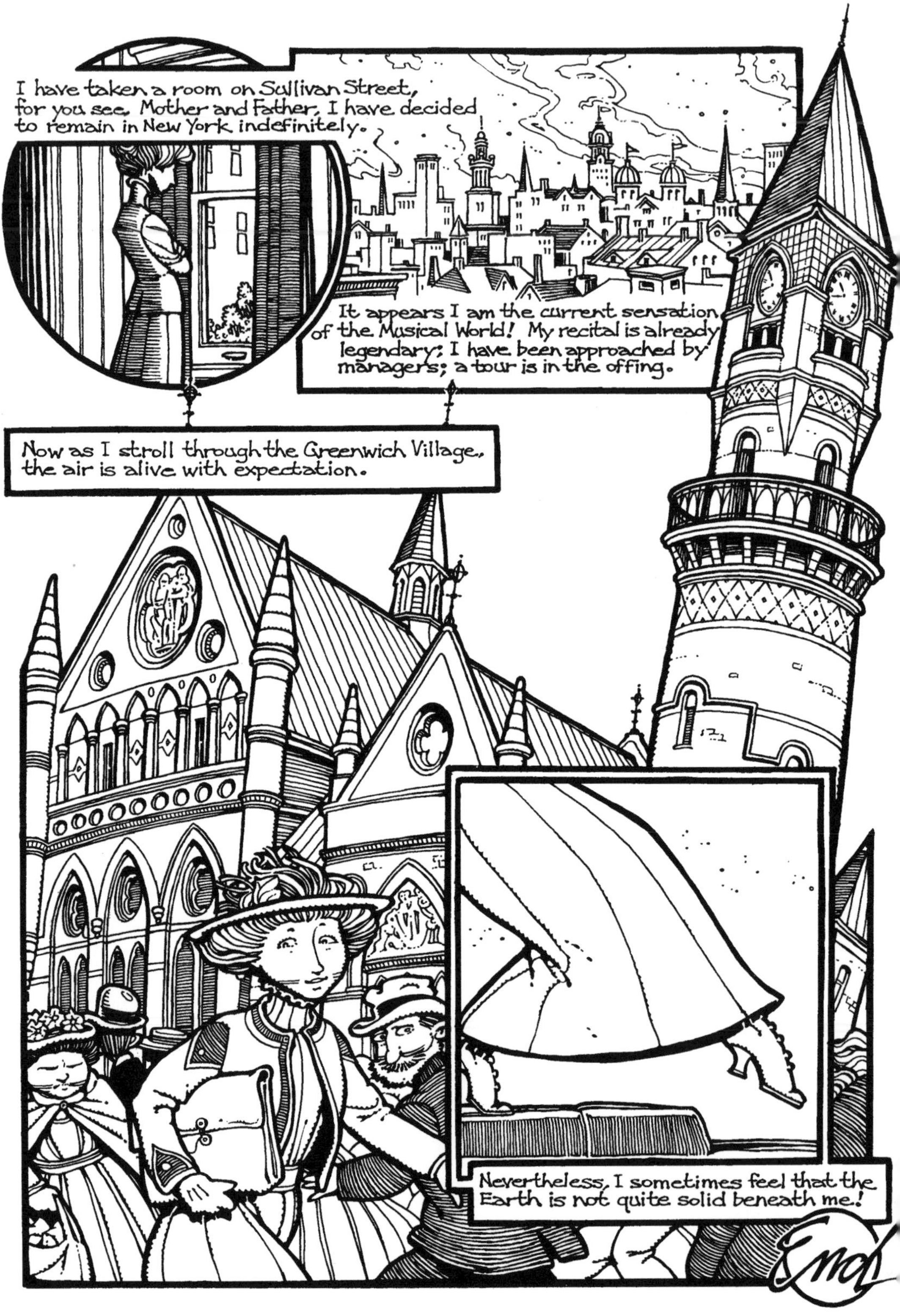
I have taken a room on Sullivan Street, for you see, Mother and Father, I have decided to remain in New York indefinitely.
It appears I am the current sensation of the Musical World! My recital is already legendary; I have been approached by managers; a tour is in the offing.
Now as I stroll through the Greenwich Village, the air is alive with expectation.
Nevertheless, I sometimes feel that the Earth is not quite solid beneath me!
End

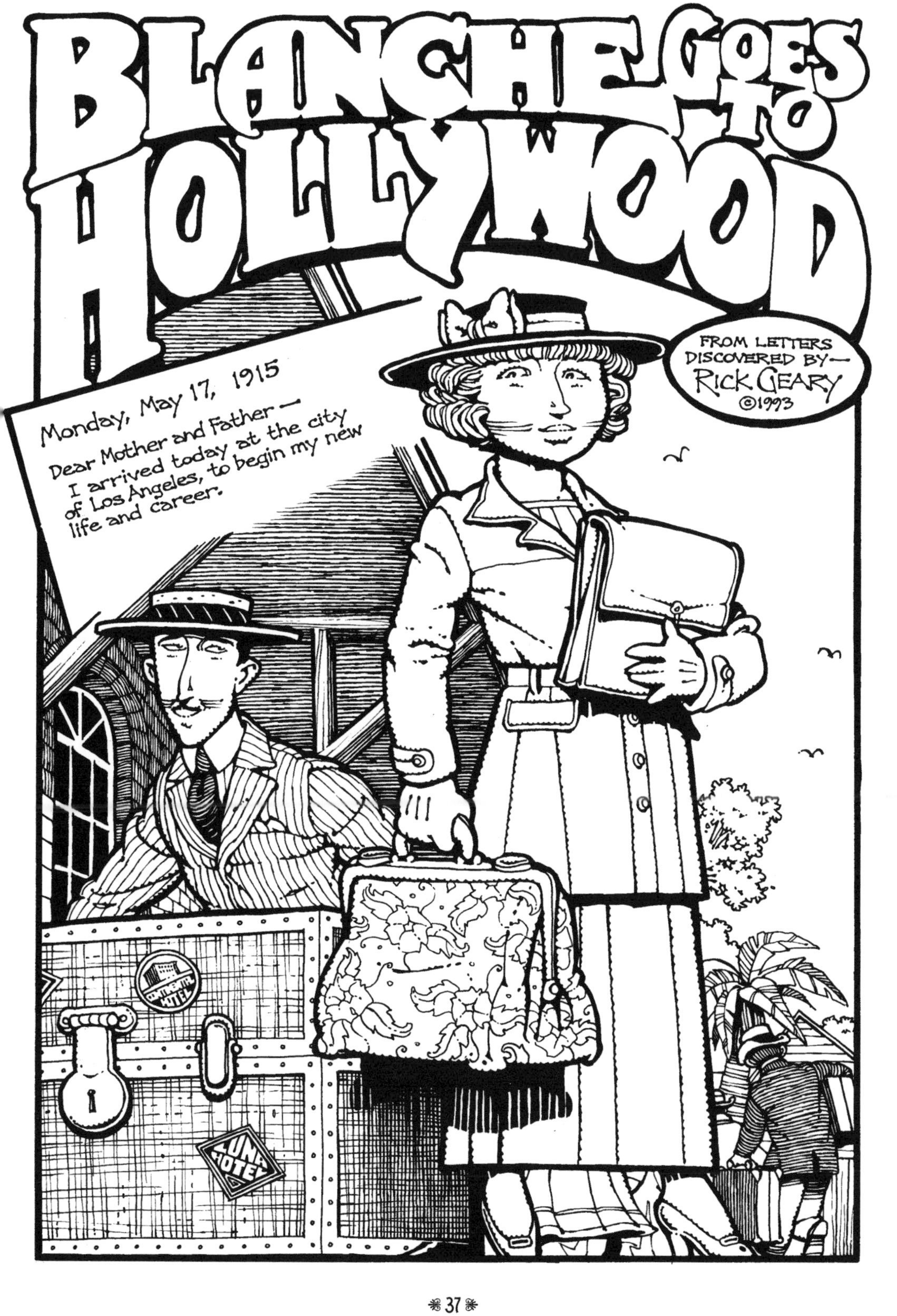
BLANCHE GOES TO HOLLYWOOD
FROM LETTERS DISCOVERED BY— RICK GEARY ©1993
Monday, May 17, 1915
Dear Mother and Father—
I arrived today at the city of Los Angeles, to begin my new life and career.
CONTINENTAL HOTEL
LUNA HOTEL

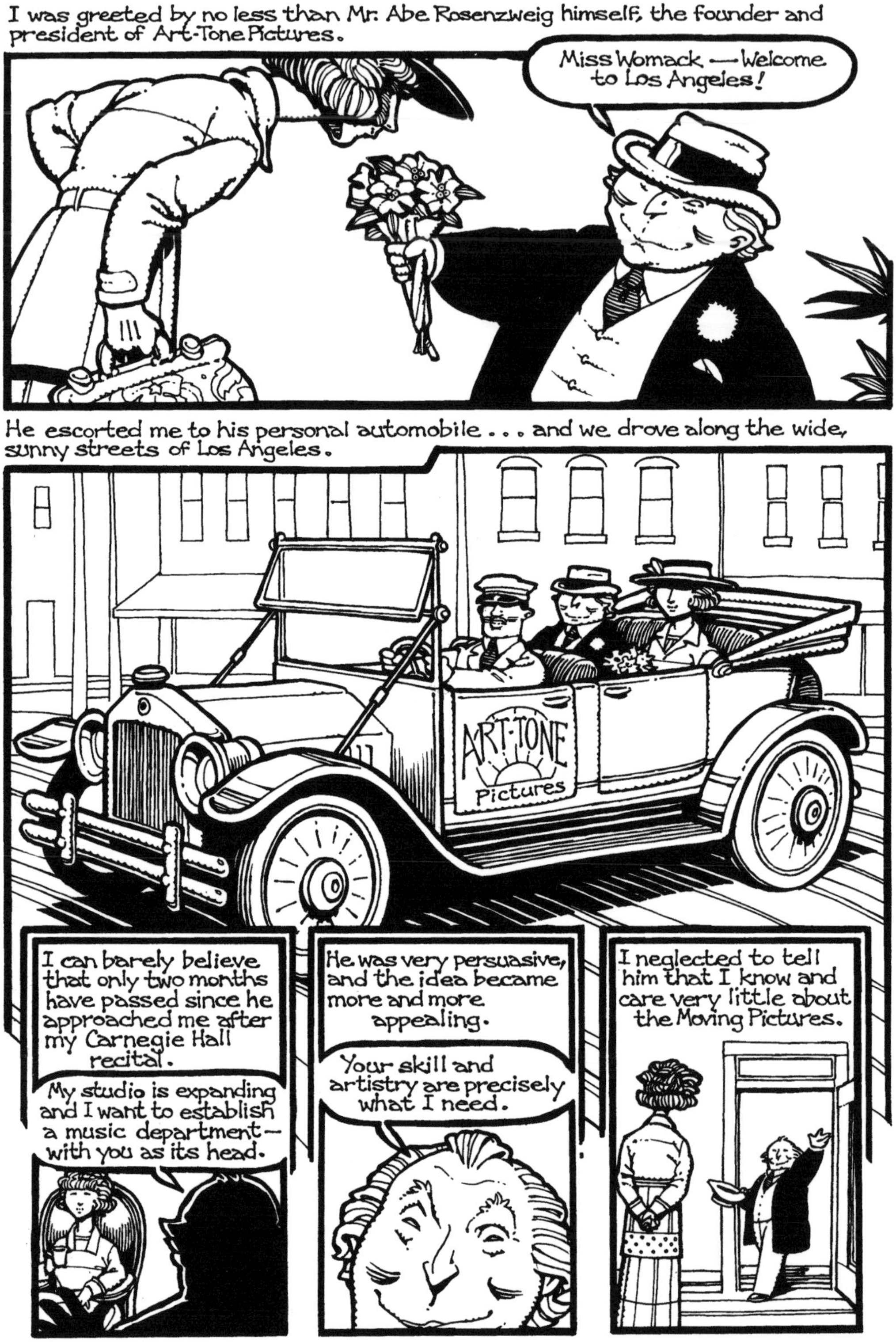
I was greeted by no less than Mr. Abe Rosenzweig himself, the founder and president of Art-Tone Pictures.
Miss Womack — Welcome to Los Angeles!
He escorted me to his personal automobile . . . and we drove along the wide, sunny streets of Los Angeles.
ART-TONE Pictures
I can barely believe that only two months have passed since he approached me after my Carnegie Hall recital.
My studio is expanding and I want to establish a music department— with you as its head.
He was very persuasive, and the idea became more and more appealing.
Your skill and artistry are precisely what I need.
I neglected to tell him that I know and care very little about the Moving Pictures.

Before long, we were in the countryside, heading North toward the foot-hill community of Hollywood.

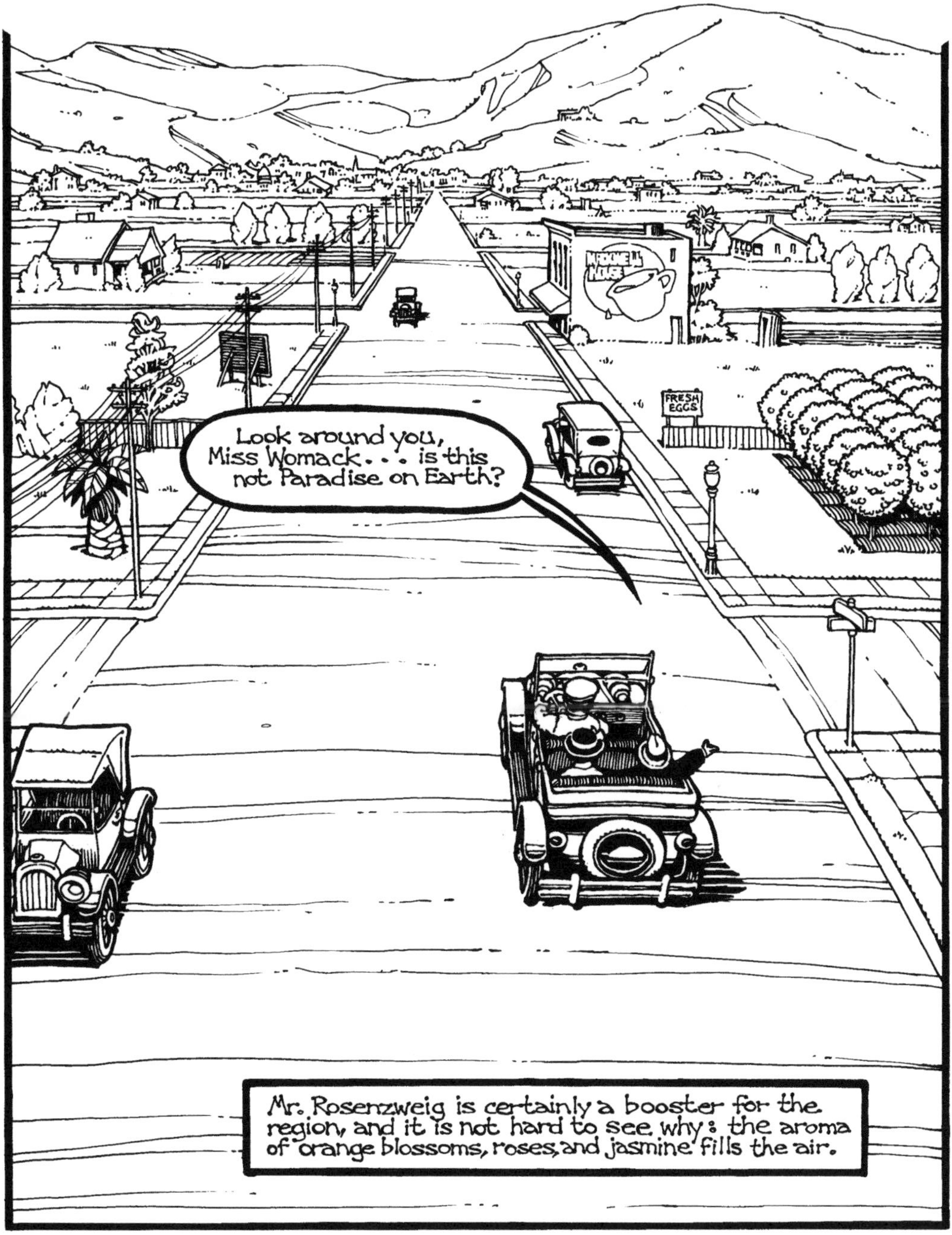
Look around you, Miss Womack . . . is this not Paradise on Earth?
FRESH EGGS
Mr. Rosenzweig is certainly a booster for the region, and it is not hard to see why: the aroma of orange blossoms, roses, and jasmine fills the air.

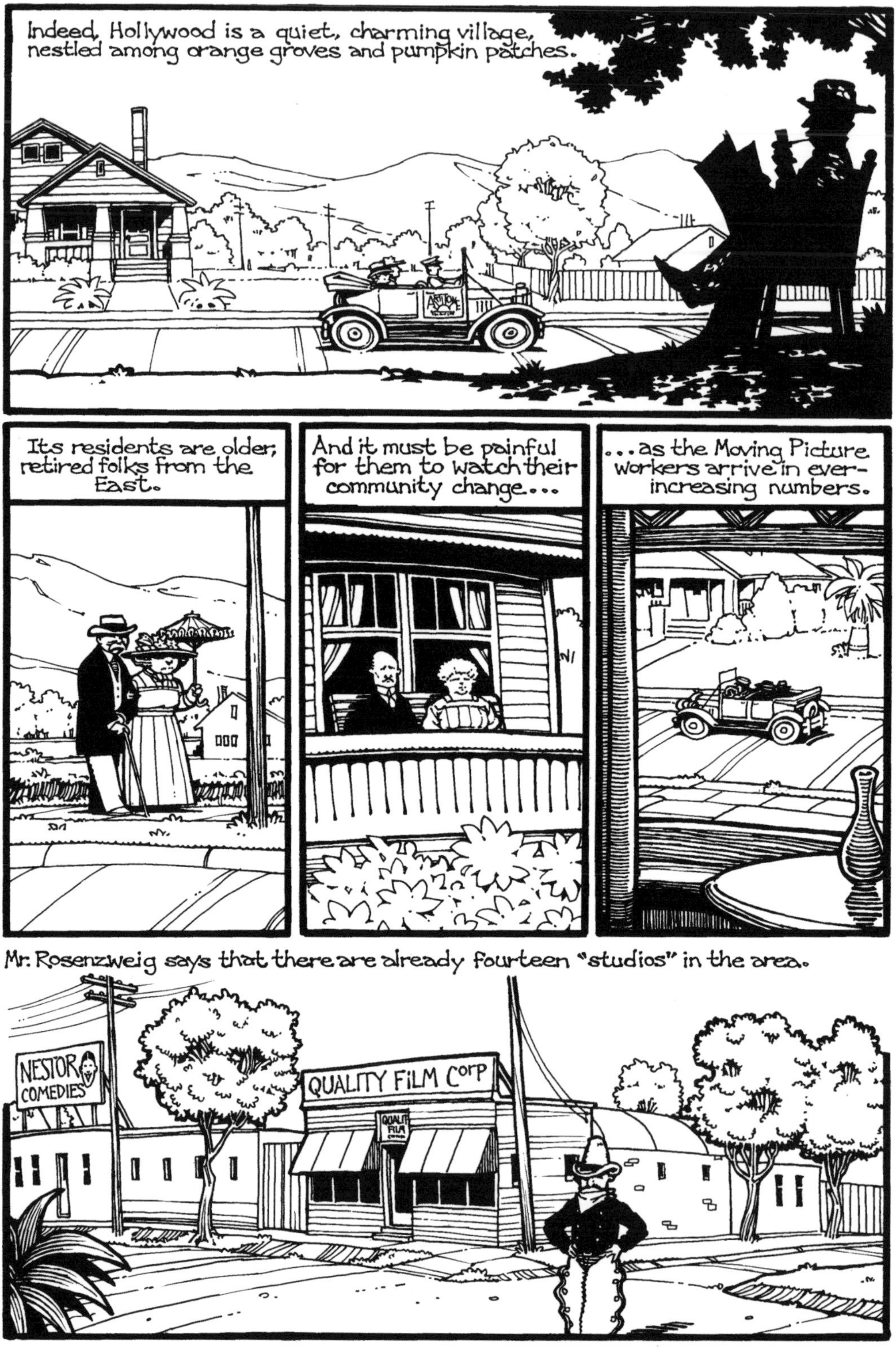
Indeed, Hollywood is a quiet, charming village, nestled among orange groves and pumpkin patches.
Its residents are older, retired folks from the East.
And it must be painful for them to watch their community change...
...as the Moving Picture workers arrive in ever-increasing numbers.
Mr. Rosenzweig says that there are already fourteen "studios" in the area.
NESTOR COMEDIES
QUALITY FILM Corp

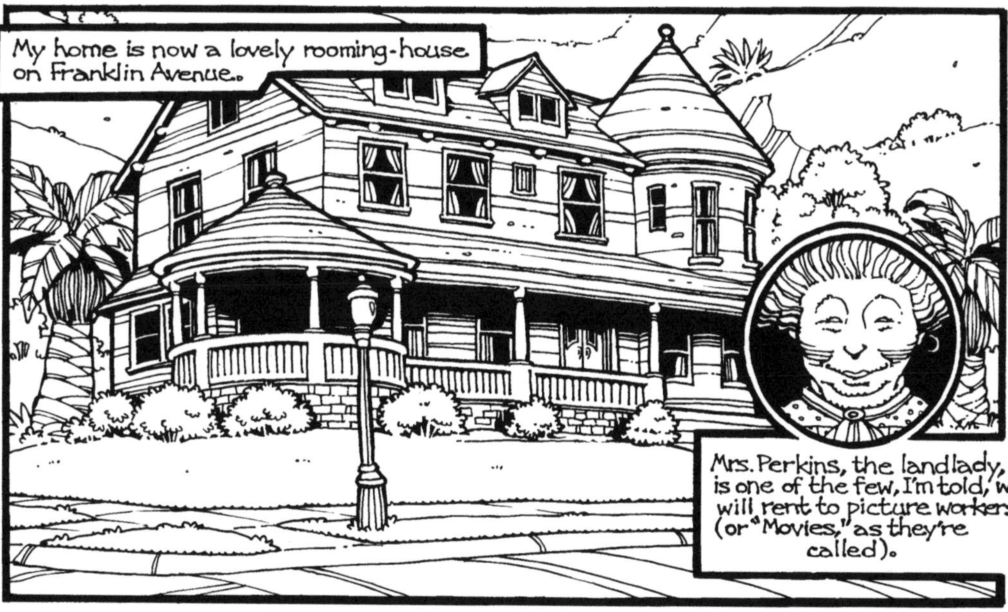
My home is now a lovely rooming-house on Franklin Avenue.
Mrs. Perkins, the landlady, is one of the few, I'm told, who will rent to picture workers (or "Movies," as they're called).

She's a widow-lady, from Oklahoma, so I know we'll have lots to talk about.

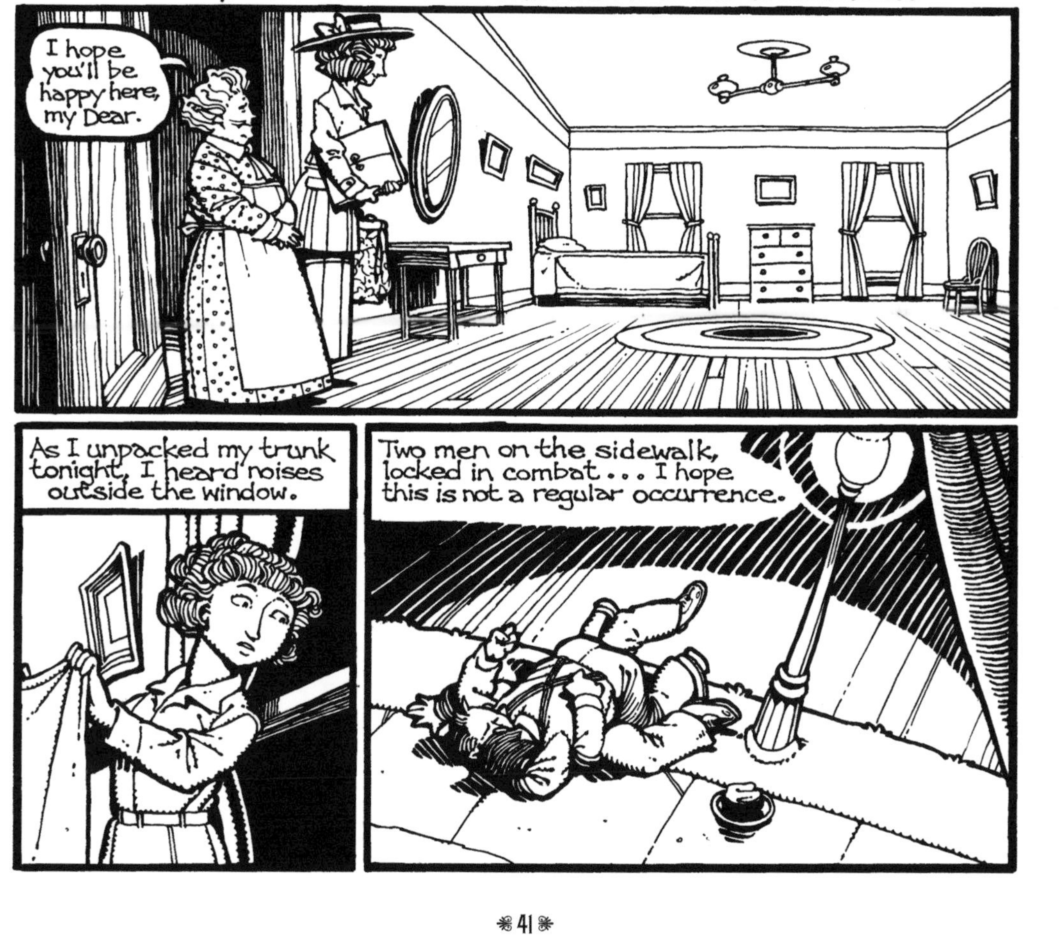
I hope you'll be happy here, my Dear.
As I unpacked my trunk tonight, I heard noises outside the window.
Two men on the sidewalk, locked in combat . . . I hope this is not a regular occurrence.

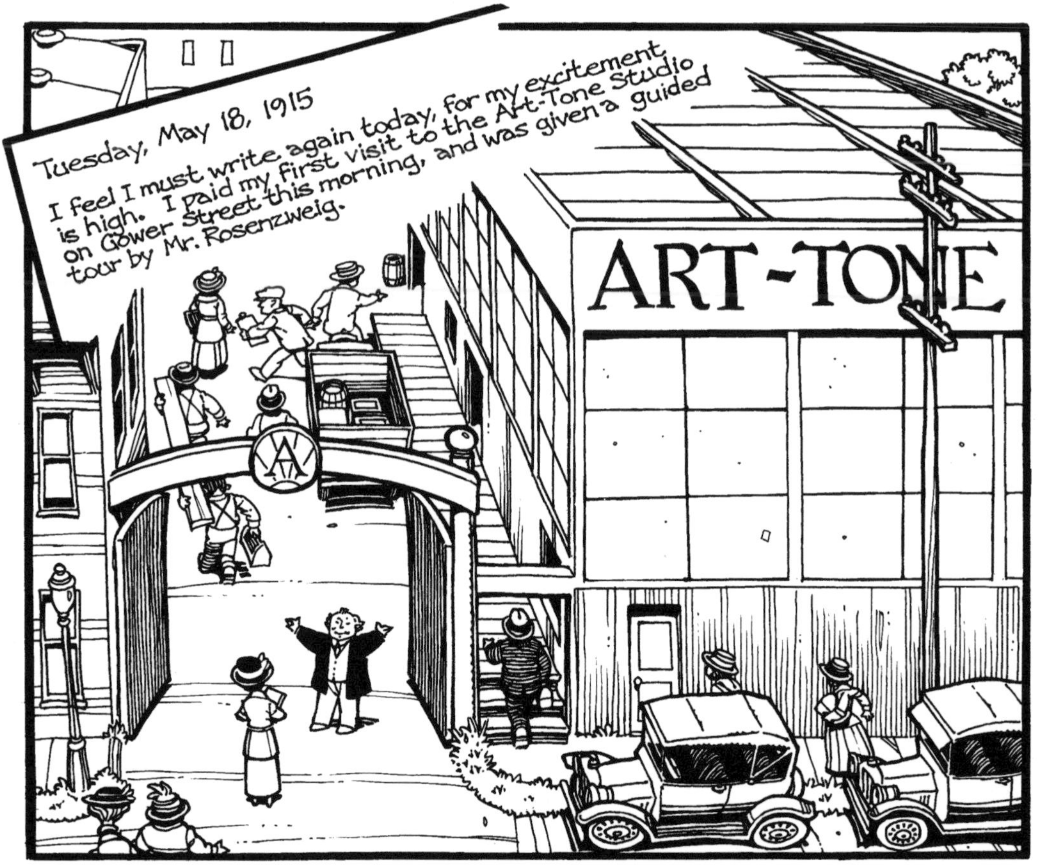
Tuesday, May 18, 1915
I feel I must write again today, for my excitement is high. I paid my first visit to the Art-Tone Studio on Gower Street this morning, and was given a guided tour by Mr. Rosenzweig.
ART-TONE

All his workers seem to love him. They call him "Uncle Abe."

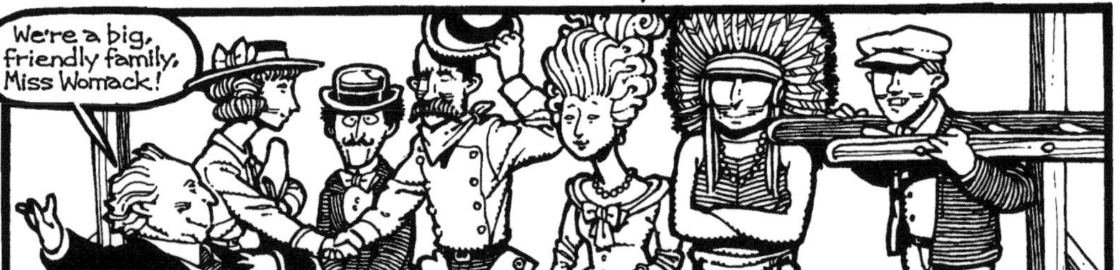
We're a big, friendly family, Miss Womack!

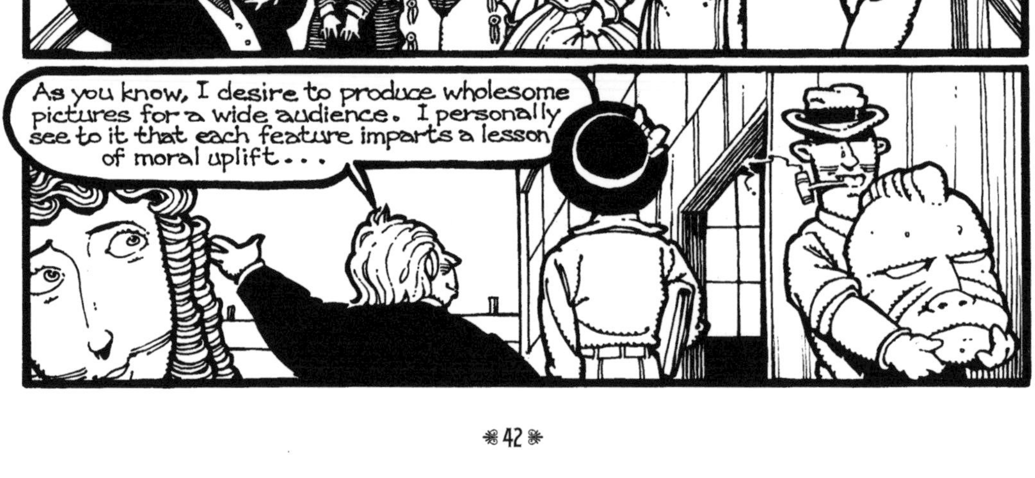
As you know, I desire to produce wholesome pictures for a wide audience. I personally see to it that each feature imparts a lesson of moral uplift . . .

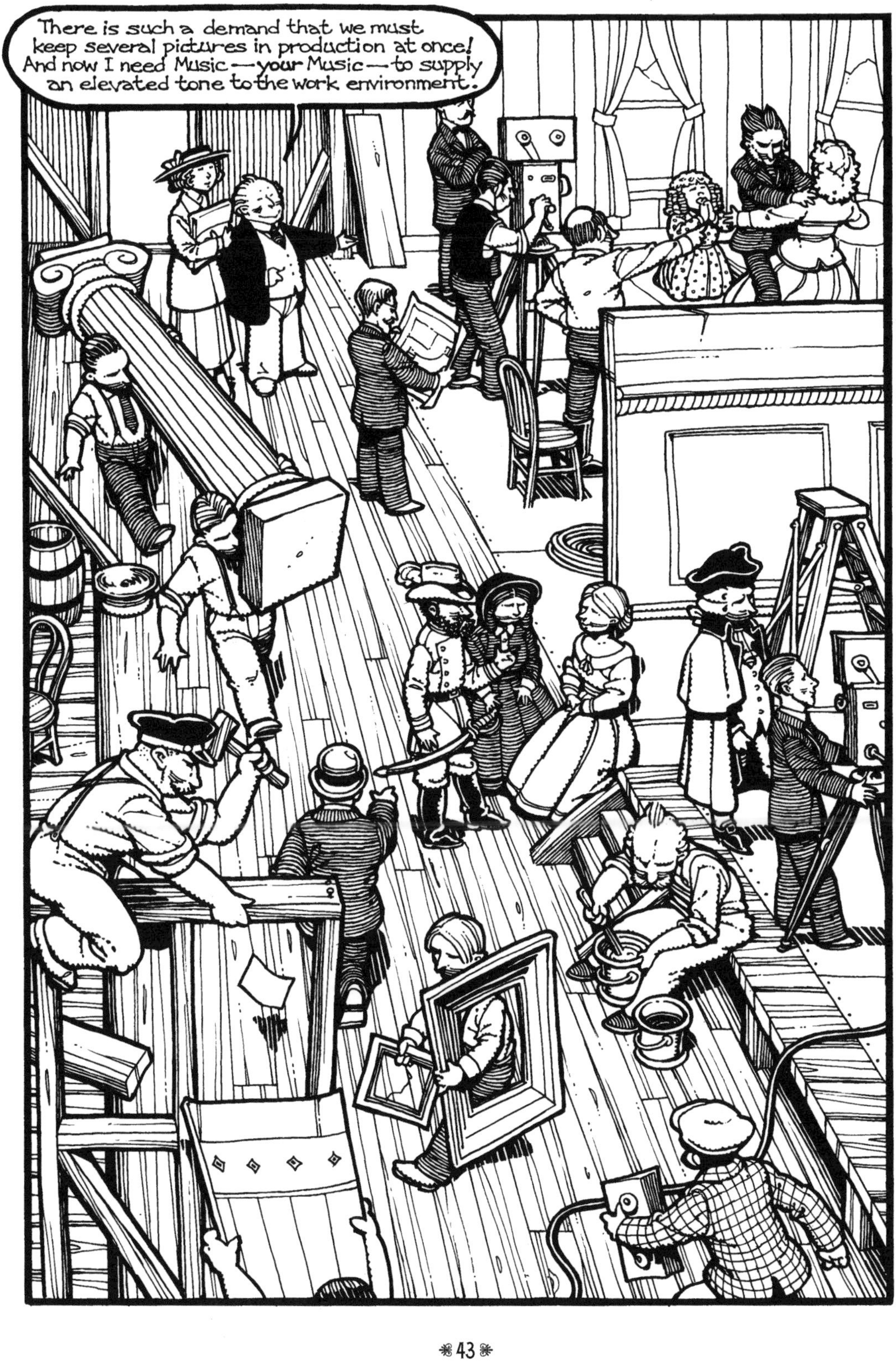
There is such a demand that we must keep several pictures in production at once! And now I need Music — **your** Music — to supply an elevated tone to the work environment.

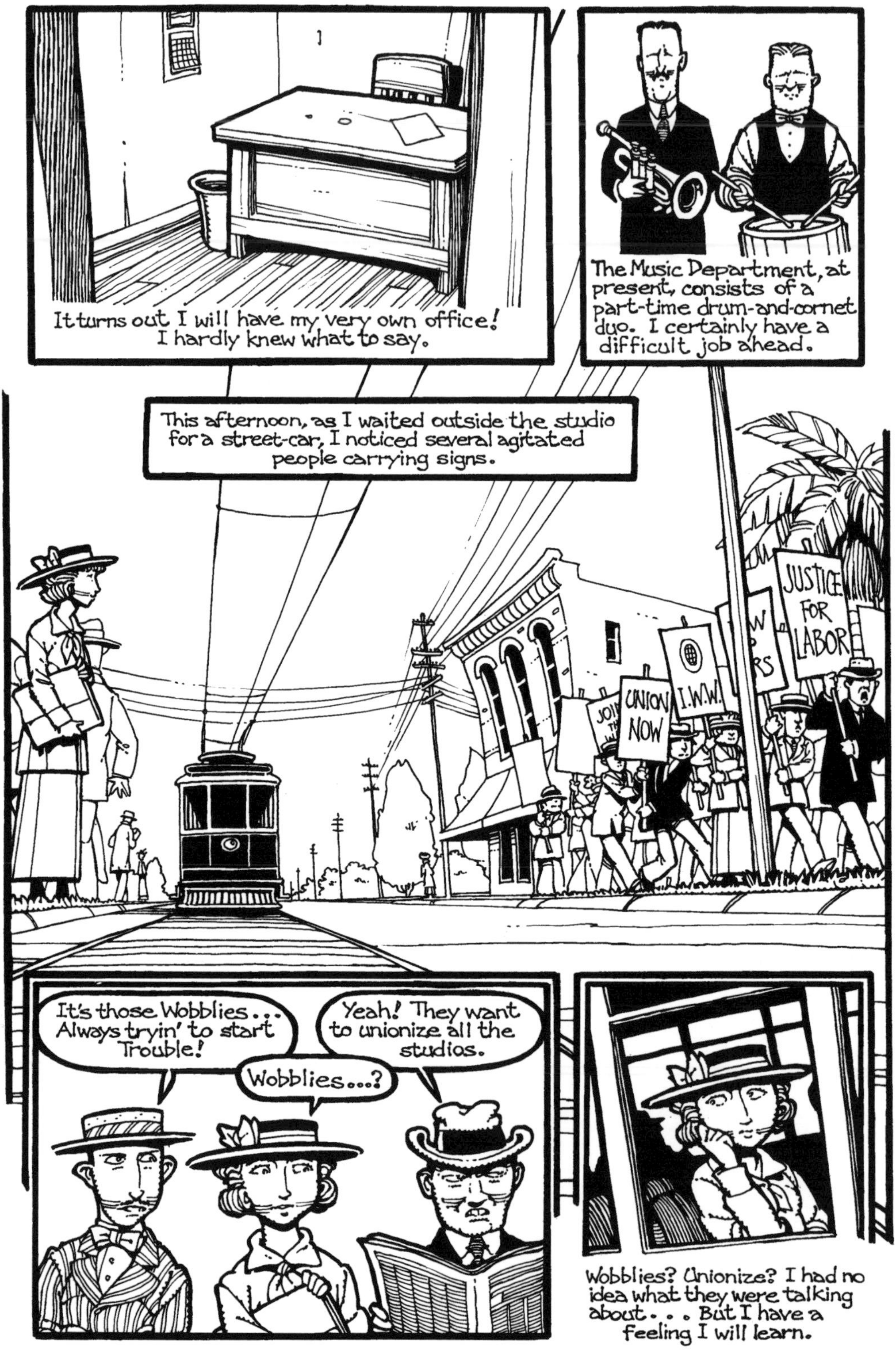
It turns out I will have my very own office! I hardly knew what to say.
The Music Department, at present, consists of a part-time drum-and-cornet duo. I certainly have a difficult job ahead.
This afternoon, as I waited outside the studio for a street-car, I noticed several agitated people carrying signs.
JUSTICE FOR LABOR
I.W.W.
UNION NOW
It's those Wobblies... Always tryin' to start Trouble!
Yeah! They want to unionize all the studios.
Wobblies...?
Wobblies? Unionize? I had no idea what they were talking about... But I have a feeling I will learn.

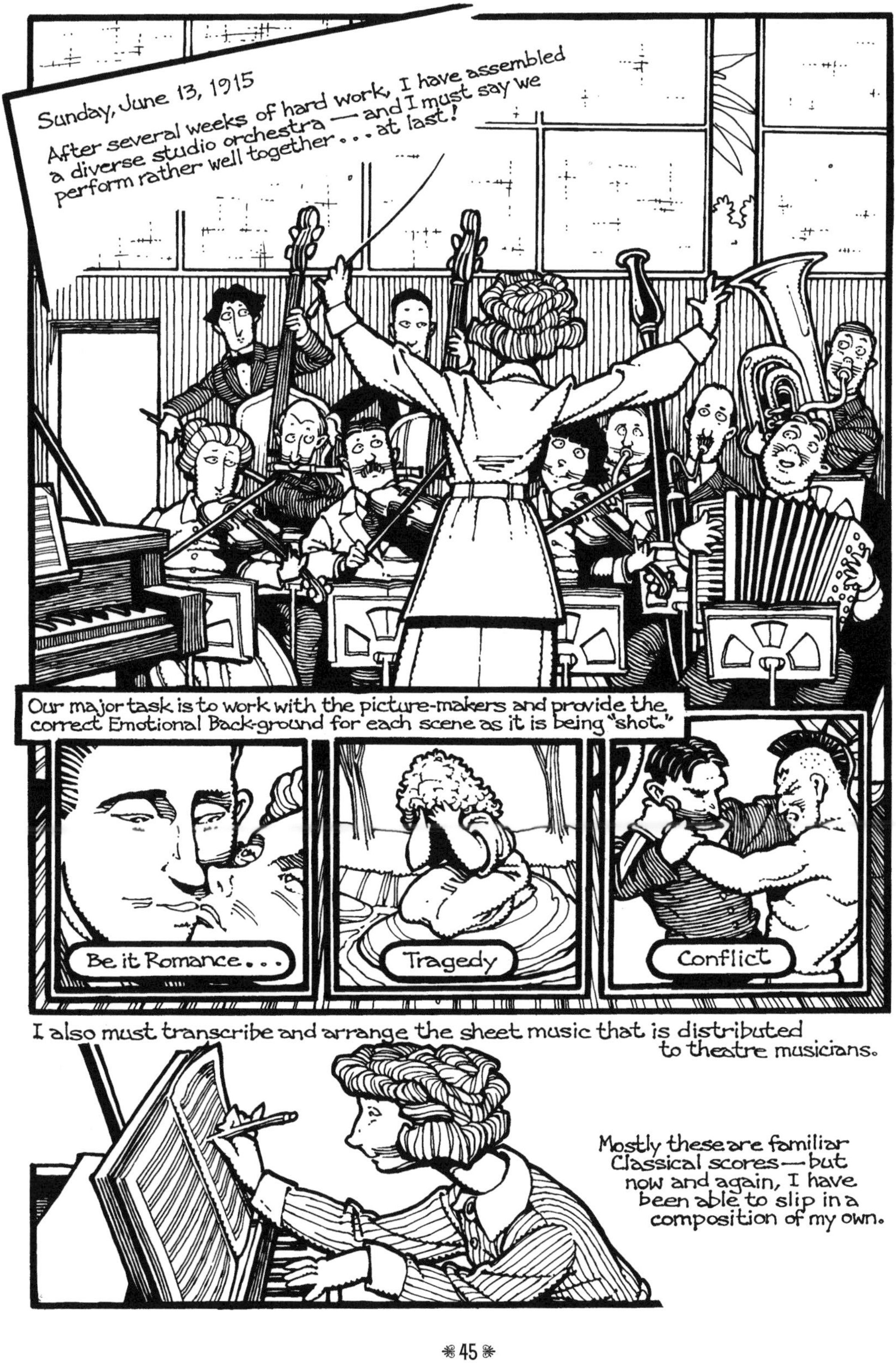
Sunday, June 13, 1915
After several weeks of hard work, I have assembled a diverse studio orchestra — and I must say we perform rather well together . . . at last!
Our major task is to work with the picture-makers and provide the correct Emotional Back-ground for each scene as it is being "shot."
Be it Romance . . .
Tragedy
Conflict
I also must transcribe and arrange the sheet music that is distributed to theatre musicians.
Mostly these are familiar Classical scores — but now and again, I have been able to slip in a composition of my own.

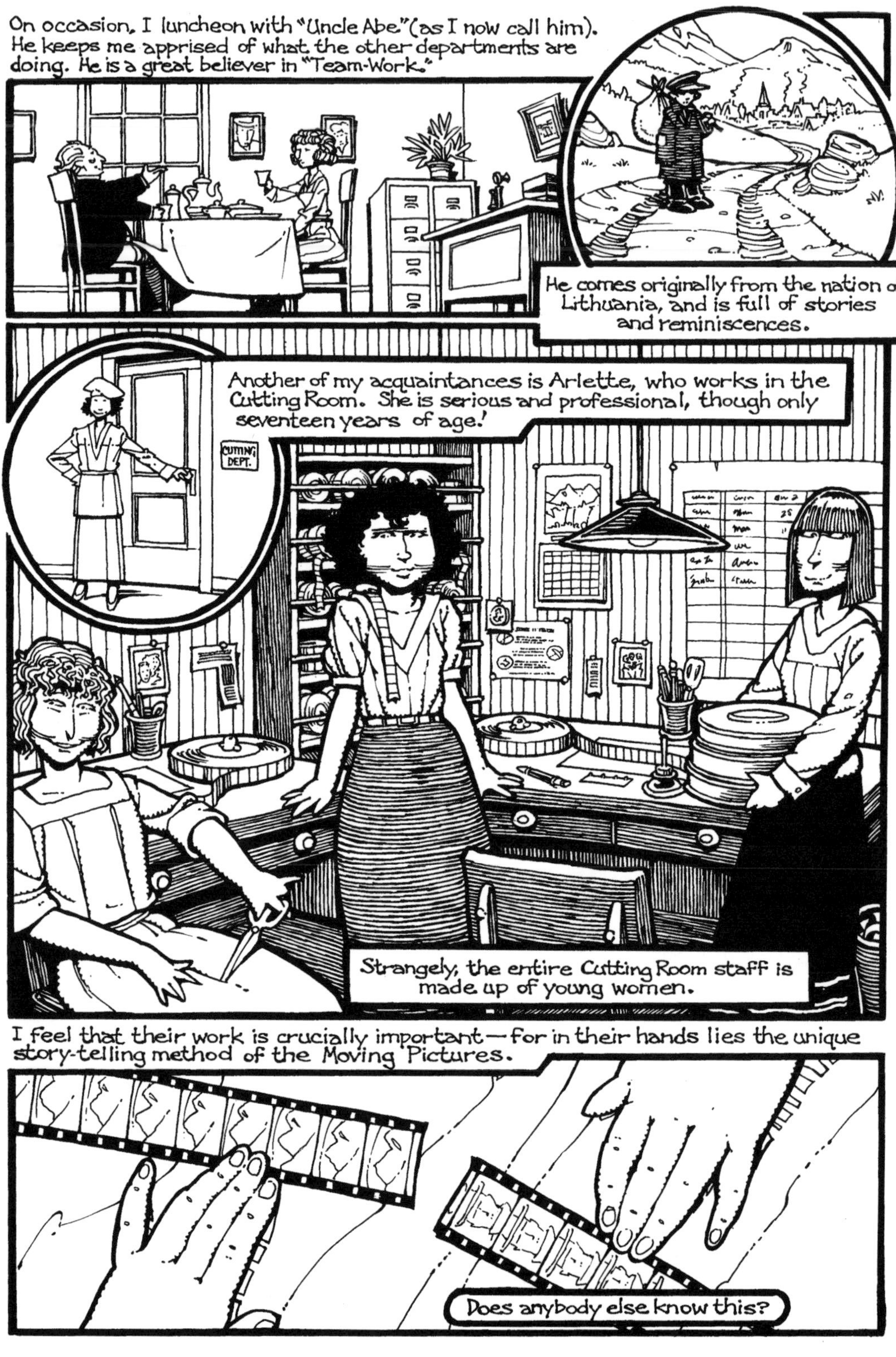
On occasion, I luncheon with "Uncle Abe" (as I now call him). He keeps me apprised of what the other departments are doing. He is a great believer in "Team-Work."
He comes originally from the nation of Lithuania, and is full of stories and reminiscences.
Another of my acquaintances is Arlette, who works in the Cutting Room. She is serious and professional, though only seventeen years of age.
CUTTING DEPT.
Strangely, the entire Cutting Room staff is made up of young women.
I feel that their work is crucially important — for in their hands lies the unique story-telling method of the Moving Pictures.
Does anybody else know this?

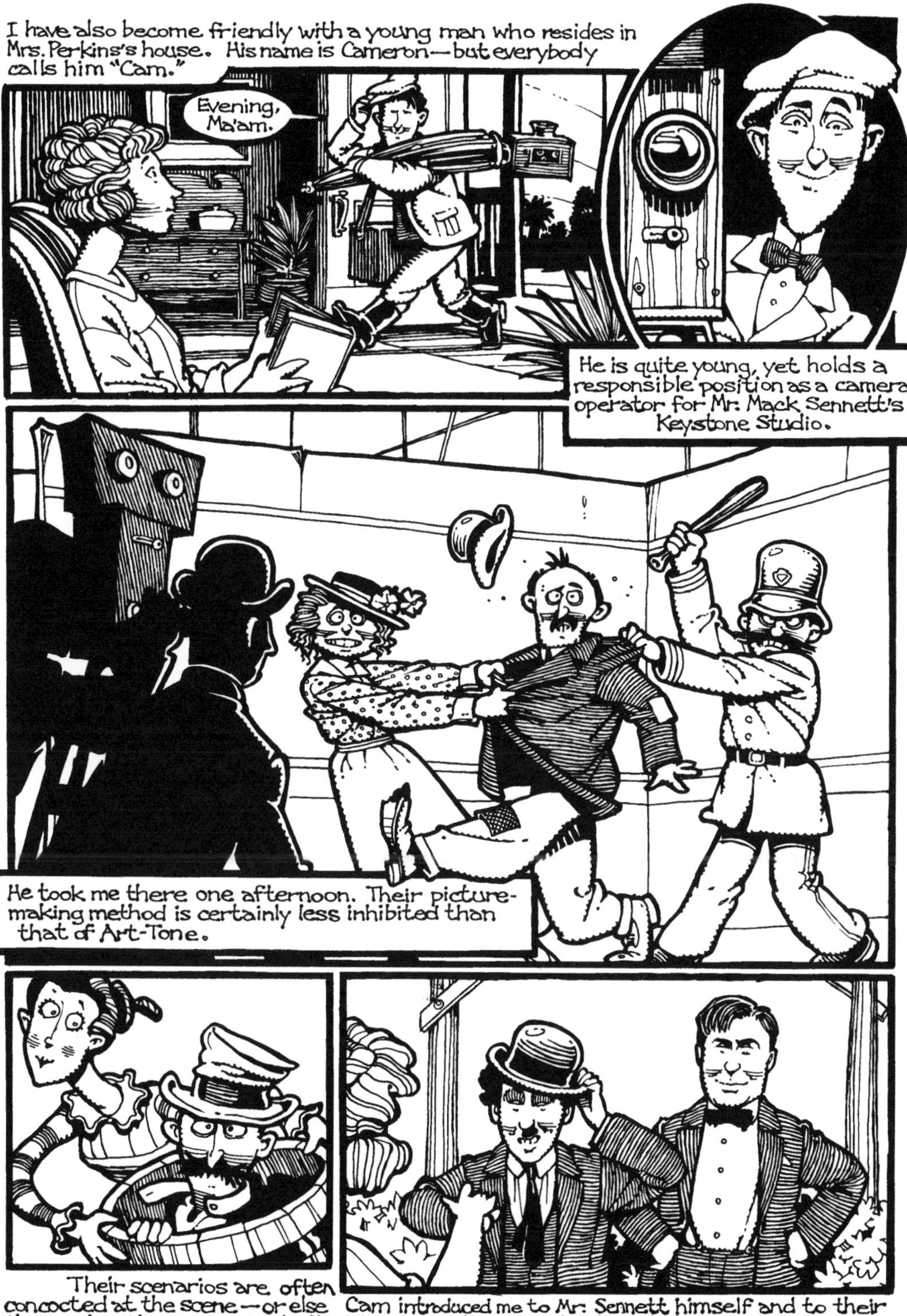
I have also become friendly with a young man who resides in Mrs. Perkins's house. His name is Cameron—but everybody calls him "Cam."
Evening, Ma'am.
He is quite young, yet holds a responsible position as a camera-operator for Mr. Mack Sennett's Keystone Studio.
He took me there one afternoon. Their picture-making method is certainly less inhibited than that of Art-Tone.
Their scenarios are often concocted at the scene—or else they work with no scenario at all! (Uncle Abe turns up his nose at this.)
Cam introduced me to Mr. Sennett himself and to their Star comedian, Mr. Chaplin, whom, I'm told, is very popular with picture-goers.

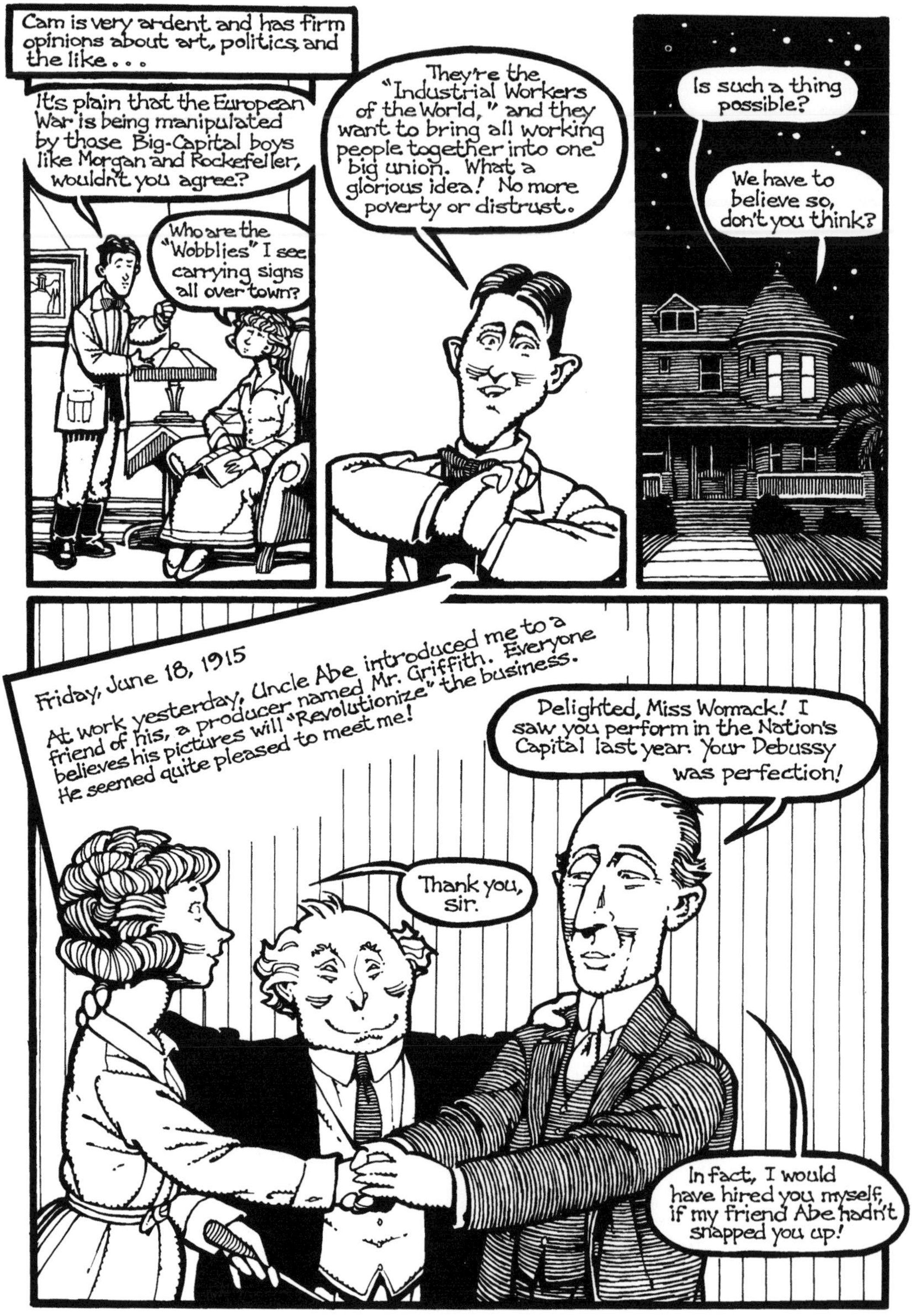
Cam is very ardent and has firm opinions about art, politics, and the like . . .
It's plain that the European War is being manipulated by those Big-Capital boys like Morgan and Rockefeller, wouldn't you agree?
Who are the "Wobblies" I see carrying signs all over town?
They're the "Industrial Workers of the World," and they want to bring all working people together into one big union. What a glorious idea! No more poverty or distrust.
Is such a thing possible?
We have to believe so, don't you think?
Friday, June 18, 1915
At work yesterday, Uncle Abe introduced me to a friend of his, a producer named Mr. Griffith. Everyone believes his pictures will "Revolutionize" the business. He seemed quite pleased to meet me!
Delighted, Miss Womack! I saw you perform in the Nation's Capital last year. Your Debussy was perfection!
Thank you, sir.
In fact, I would have hired you myself, if my friend Abe hadn't snapped you up!

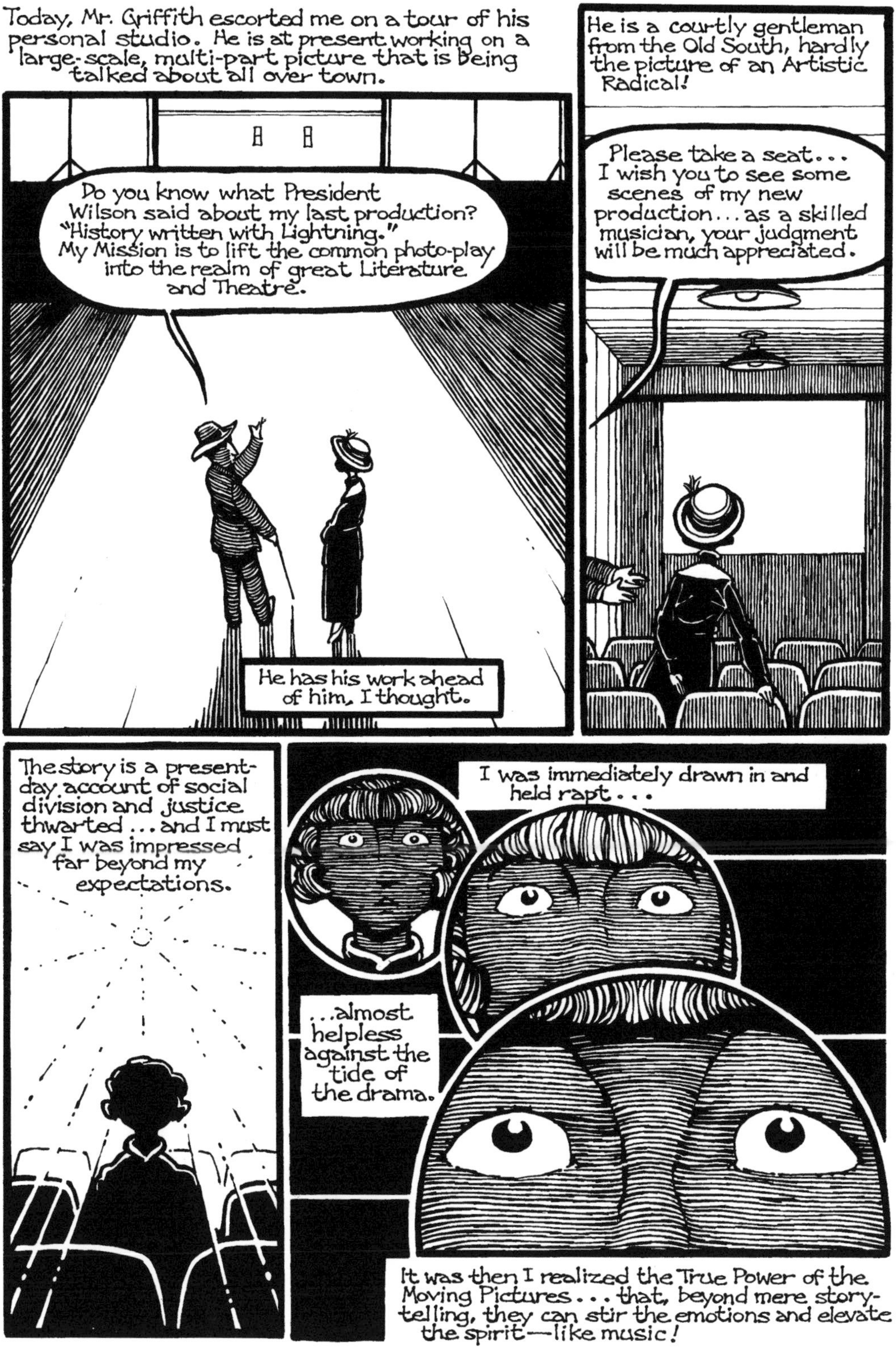
Today, Mr. Griffith escorted me on a tour of his personal studio. He is at present working on a large-scale, multi-part picture that is being talked about all over town.
Do you know what President Wilson said about my last production? "History written with Lightning." My Mission is to lift the common photo-play into the realm of great Literature and Theatre.
He has his work ahead of him, I thought.
He is a courtly gentleman from the Old South, hardly the picture of an Artistic Radical!
Please take a seat... I wish you to see some scenes of my new production... as a skilled musician, your judgment will be much appreciated.
The story is a present-day account of social division and justice thwarted ... and I must say I was impressed far beyond my expectations.
I was immediately drawn in and held rapt...
...almost helpless against the tide of the drama.
It was then I realized the True Power of the Moving Pictures... that, beyond mere story-telling, they can stir the emotions and elevate the spirit—like music!

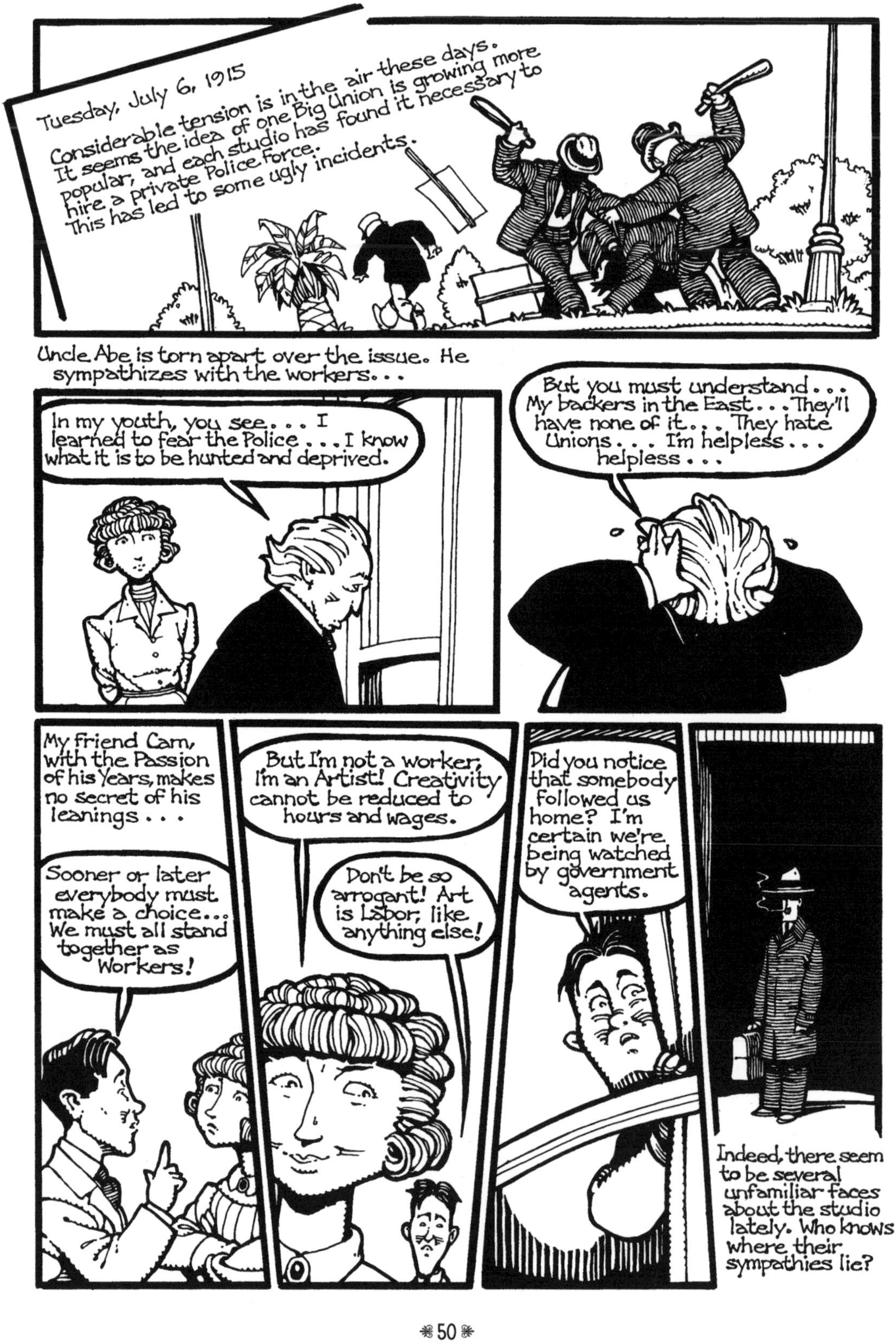
Tuesday, July 6, 1915
Considerable tension is in the air these days. It seems the idea of one Big Union is growing more popular, and each studio has found it necessary to hire a private Police force. This has led to some ugly incidents.
Uncle Abe is torn apart over the issue. He sympathizes with the workers...
In my youth, you see... I learned to fear the Police ...I know what it is to be hunted and deprived.
But you must understand... My backers in the East... They'll have none of it... They hate Unions... I'm helpless... helpless...
My friend Cam, with the Passion of his Years, makes no secret of his leanings...
Sooner or later everybody must make a choice... We must all stand together as Workers!
But I'm not a worker, I'm an Artist! Creativity cannot be reduced to hours and wages.
Don't be so arrogant! Art is Labor, like anything else!
Did you notice that somebody followed us home? I'm certain we're being watched by government agents.
Indeed, there seem to be several unfamiliar faces about the studio lately. Who knows where their sympathies lie?

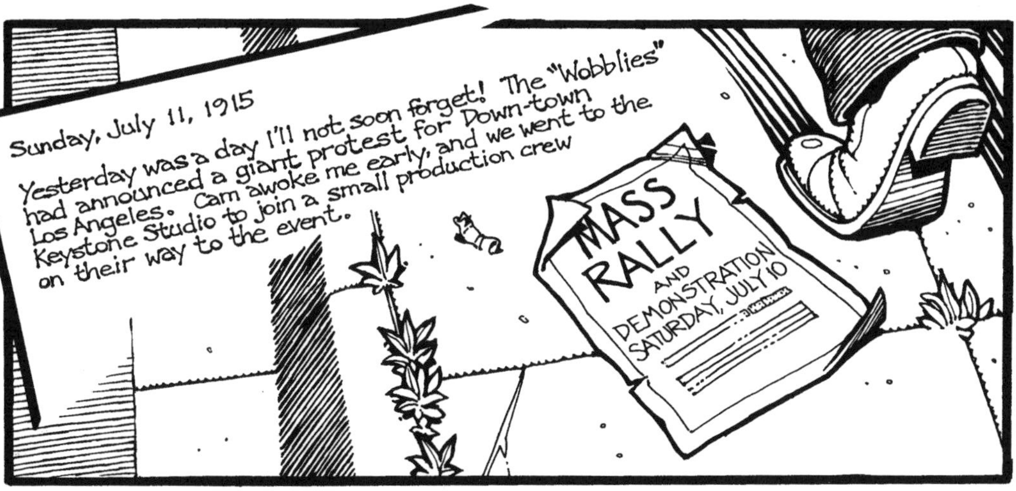
Sunday, July 11, 1915
Yesterday was a day I'll not soon forget! The "Wobblies" had announced a giant protest for Down-town Los Angeles. Cam awoke me early, and we went to the Keystone Studio to join a small production crew on their way to the event.
MASS RALLY AND DEMONSTRATION SATURDAY, JULY 10

Their scheme was to use the actual demonstration as background for a comedy scenario!

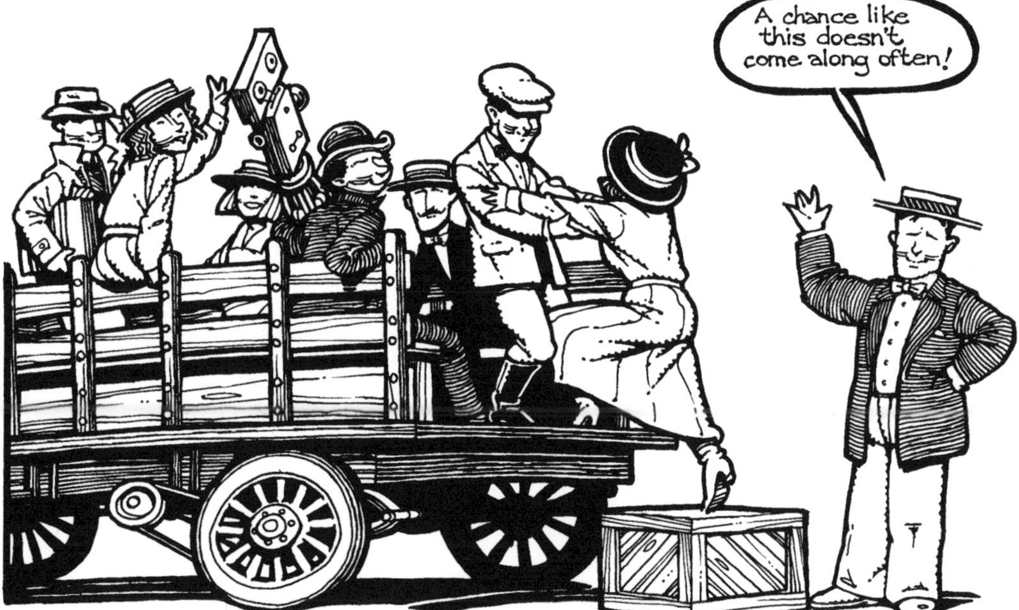
A chance like this doesn't come along often!

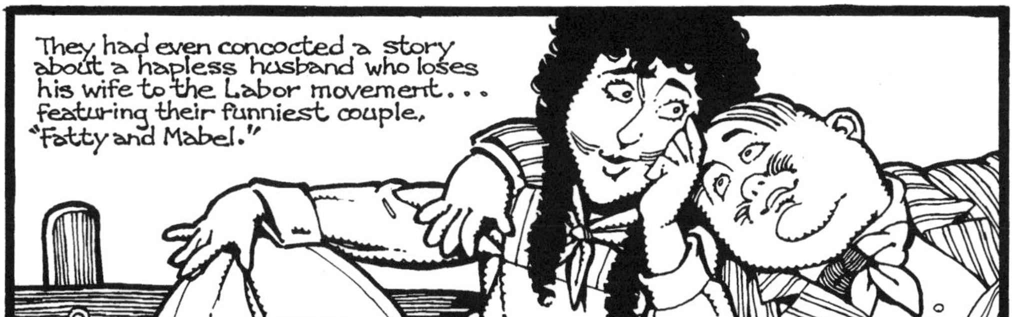
They had even concocted a story about a hapless husband who loses his wife to the Labor movement... featuring their funniest couple, "Fatty and Mabel."

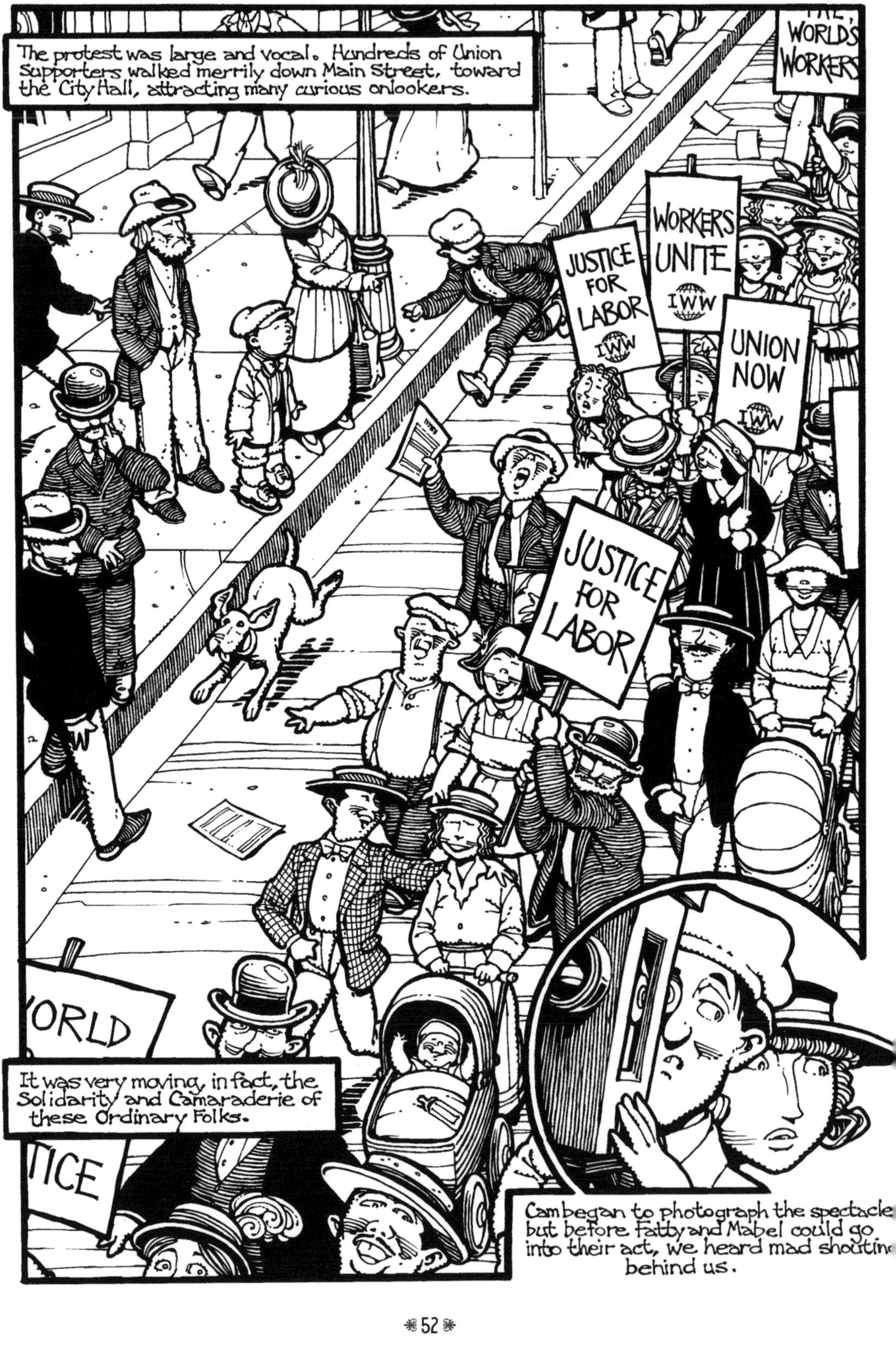

The protest was large and vocal. Hundreds of Union Supporters walked merrily down Main Street, toward the City Hall, attracting many curious onlookers.
WORLD'S WORKERS
WORKERS UNITE IWW
JUSTICE FOR LABOR IWW
UNION NOW IWW
JUSTICE FOR LABOR
ORLD
It was very moving, in fact, the Solidarity and Camaraderie of these Ordinary Folks.
TICE
Cam began to photograph the spectacle but before Fatty and Mabel could go into their act, we heard mad shouting behind us.

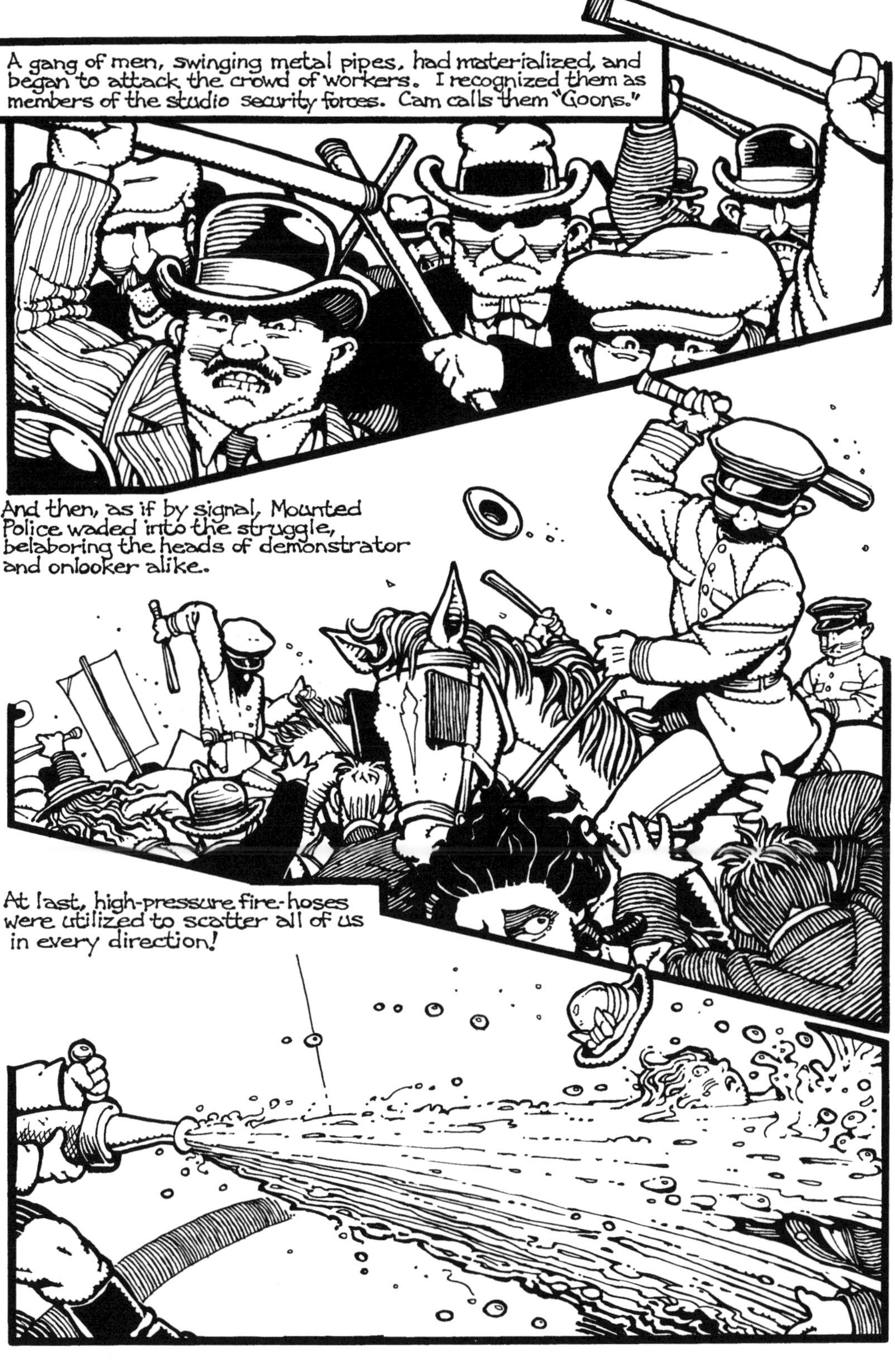
A gang of men, swinging metal pipes, had materialized, and began to attack the crowd of workers. I recognized them as members of the studio security forces. Cam calls them "Goons."
And then, as if by signal, Mounted Police waded into the struggle, belaboring the heads of demonstrator and onlooker alike.
At last, high-pressure fire-hoses were utilized to scatter all of us in every direction!

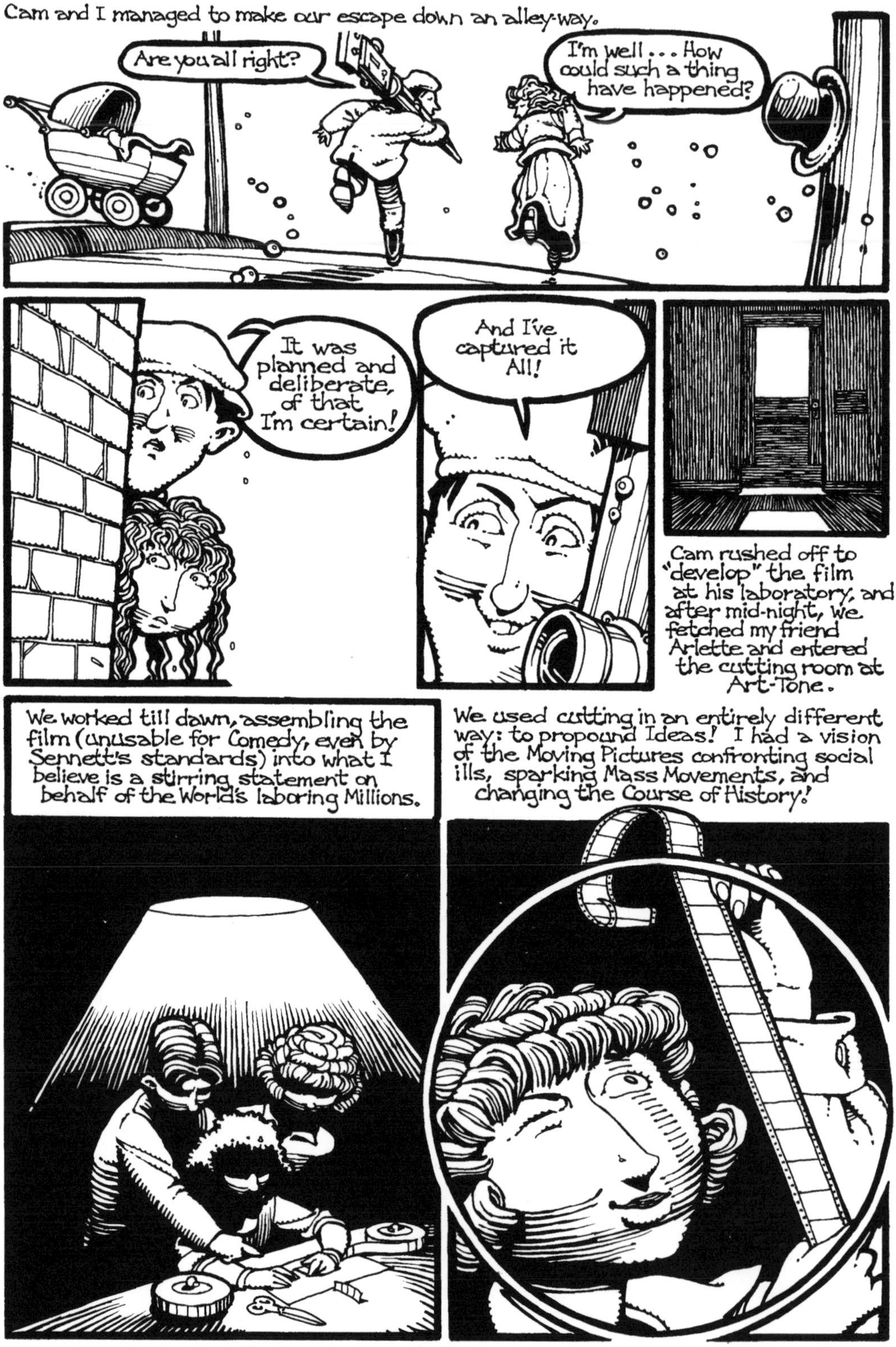
Cam and I managed to make our escape down an alley-way.
Are you all right?
I'm well . . . How could such a thing have happened?
It was planned and deliberate, of that I'm certain!
And I've captured it All!
Cam rushed off to "develop" the film at his laboratory, and after mid-night, we fetched my friend Arlette and entered the cutting room at Art-Tone.
We worked till dawn, assembling the film (unusable for Comedy, even by Sennett's standards) into what I believe is a stirring statement on behalf of the World's laboring Millions.
We used cutting in an entirely different way: to propound Ideas! I had a vision of the Moving Pictures confronting social ills, sparking Mass Movements, and changing the Course of History!

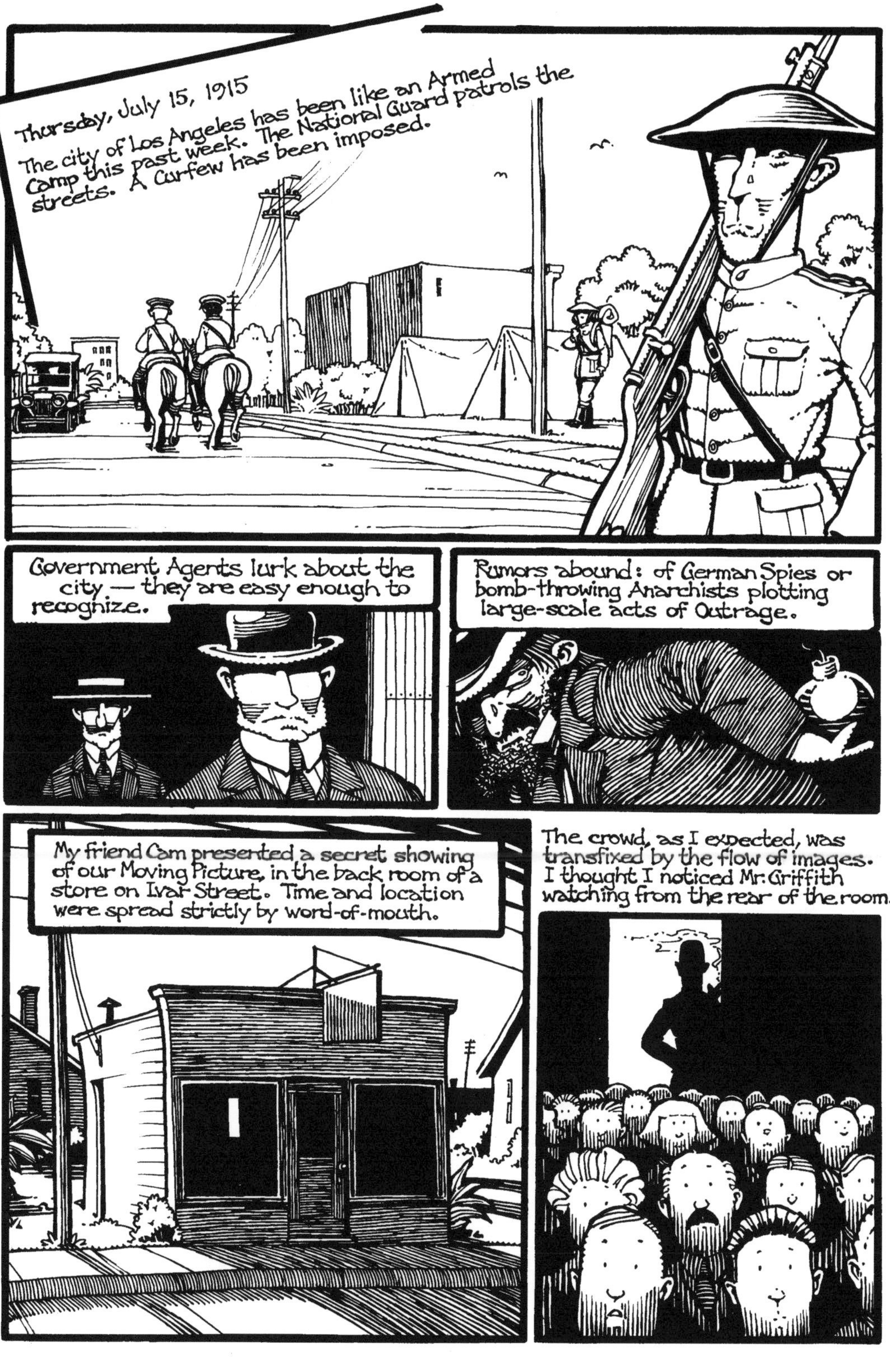
Thursday, July 15, 1915
The city of Los Angeles has been like an Armed Camp this past week. The National Guard patrols the streets. A Curfew has been imposed.
Government Agents lurk about the city — they are easy enough to recognize.
Rumors abound: of German Spies or bomb-throwing Anarchists plotting large-scale acts of Outrage.
My friend Cam presented a secret showing of our Moving Picture, in the back room of a store on Ivar Street. Time and location were spread strictly by word-of-mouth.
The crowd, as I expected, was transfixed by the flow of images. I thought I noticed Mr. Griffith watching from the rear of the room.

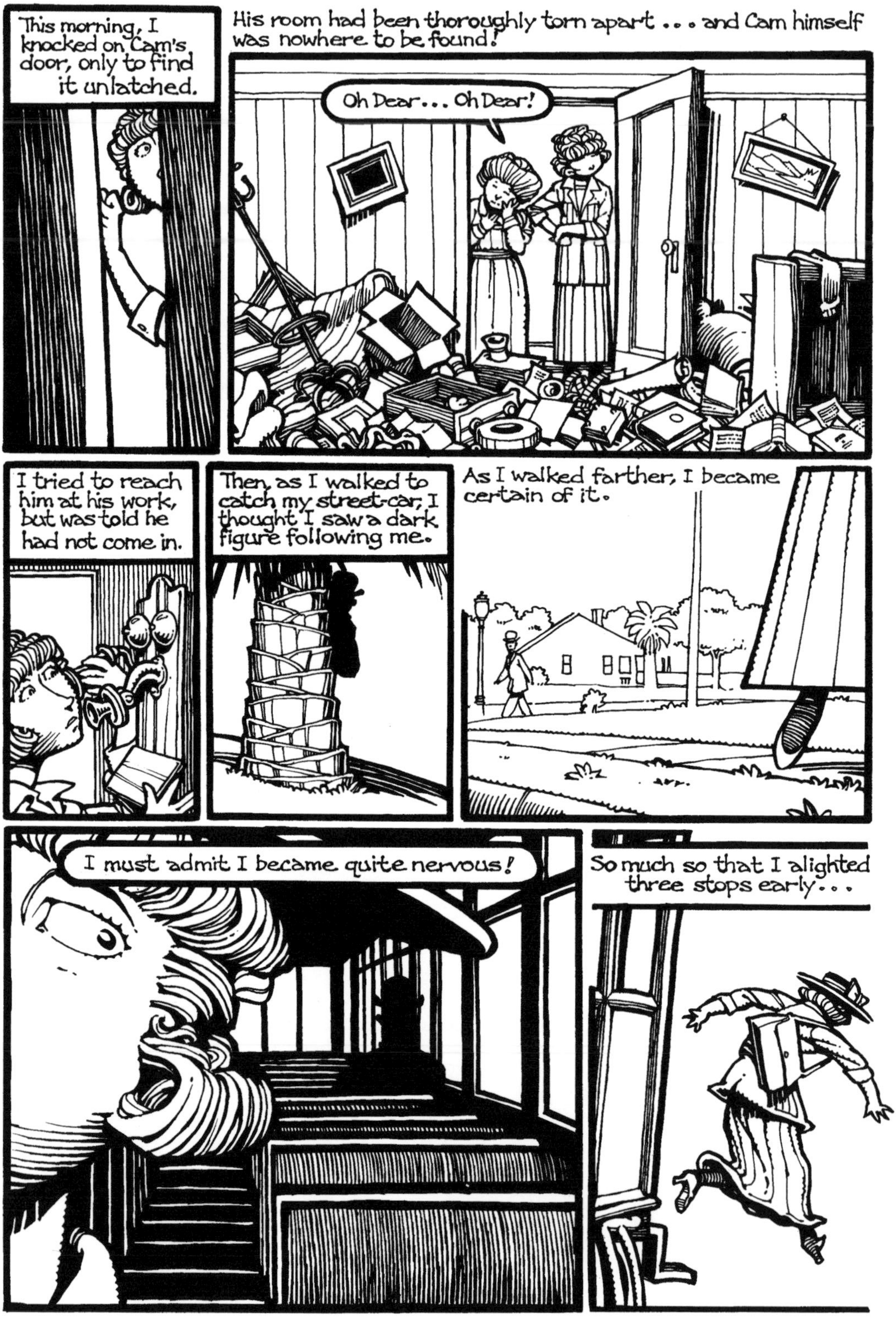
This morning, I knocked on Cam's door, only to find it unlatched.
His room had been thoroughly torn apart . . . and Cam himself was nowhere to be found!
Oh Dear . . . Oh Dear!
I tried to reach him at his work, but was told he had not come in.
Then, as I walked to catch my street-car, I thought I saw a dark figure following me.
As I walked farther, I became certain of it.
I must admit I became quite nervous!
So much so that I alighted three stops early . . .

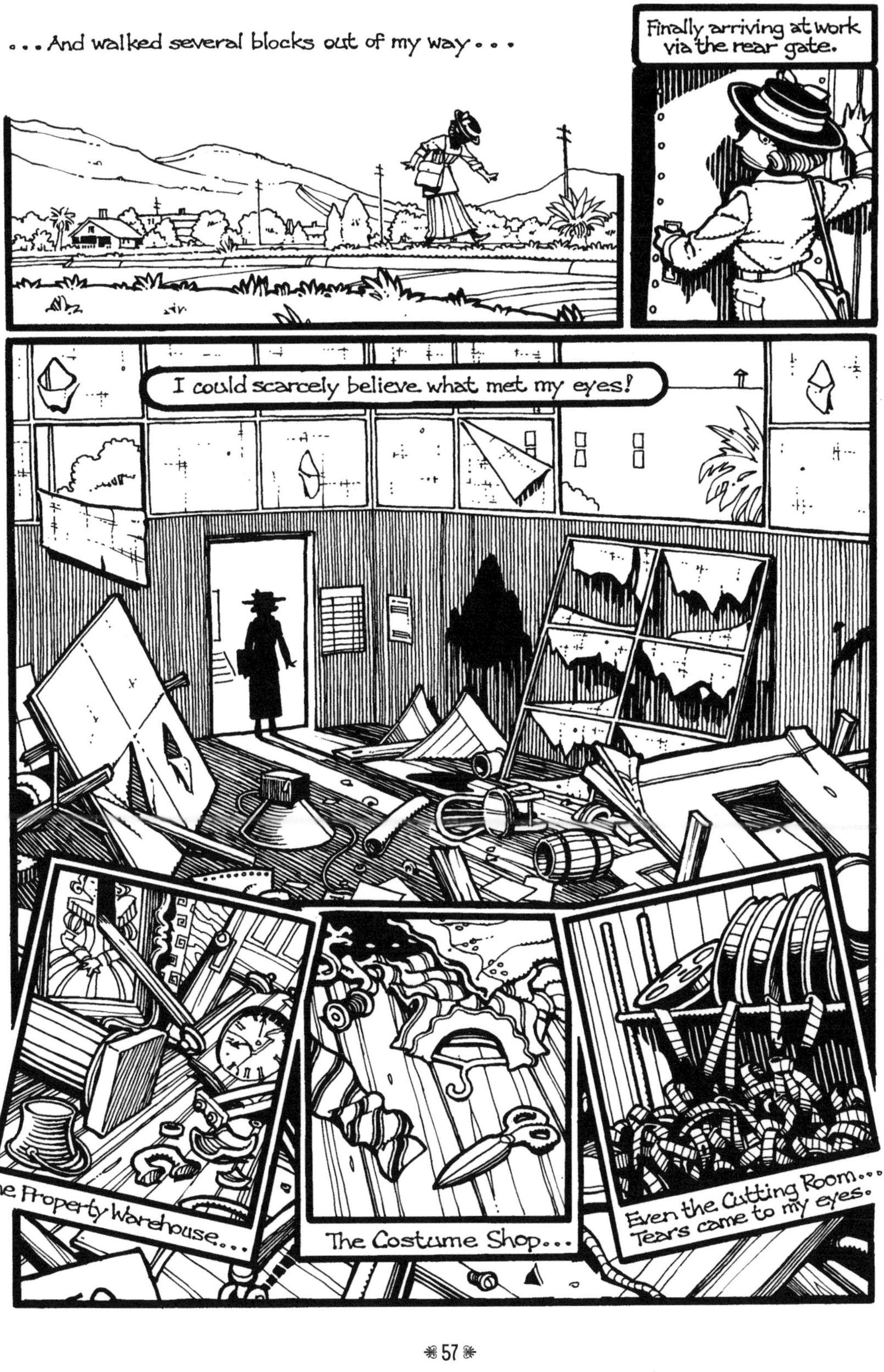
...And walked several blocks out of my way...
Finally arriving at work via the rear gate.
I could scarcely believe what met my eyes!
The Property Warehouse...
The Costume Shop...
Even the Cutting Room...
Tears came to my eyes.

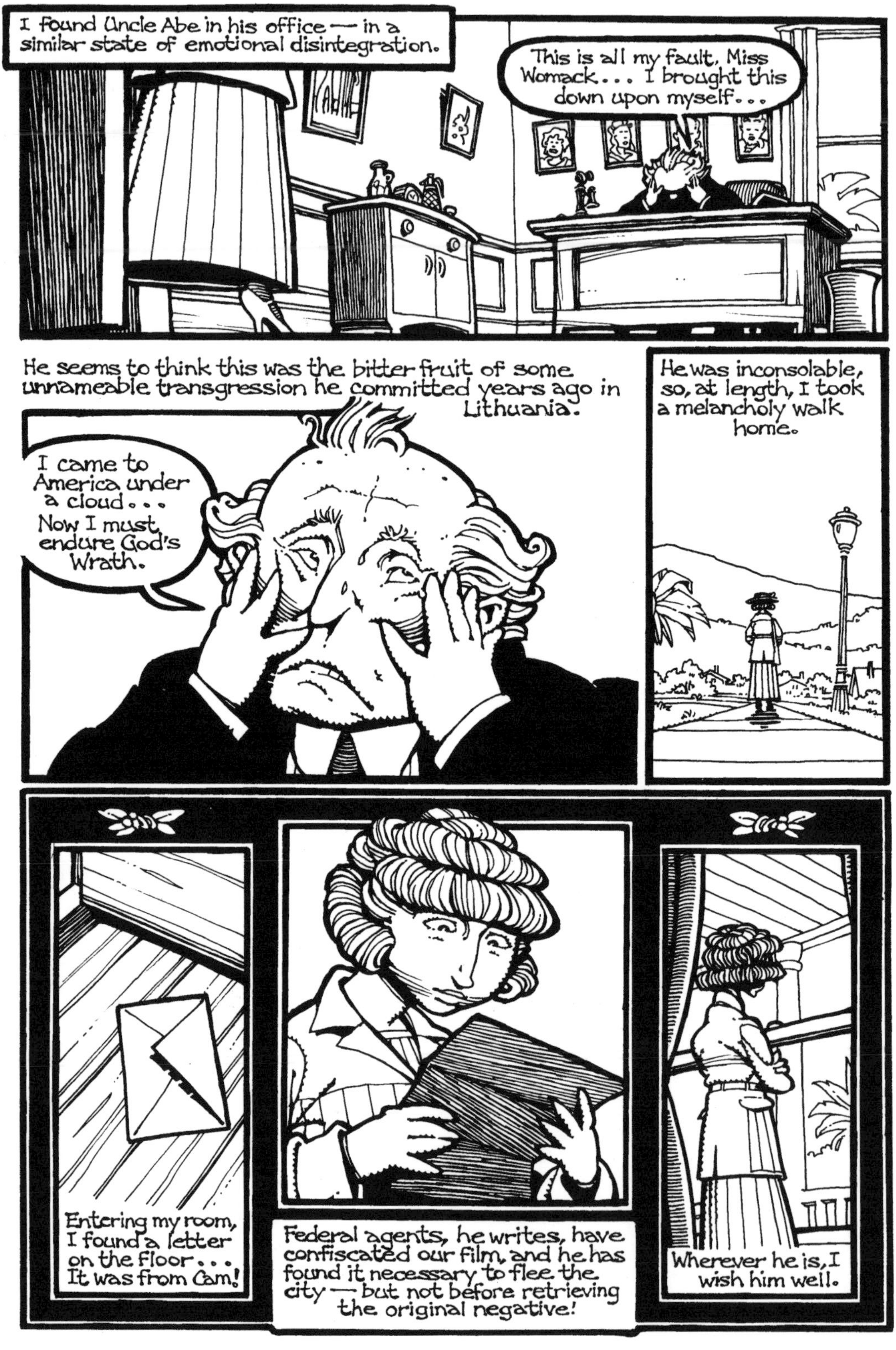
I found Uncle Abe in his office — in a similar state of emotional disintegration.
This is all my fault, Miss Womack... I brought this down upon myself...
He seems to think this was the bitter fruit of some unnameable transgression he committed years ago in Lithuania.
I came to America under a cloud... Now I must endure God's Wrath.
He was inconsolable, so, at length, I took a melancholy walk home.
Entering my room, I found a letter on the floor... It was from Cam!
Federal agents, he writes, have confiscated our film, and he has found it necessary to flee the city — but not before retrieving the original negative!
Wherever he is, I wish him well.

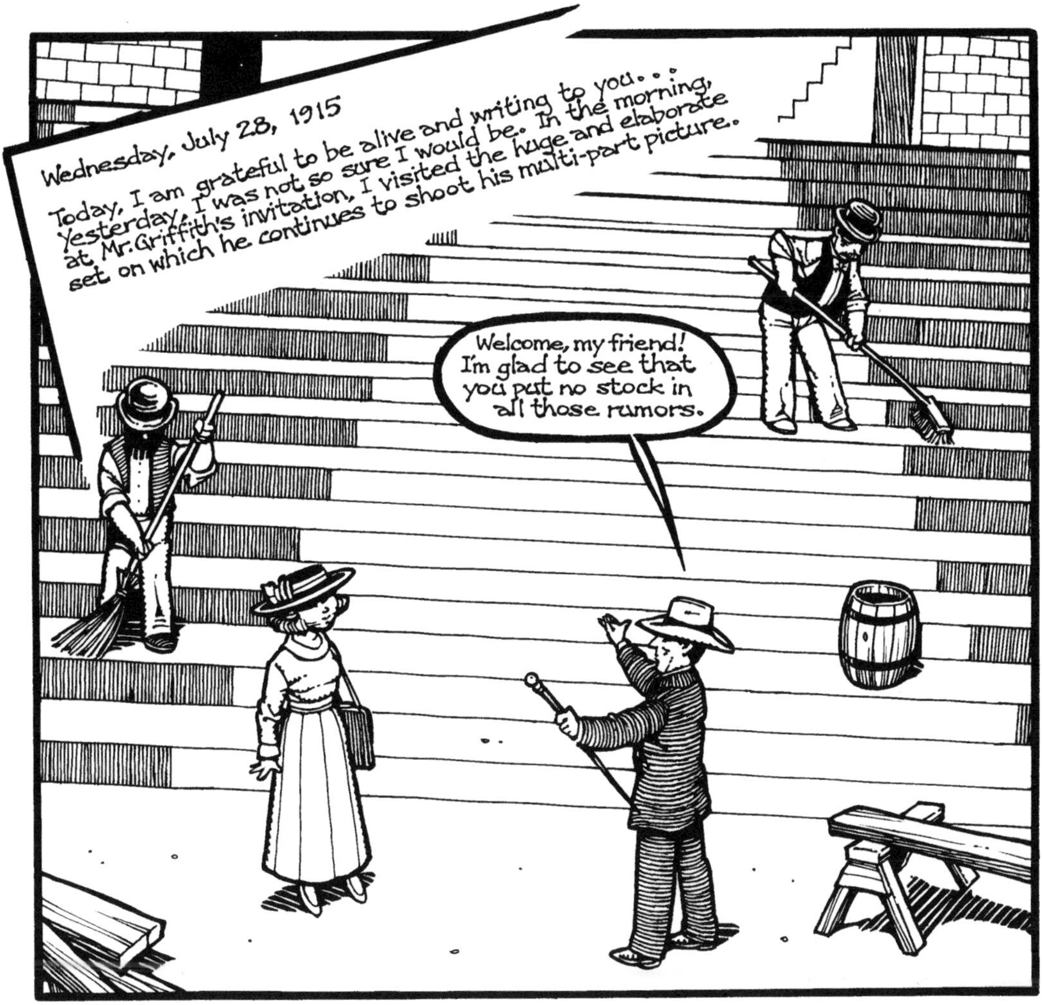
Wednesday, July 28, 1915
Today, I am grateful to be alive and writing to you... Yesterday, I was not so sure I would be. In the morning, at Mr. Griffith's invitation, I visited the huge and elaborate set on which he continues to shoot his multi-part picture.
Welcome, my friend! I'm glad to see that you put no stock in all those rumors.

Since the Outrage at Art-Tone, the town has been heavy with the expectation of further sabotage. Mr. Griffith appears especially vulnerable because of the Pacifist sentiments of this new picture... to be titled "Intolerance."

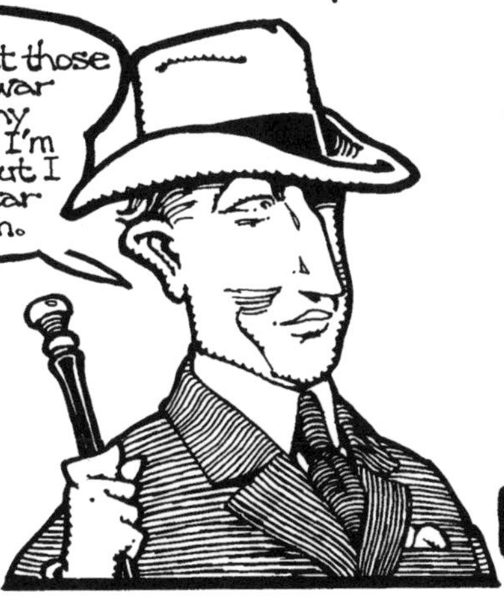
It seems that those who wish a war with Germany dislike what I'm doing... But I have no fear of them.

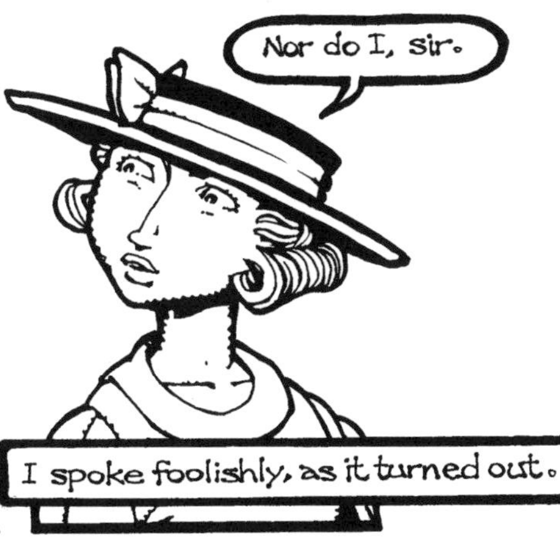
Nor do I, sir.
I spoke foolishly, as it turned out.

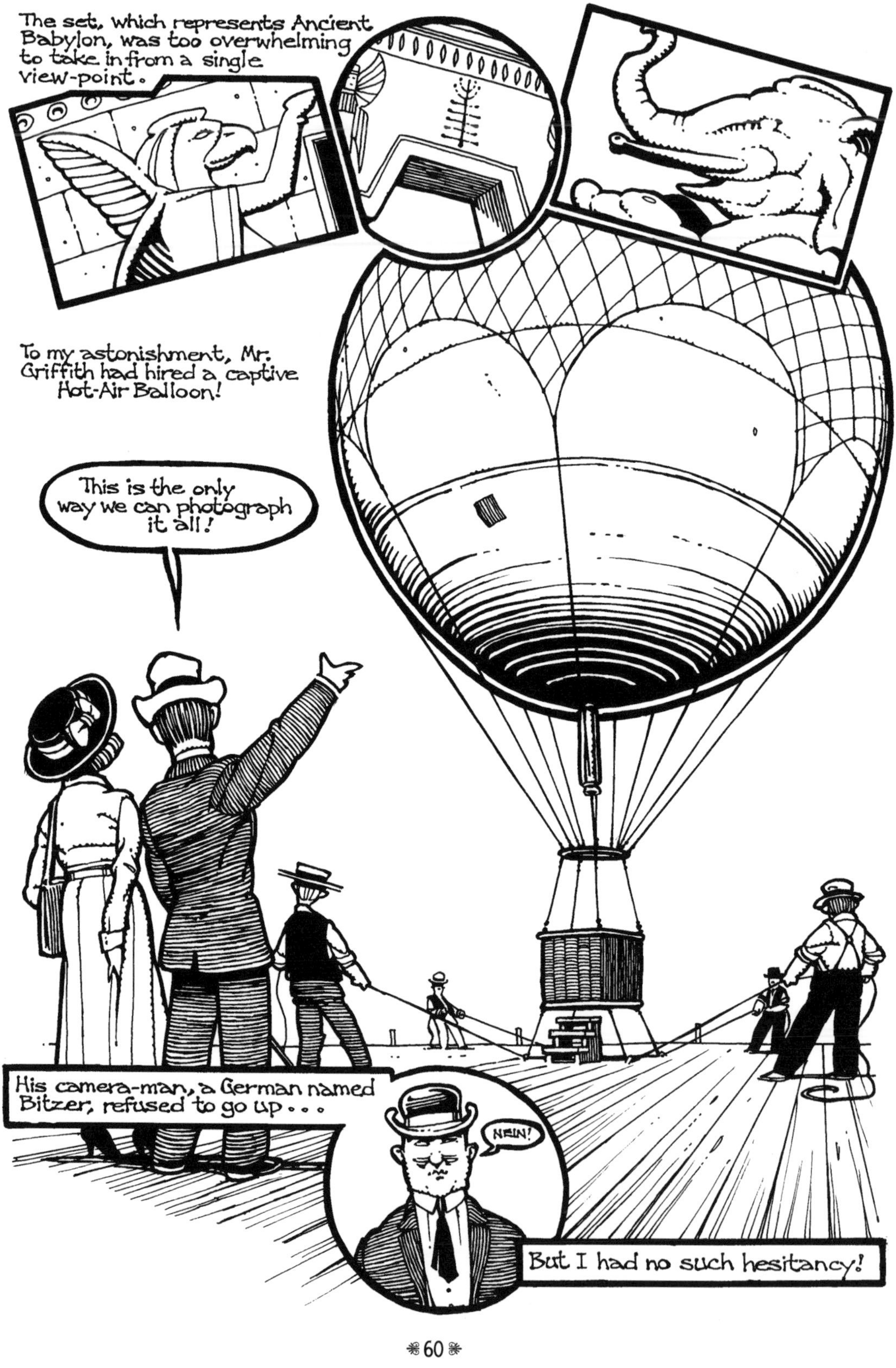

The set, which represents Ancient Babylon, was too overwhelming to take in from a single view-point.
To my astonishment, Mr. Griffith had hired a captive Hot-Air Balloon!
This is the only way we can photograph it all!
His camera-man, a German named Bitzer, refused to go up . . .
NEIN!
But I had no such hesitancy!

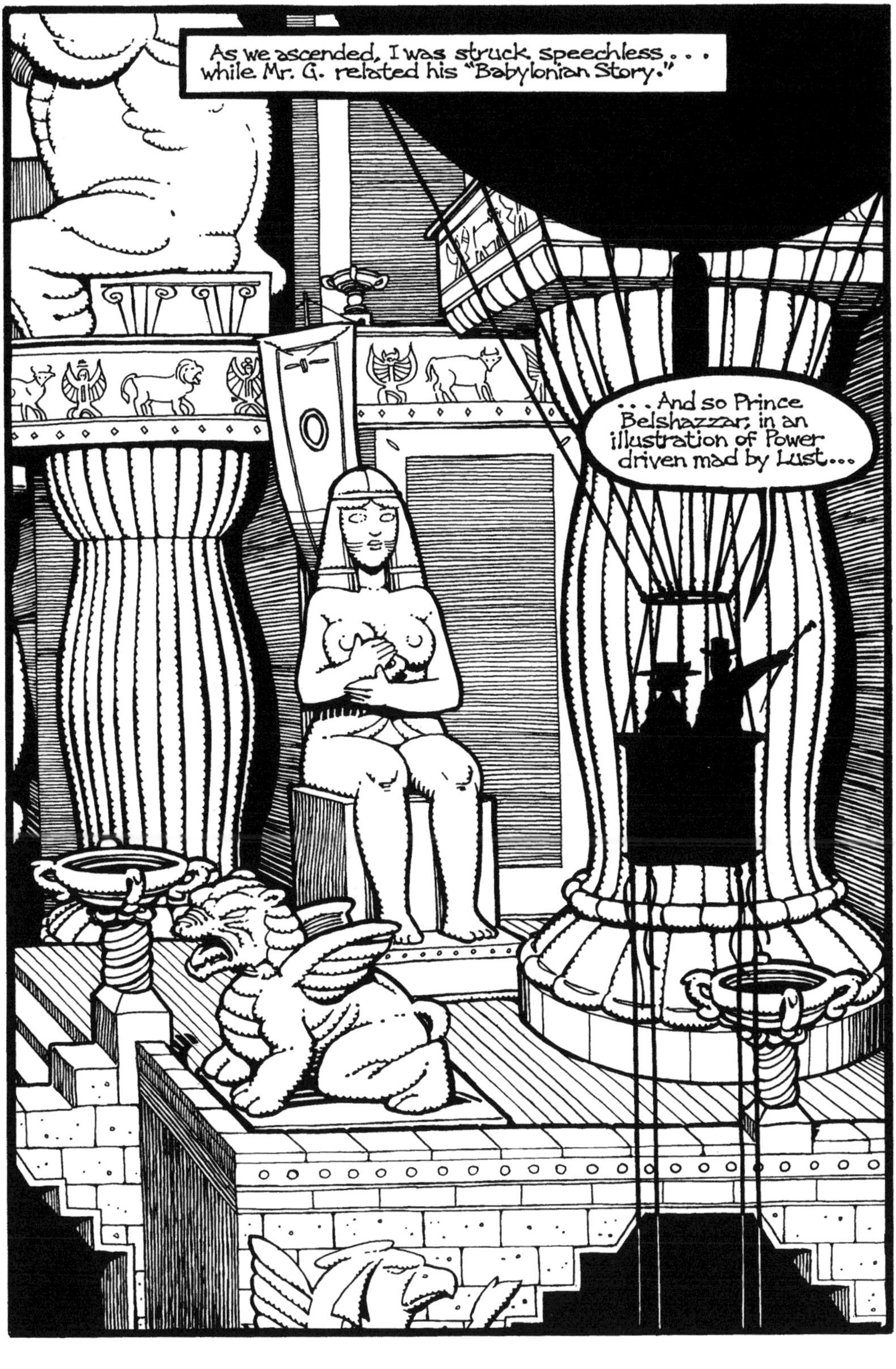
As we ascended, I was struck speechless . . . while Mr. G. related his "Babylonian Story."
. . . And so Prince Belshazzar, in an illustration of Power driven mad by Lust . . .

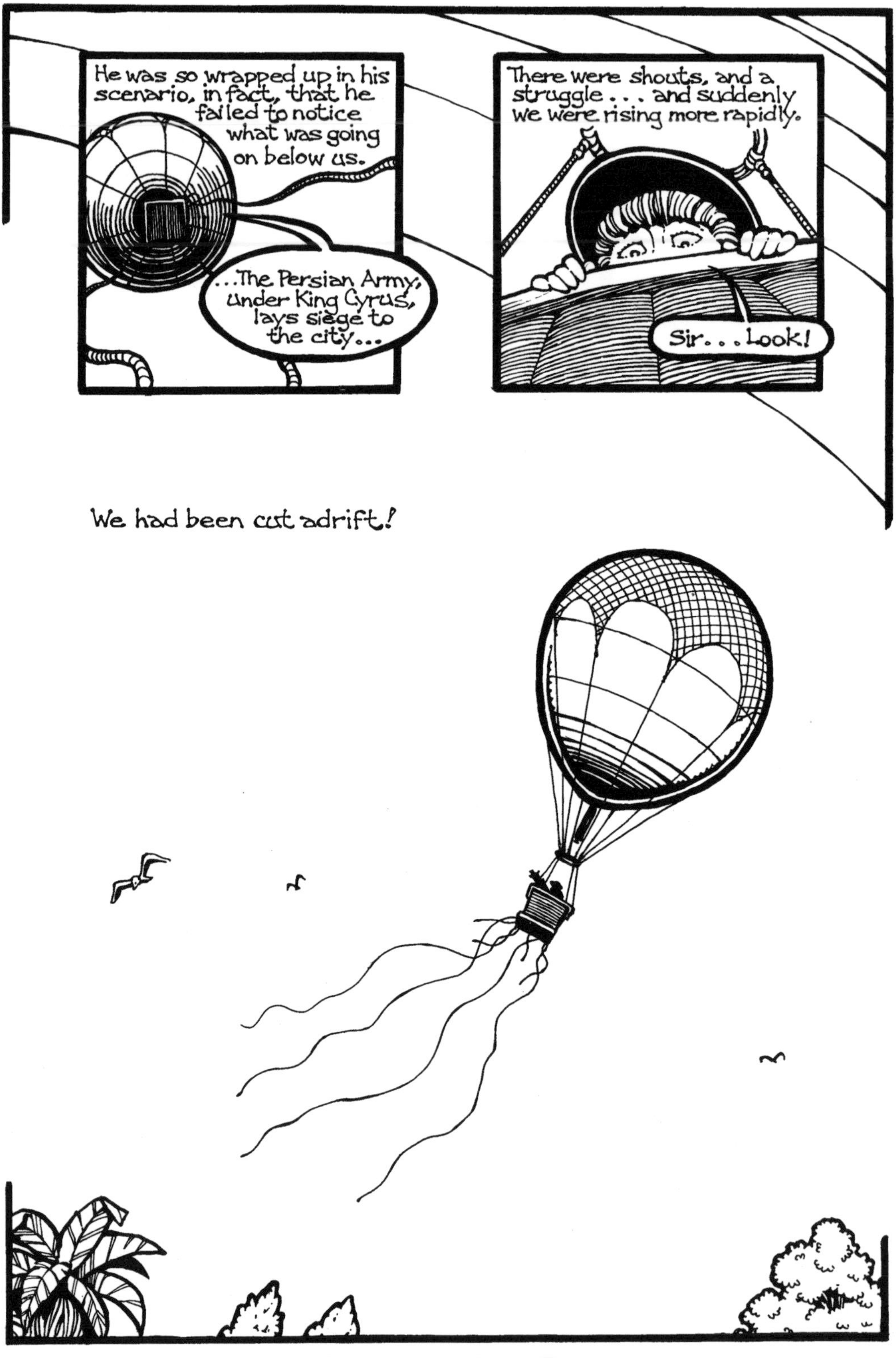

He was so wrapped up in his scenario, in fact, that he failed to notice what was going on below us.
...The Persian Army, under King Cyrus, lays siege to the city...
There were shouts, and a struggle . . . and suddenly we were rising more rapidly.
Sir. . . Look!
We had been cut adrift!

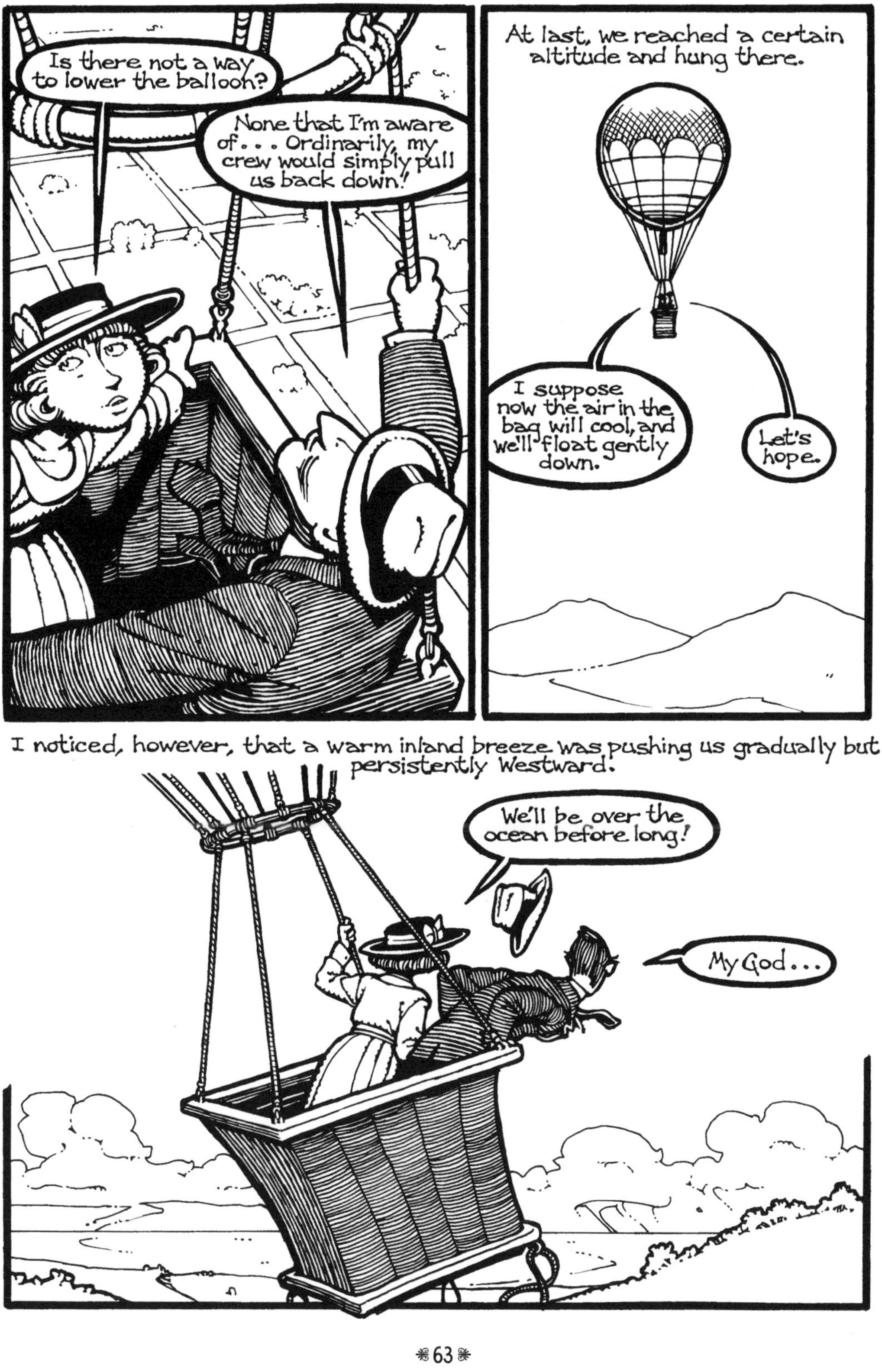
Is there not a way to lower the balloon?
None that I'm aware of . . . Ordinarily, my crew would simply pull us back down!
At last, we reached a certain altitude and hung there.
I suppose now the air in the bag will cool, and we'll float gently down.
Let's hope.
I noticed, however, that a warm inland breeze was pushing us gradually but persistently Westward.
We'll be over the ocean before long!
My God . . .

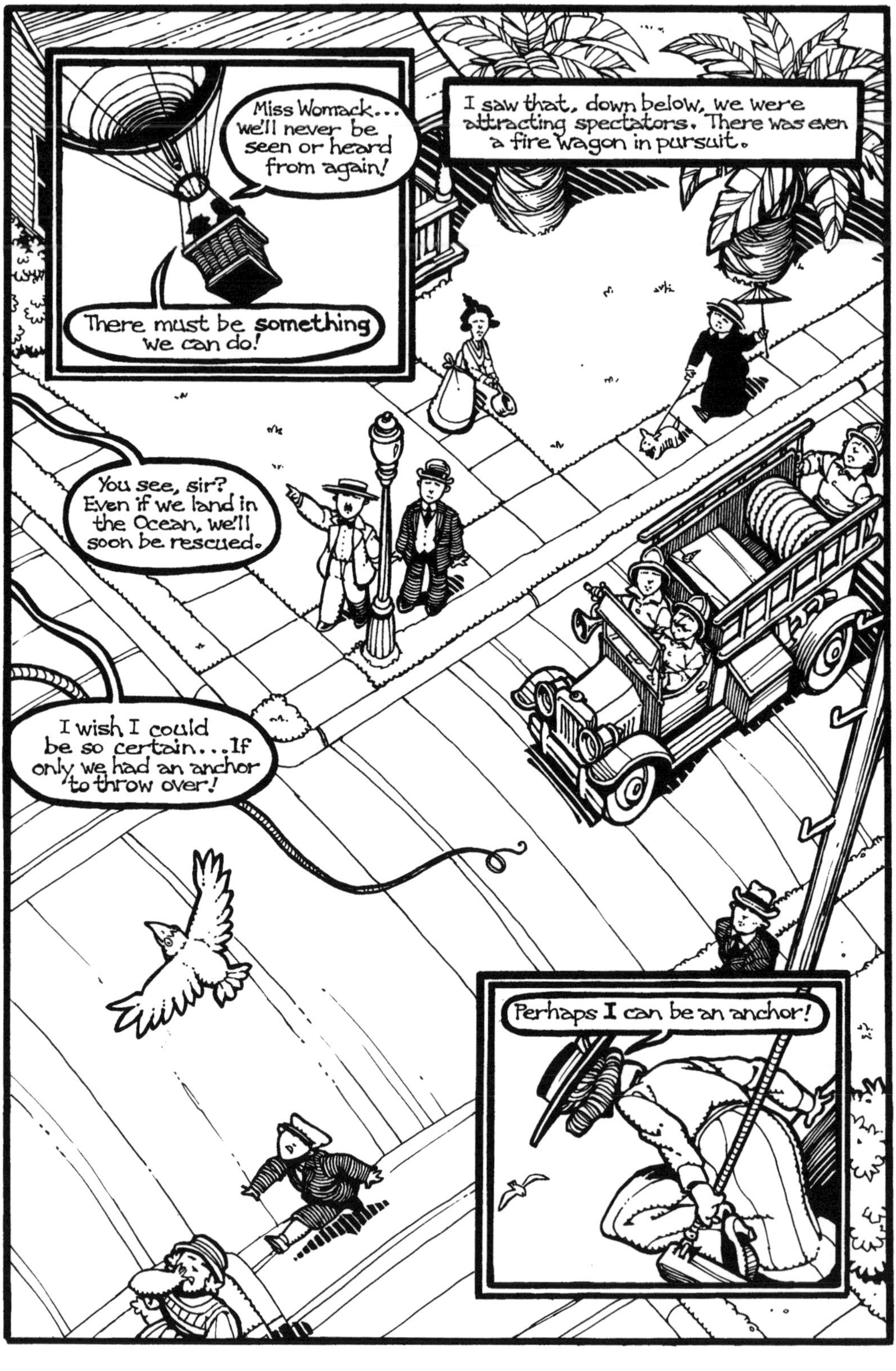
Miss Womack... we'll never be seen or heard from again!
There must be something we can do!
I saw that, down below, we were attracting spectators. There was even a fire wagon in pursuit.
You see, sir? Even if we land in the Ocean, we'll soon be rescued.
I wish I could be so certain...If only we had an anchor to throw over!
Perhaps I can be an anchor!

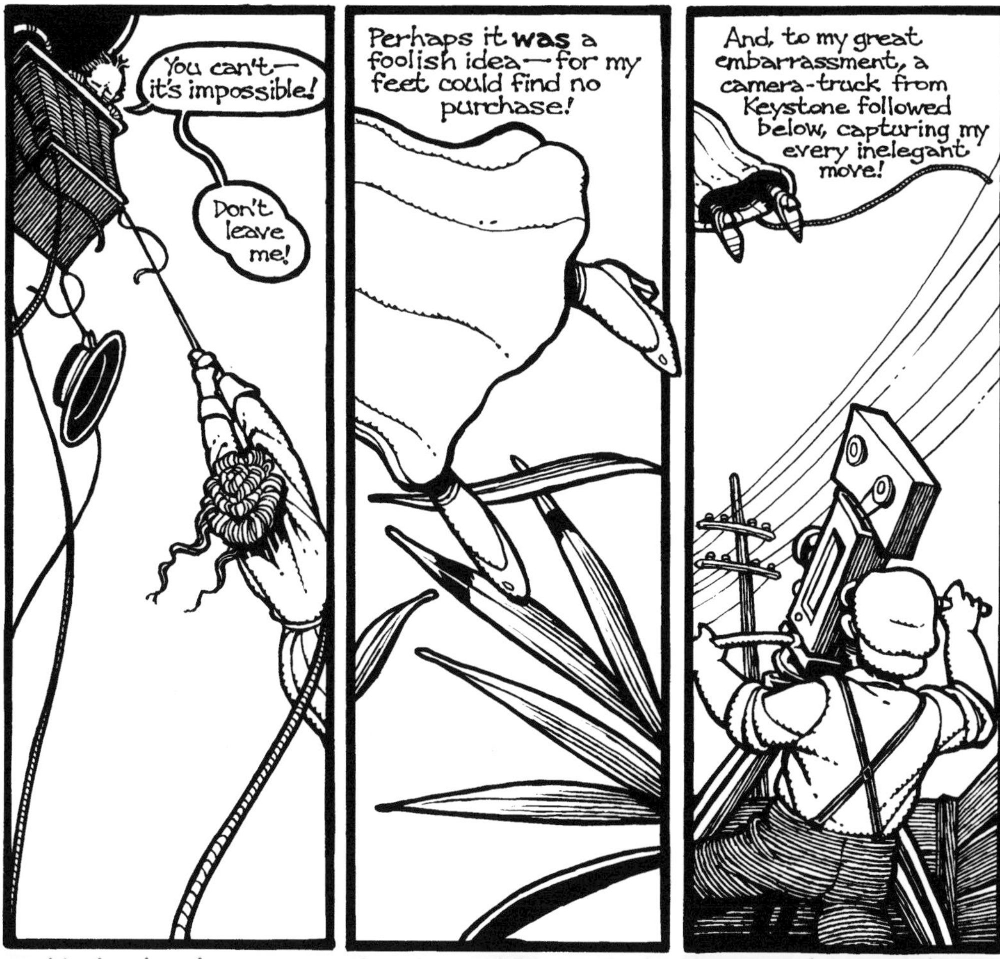
You can't— it's impossible!
Don't leave me!
Perhaps it **was** a foolish idea—for my feet could find no purchase!
And, to my great embarrassment, a camera-truck from Keystone followed below, capturing my every inelegant move!

Suddenly ahead of us were the steep cliffs of Santa-Monica and, beyond them, the Limitless Pacific.

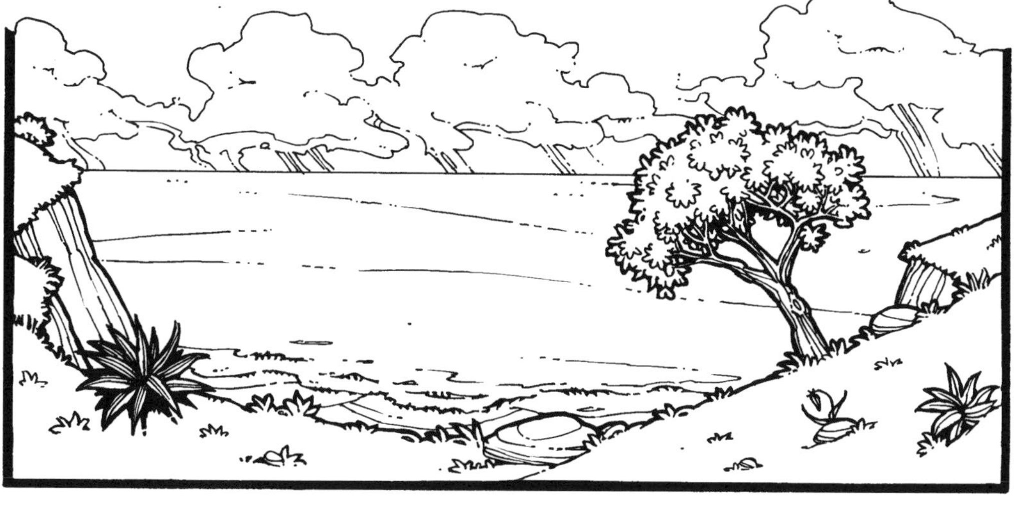

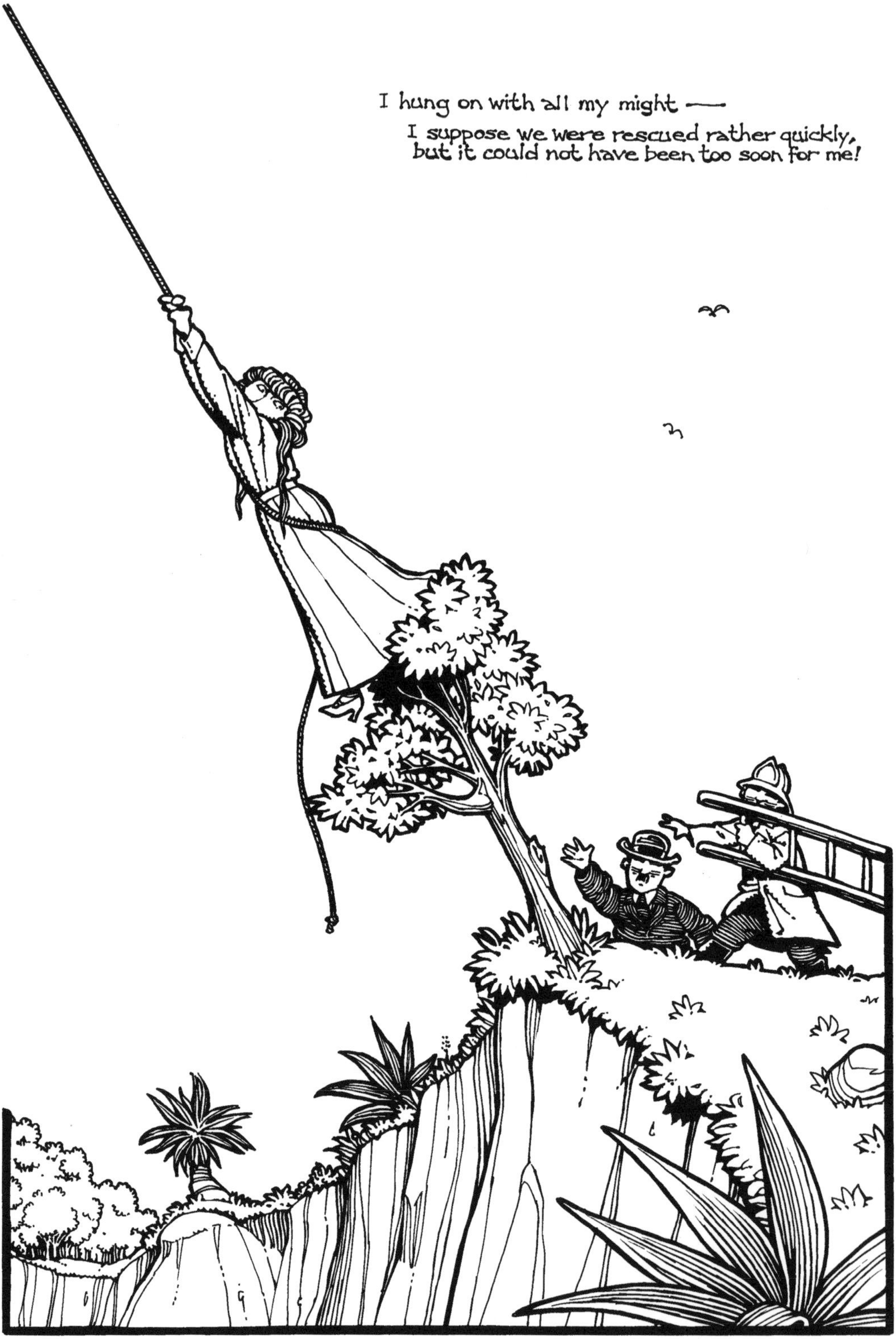
I hung on with all my might ——
I suppose we were rescued rather quickly, but it could not have been too soon for me!

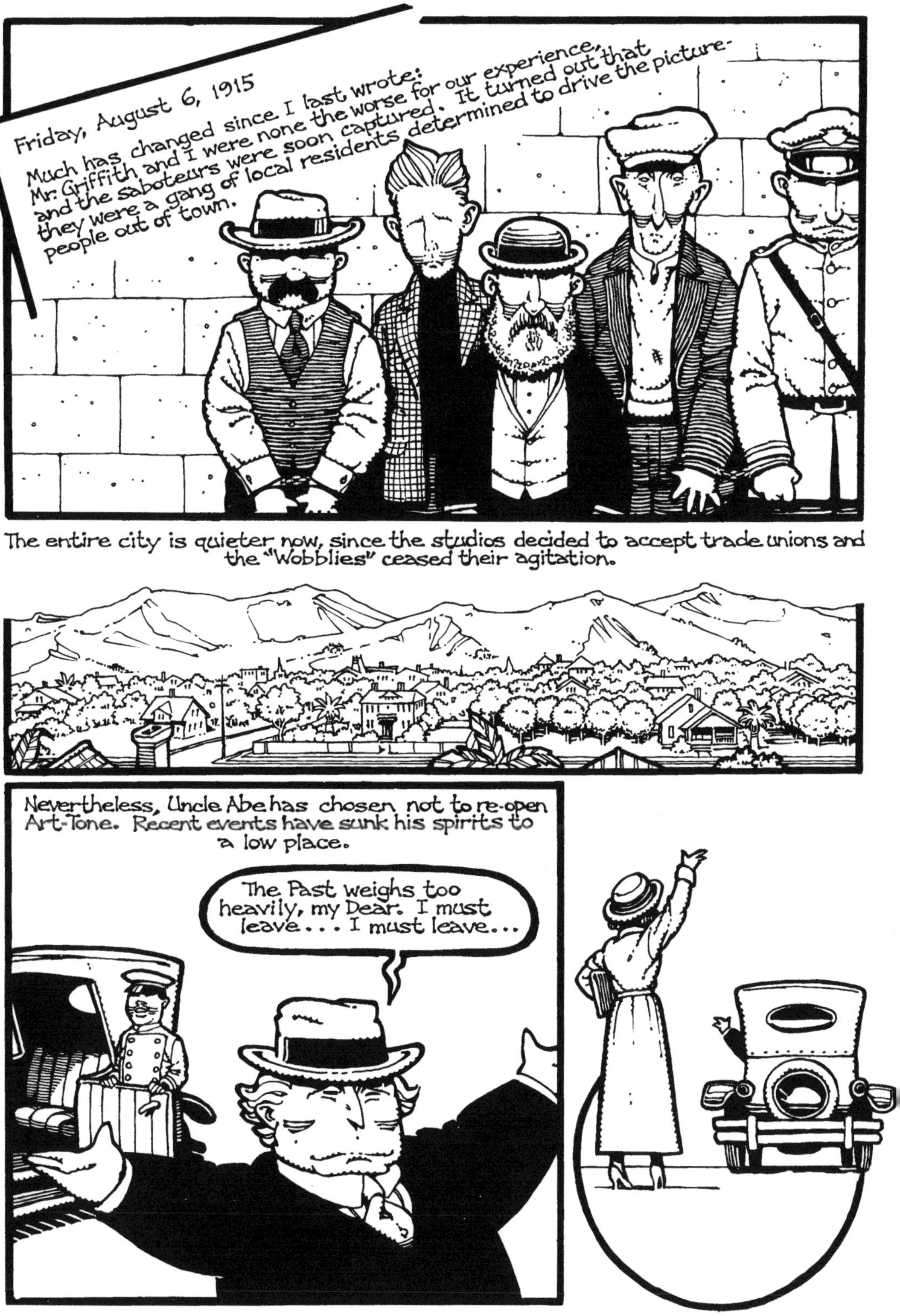
Friday, August 6, 1915
Much has changed since I last wrote: Mr. Griffith and I were none the worse for our experience, and the saboteurs were soon captured. It turned out that they were a gang of local residents determined to drive the picture-people out of town.
The entire city is quieter now, since the studios decided to accept trade unions and the "Wobblies" ceased their agitation.
Nevertheless, Uncle Abe has chosen not to re-open Art-Tone. Recent events have sunk his spirits to a low place.
The Past weighs too heavily, my Dear. I must leave . . . I must leave . . .

I did not remain unemployed for long: Mr. Griffith has hired me as an apprentice in his Cutting Dept..!

In addition, I play the organ accompaniment nightly at a picturehouse in Down-town Los Angeles.

Nevertheless, I feel that my time in Hollywood may be coming to an end.

Just this morning, I received a picture-postal-card from Cam... He is in Paris!

He says he is doing quite well and feels at home in the European Culture.

He has shown our film to various groups to much acclaim. Most enthusiastic were a band of Russian exiles who wish to over-throw their Tzar.

It's certainly a Big World... And I feel ever more a part of it.

End

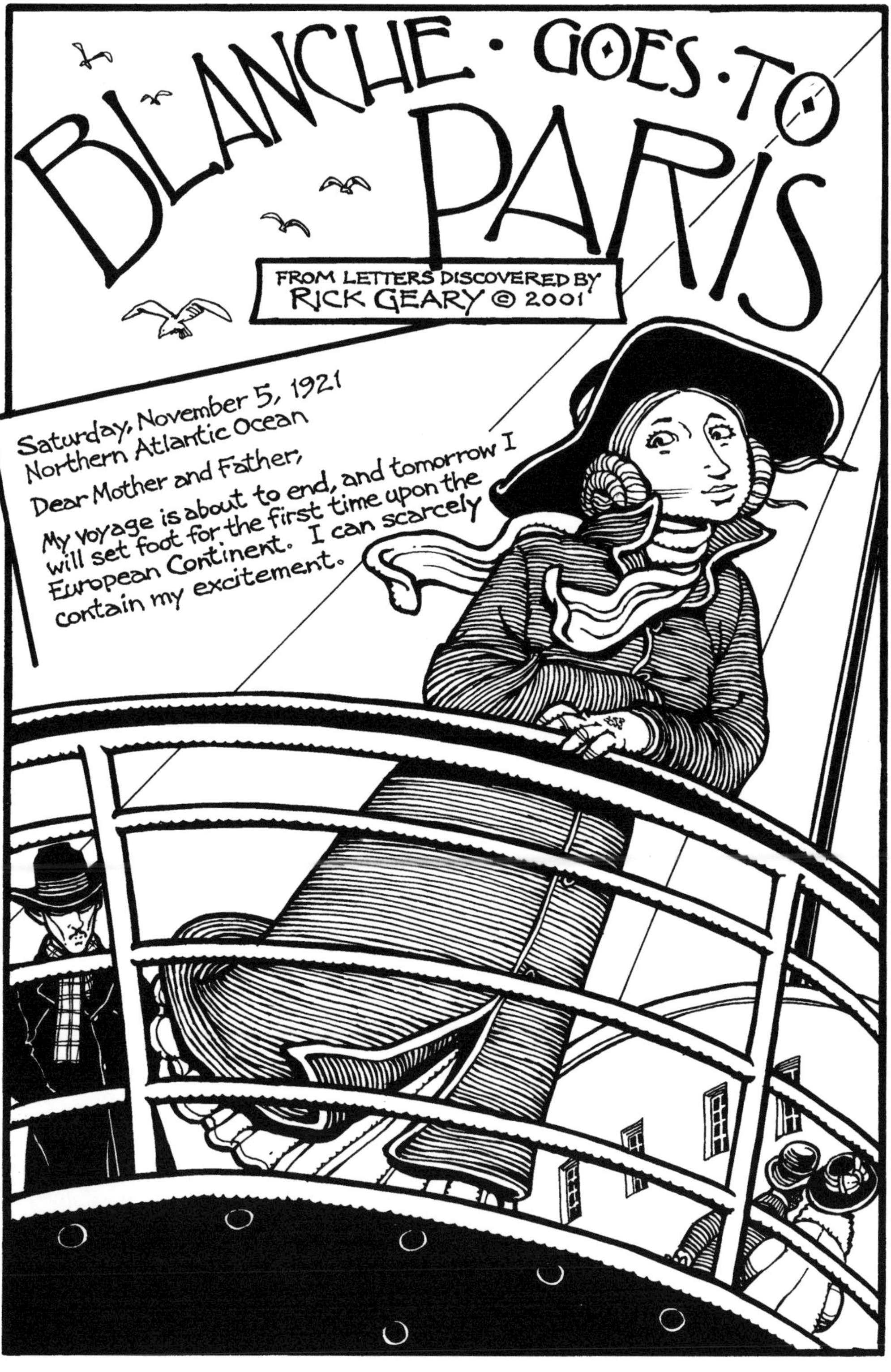
BLANCHE · GOES · TO PARIS
FROM LETTERS DISCOVERED BY RICK GEARY © 2001
Saturday, November 5, 1921
Northern Atlantic Ocean
Dear Mother and Father,
My voyage is about to end, and tomorrow I will set foot for the first time upon the European Continent. I can scarcely contain my excitement.

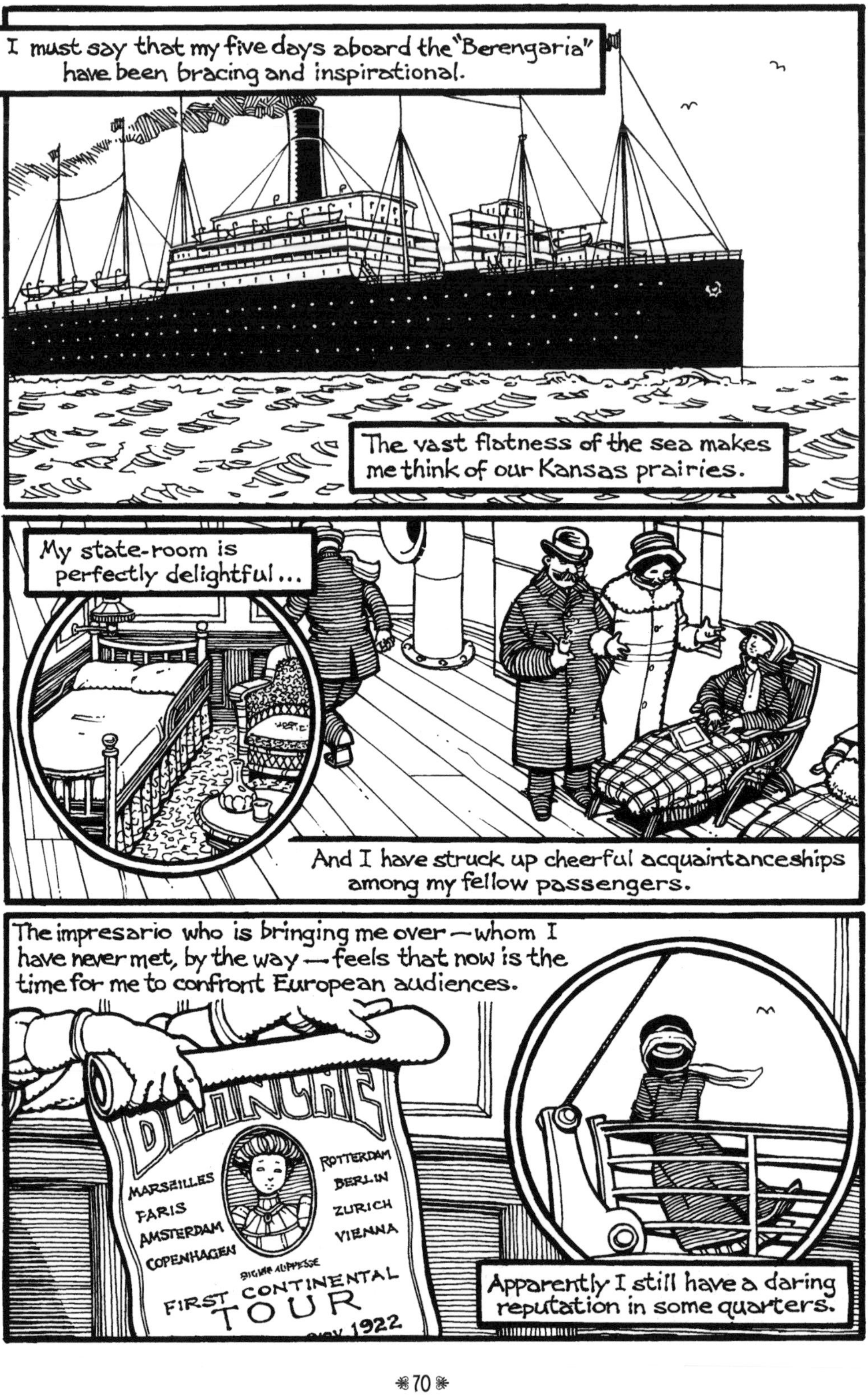
I must say that my five days aboard the "Berengaria" have been bracing and inspirational.
The vast flatness of the sea makes me think of our Kansas prairies.
My state-room is perfectly delightful...
And I have struck up cheerful acquaintanceships among my fellow passengers.
The impresario who is bringing me over — whom I have never met, by the way — feels that now is the time for me to confront European audiences.
MARSEILLES
PARIS
AMSTERDAM
COPENHAGEN
ROTTERDAM
BERLIN
ZURICH
VIENNA
FIRST CONTINENTAL TOUR
Apparently I still have a daring reputation in some quarters.

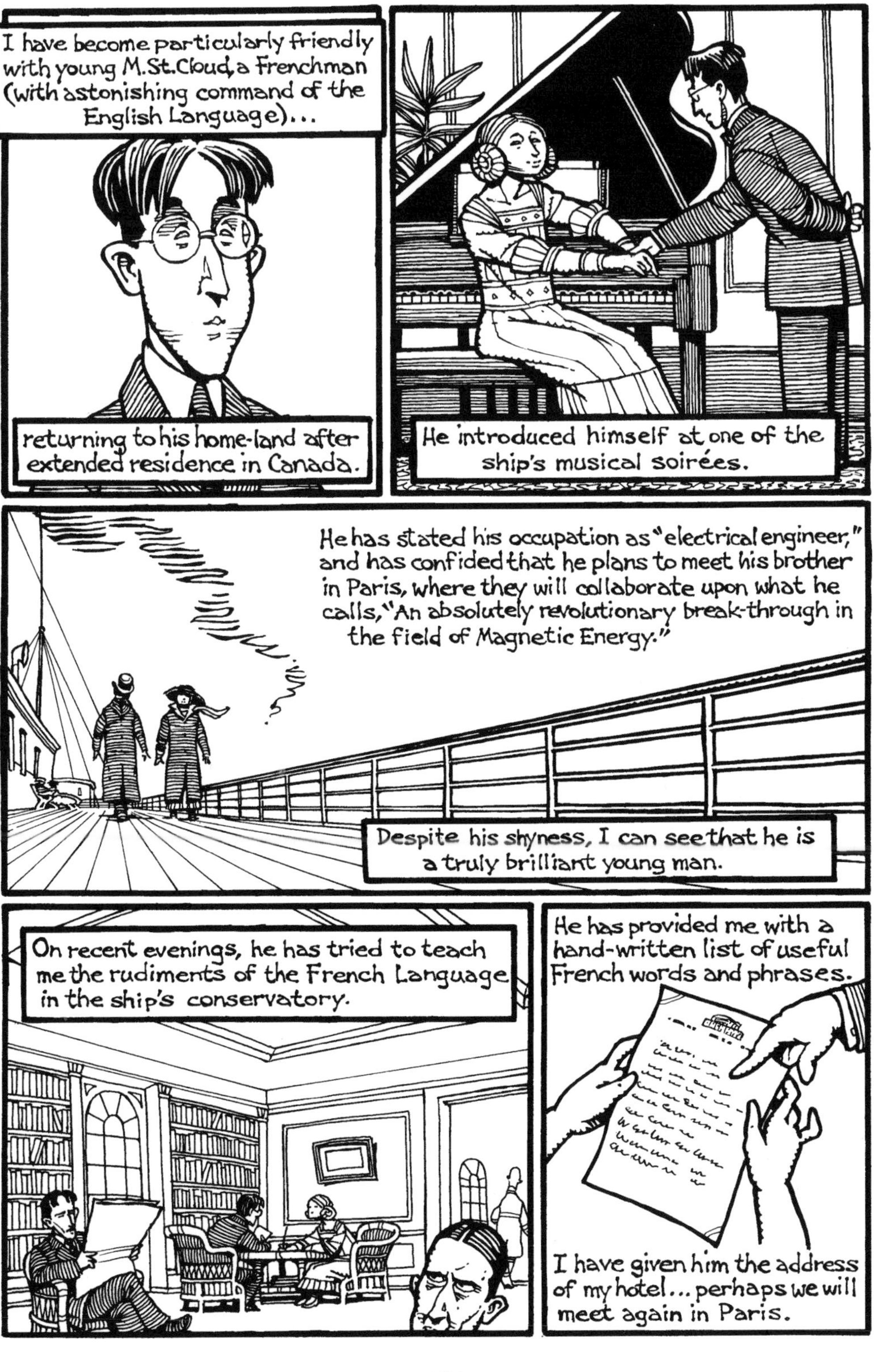

I have become particularly friendly with young M. St. Cloud, a Frenchman (with astonishing command of the English Language)...
returning to his home-land after extended residence in Canada.
He introduced himself at one of the ship's musical soirées.
He has stated his occupation as "electrical engineer," and has confided that he plans to meet his brother in Paris, where they will collaborate upon what he calls, "An absolutely revolutionary break-through in the field of Magnetic Energy."
Despite his shyness, I can see that he is a truly brilliant young man.
On recent evenings, he has tried to teach me the rudiments of the French Language in the ship's conservatory.
He has provided me with a hand-written list of useful French words and phrases.
I have given him the address of my hotel... perhaps we will meet again in Paris.

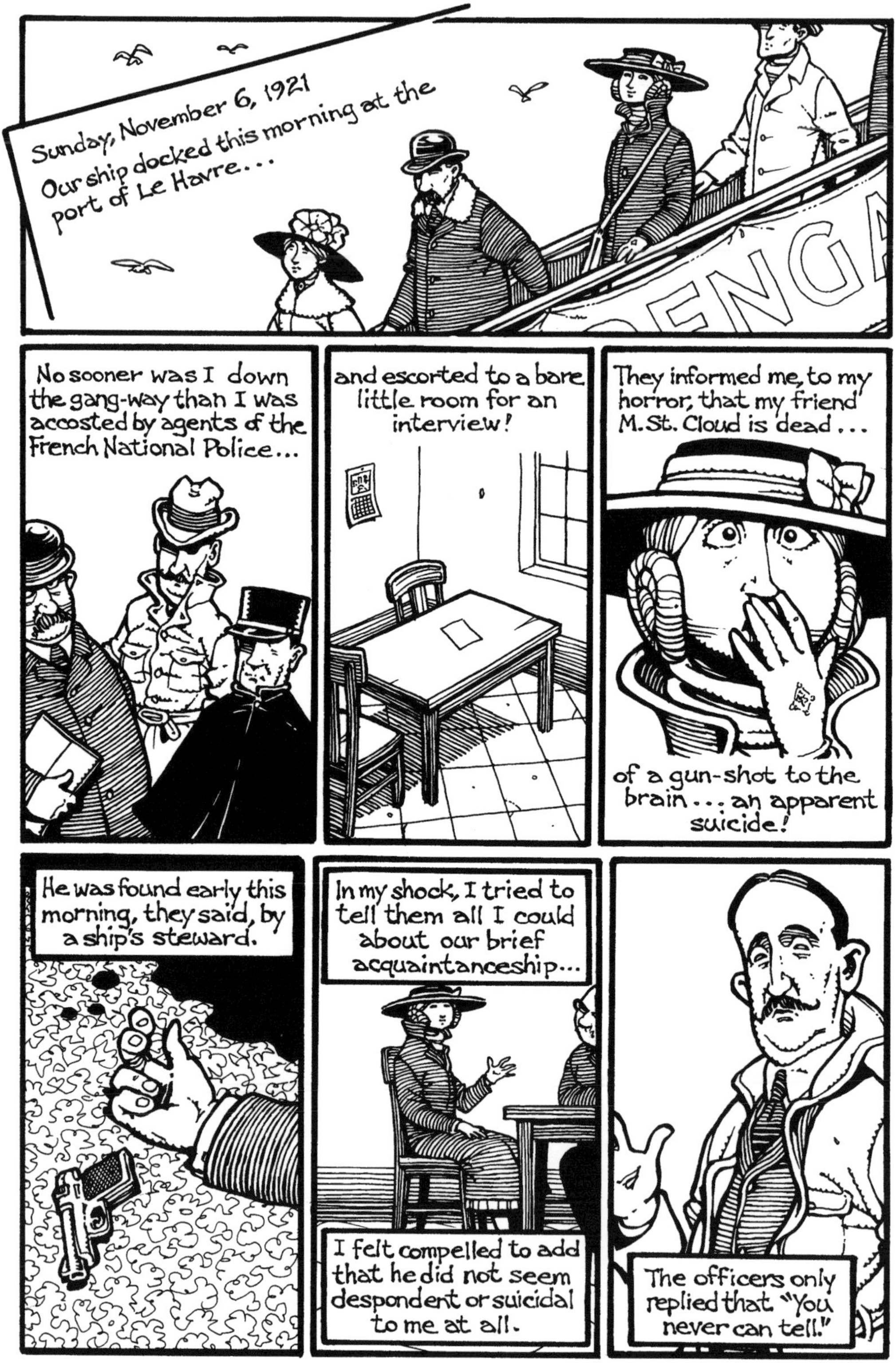
Sunday, November 6, 1921
Our ship docked this morning at the port of Le Havre...
ENGA
No sooner was I down the gang-way than I was accosted by agents of the French National Police...
and escorted to a bare little room for an interview!
They informed me, to my horror, that my friend M. St. Cloud is dead...
of a gun-shot to the brain... an apparent suicide!
He was found early this morning, they said, by a ship's steward.
In my shock, I tried to tell them all I could about our brief acquaintanceship...
I felt compelled to add that he did not seem despondent or suicidal to me at all.
The officers only replied that "You never can tell."

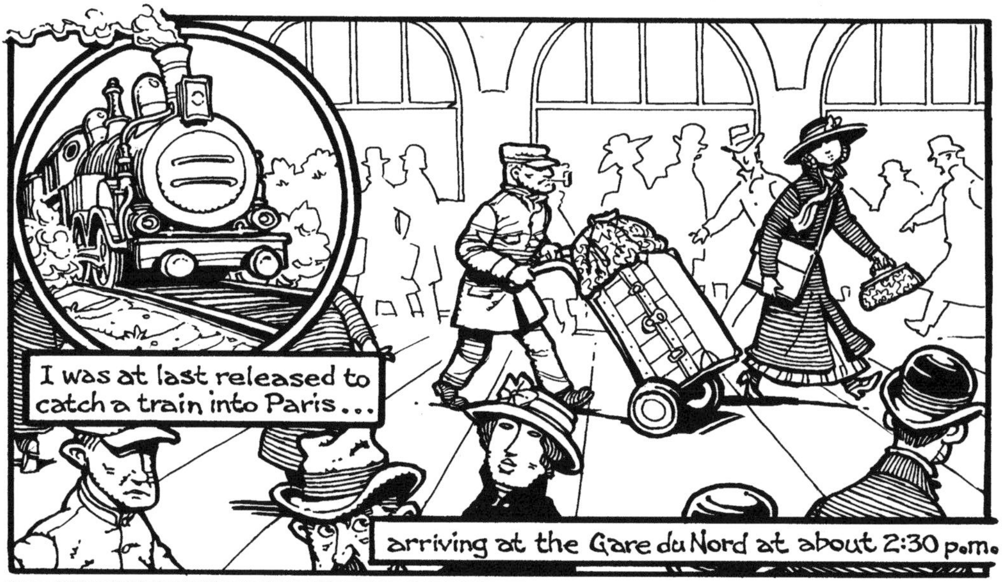
I was at last released to catch a train into Paris...
arriving at the Gare du Nord at about 2:30 p.m.

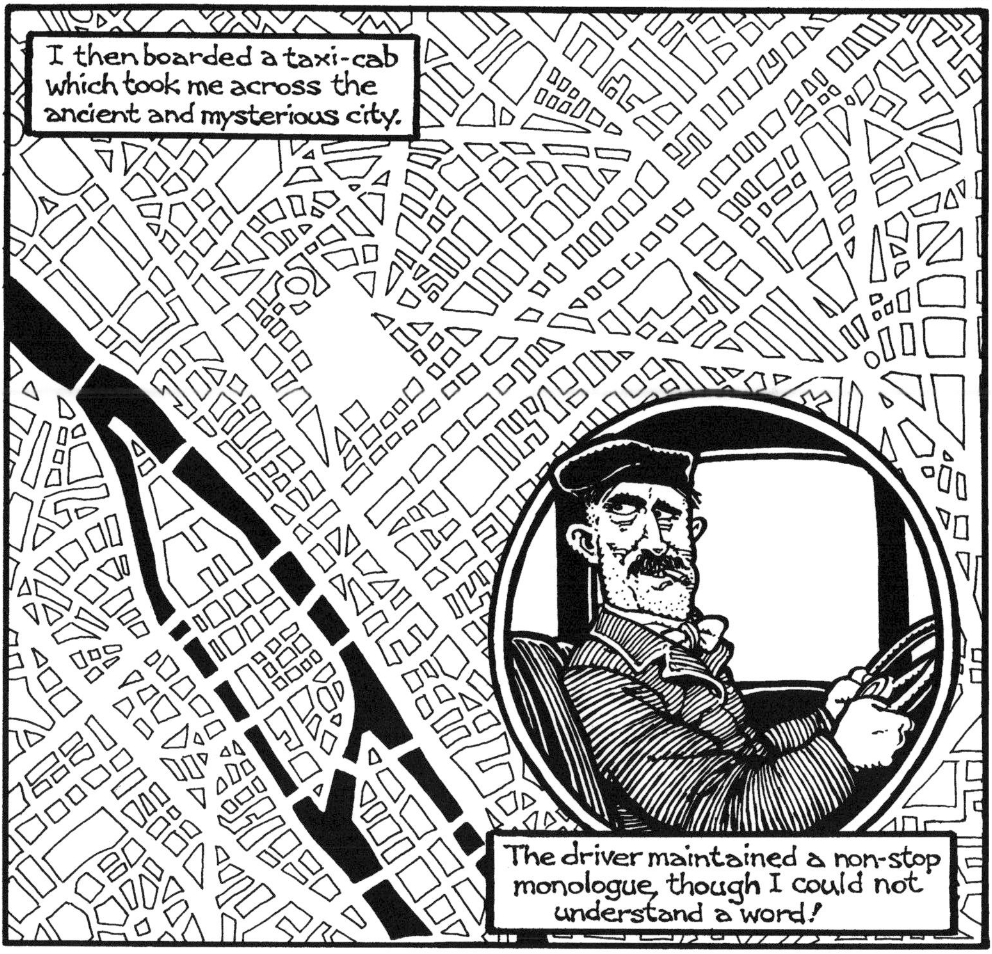
I then boarded a taxi-cab which took me across the ancient and mysterious city.
The driver maintained a non-stop monologue, though I could not understand a word!

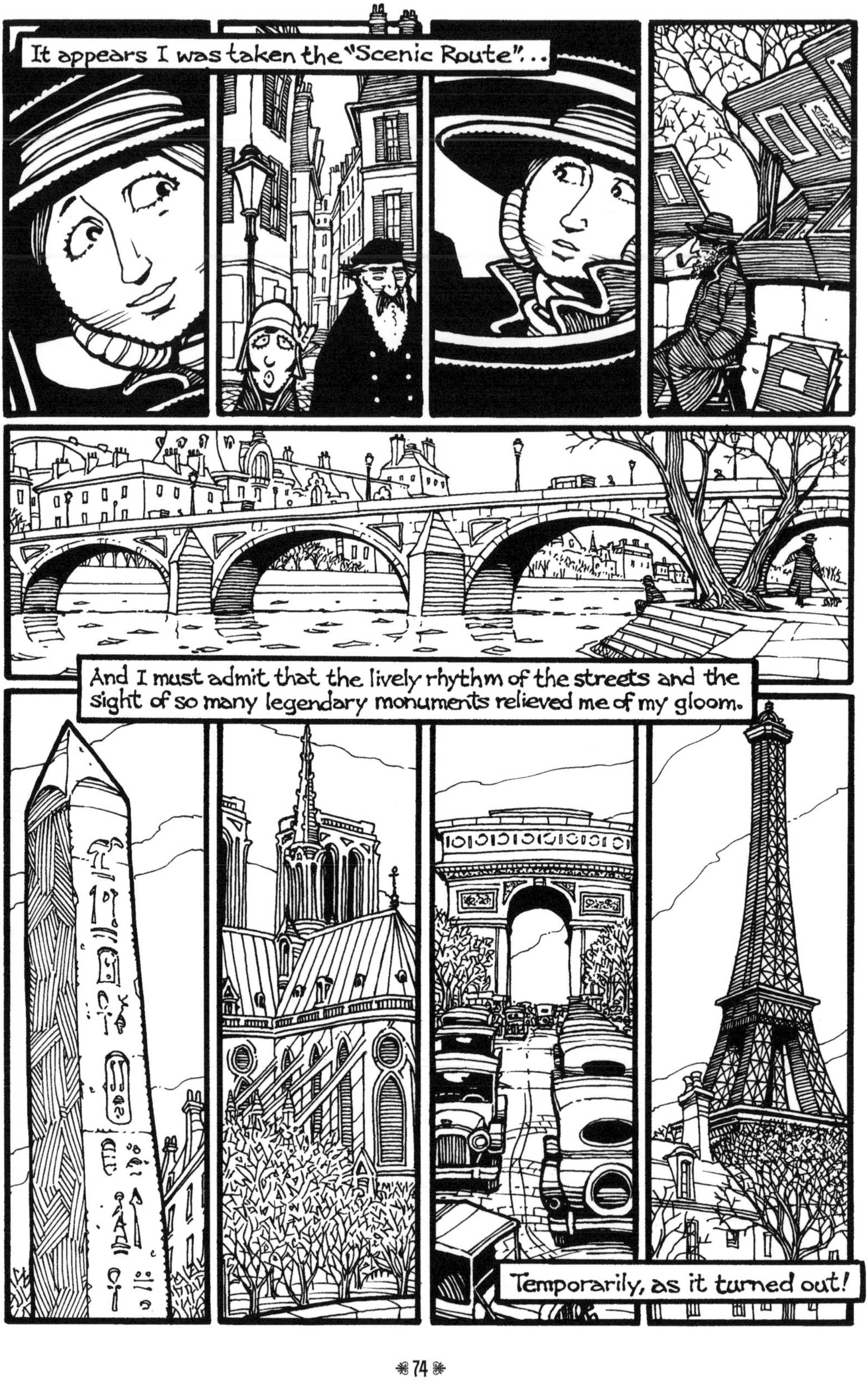
It appears I was taken the "Scenic Route"...
And I must admit that the lively rhythm of the streets and the sight of so many legendary monuments relieved me of my gloom.
Temporarily, as it turned out!

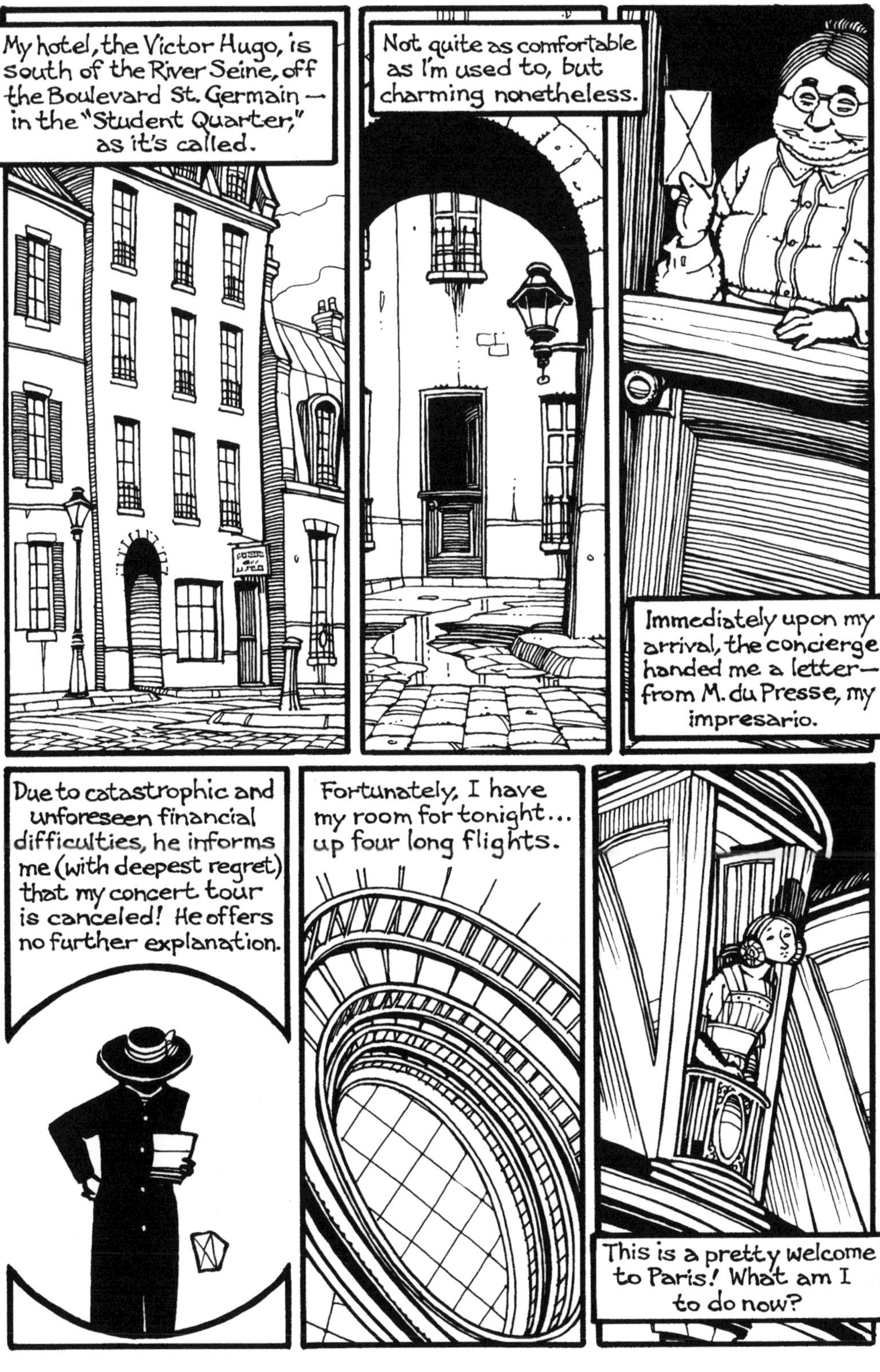
My hotel, the Victor Hugo, is south of the River Seine, off the Boulevard St. Germain — in the "Student Quarter," as it's called.
Not quite as comfortable as I'm used to, but charming nonetheless.
Immediately upon my arrival, the concierge handed me a letter— from M. du Presse, my impresario.
Due to catastrophic and unforeseen financial difficulties, he informs me (with deepest regret) that my concert tour is canceled! He offers no further explanation.
Fortunately, I have my room for tonight... up four long flights.
This is a pretty welcome to Paris! What am I to do now?

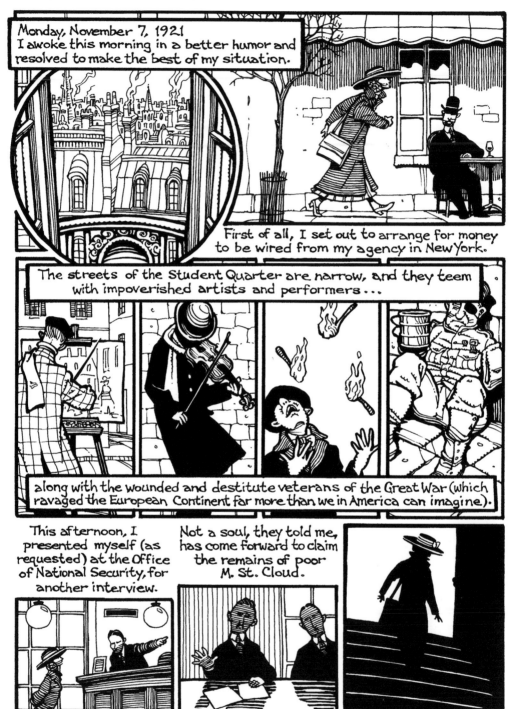

Monday, November 7, 1921
I awoke this morning in a better humor and resolved to make the best of my situation.

First of all, I set out to arrange for money to be wired from my agency in New York.

The streets of the Student Quarter are narrow, and they teem with impoverished artists and performers...

along with the wounded and destitute veterans of the Great War (which ravaged the European Continent far more than we in America can imagine).

This afternoon, I presented myself (as requested) at the Office of National Security, for another interview.

Not a soul, they told me, has come forward to claim the remains of poor M. St. Cloud.

Regretfully, there was nothing I could add to what I had told the agents yesterday.

No brother or relative of any kind is to be found in Paris or its environs.

What, I wondered, can the government's interest be in a young electrical engineer?

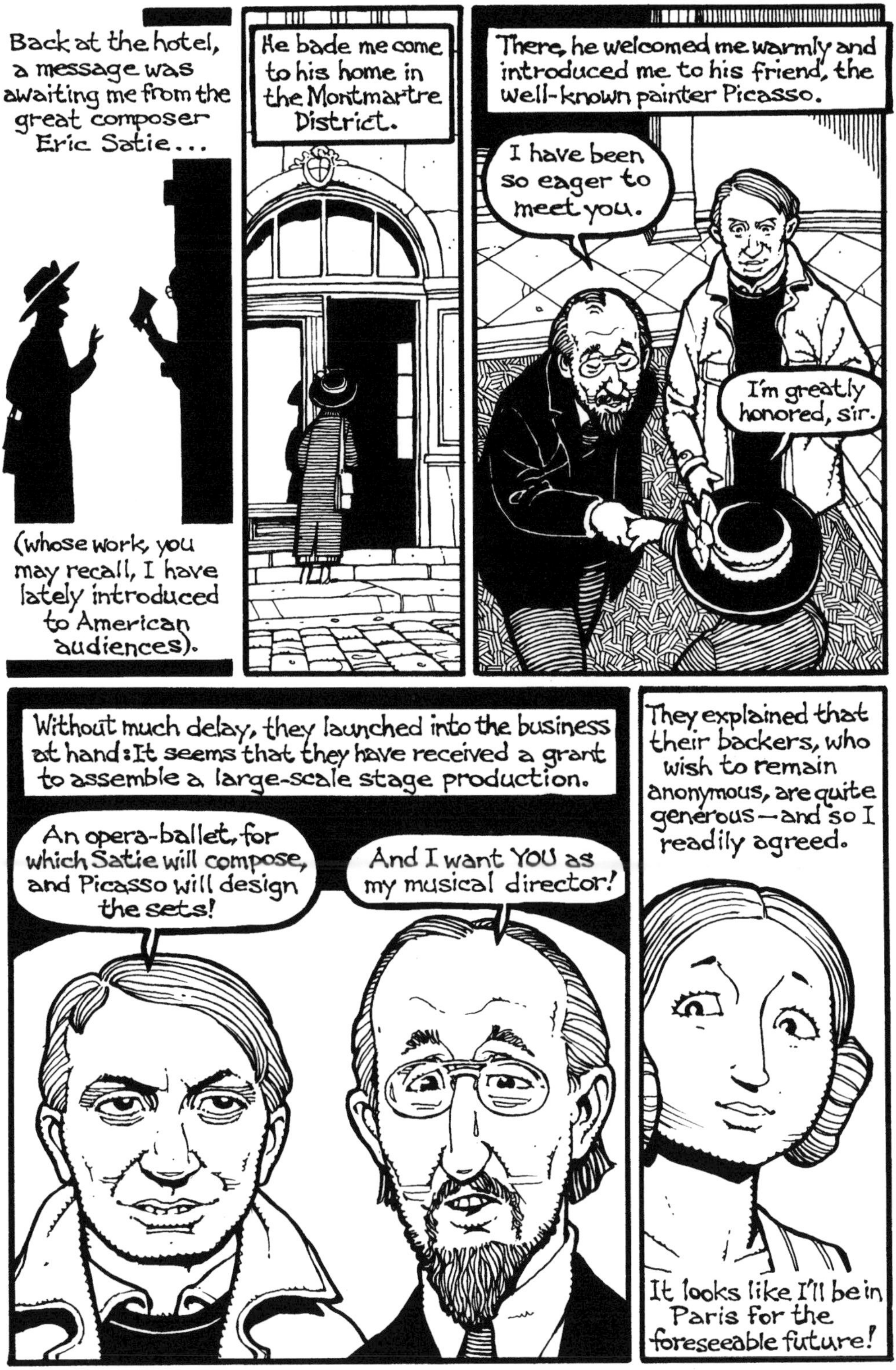
Back at the hotel, a message was awaiting me from the great composer Eric Satie...
(whose work, you may recall, I have lately introduced to American audiences).
He bade me come to his home in the Montmartre District.
There, he welcomed me warmly and introduced me to his friend, the well-known painter Picasso.
I have been so eager to meet you.
I'm greatly honored, sir.
Without much delay, they launched into the business at hand: It seems that they have received a grant to assemble a large-scale stage production.
An opera-ballet, for which Satie will compose, and Picasso will design the sets!
And I want YOU as my musical director!
They explained that their backers, who wish to remain anonymous, are quite generous—and so I readily agreed.
It looks like I'll be in Paris for the foreseeable future!

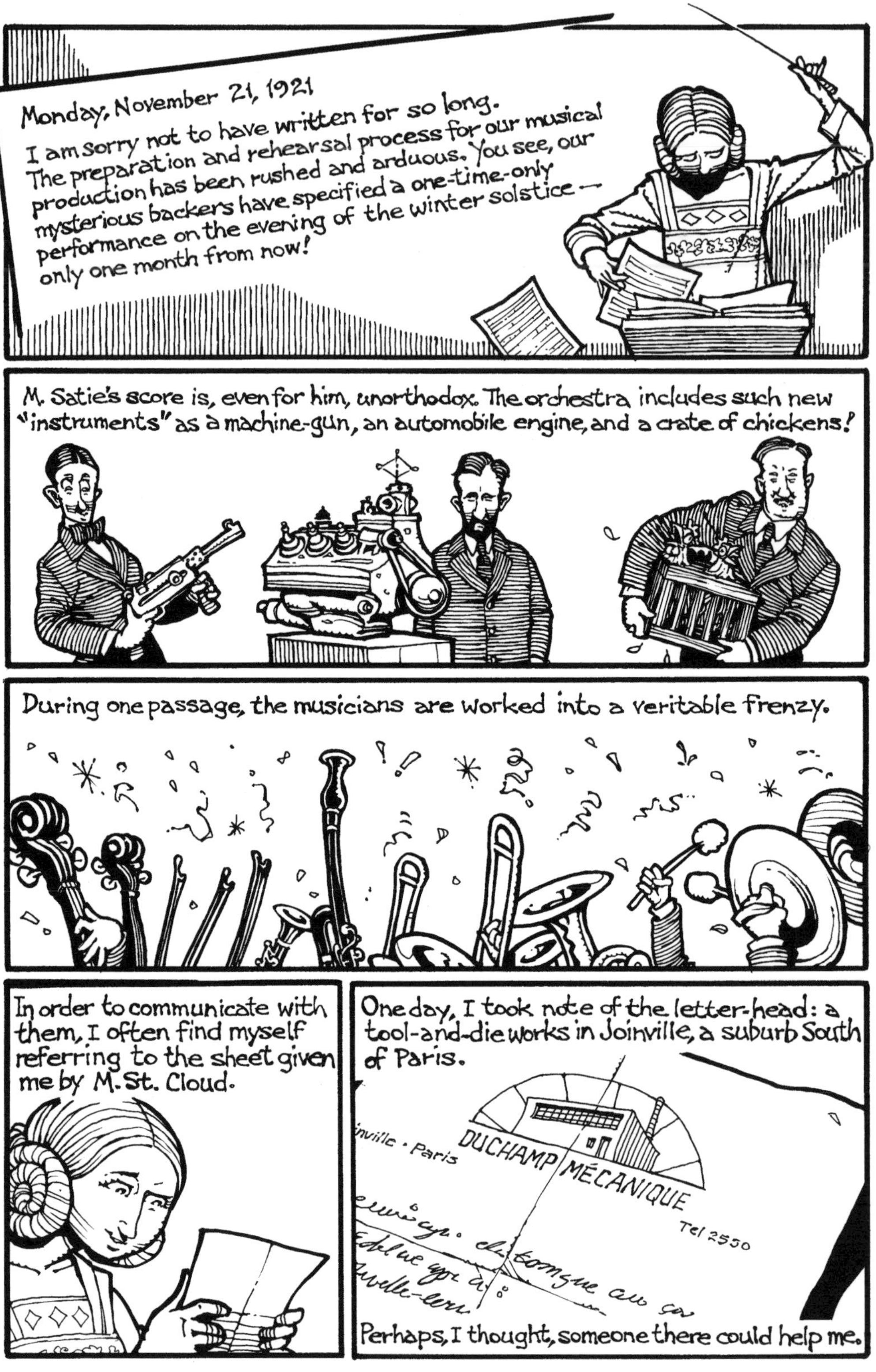
Monday, November 21, 1921
I am sorry not to have written for so long. The preparation and rehearsal process for our musical production has been rushed and arduous. You see, our mysterious backers have specified a one-time-only performance on the evening of the winter solstice — only one month from now!
M. Satie's score is, even for him, unorthodox. The orchestra includes such new "instruments" as a machine-gun, an automobile engine, and a crate of chickens!
During one passage, the musicians are worked into a veritable frenzy.
In order to communicate with them, I often find myself referring to the sheet given me by M. St. Cloud.
One day, I took note of the letter-head: a tool-and-die works in Joinville, a suburb South of Paris.
DUCHAMP MÉCANIQUE
inville • Paris
Tel 2550
Perhaps, I thought, someone there could help me.

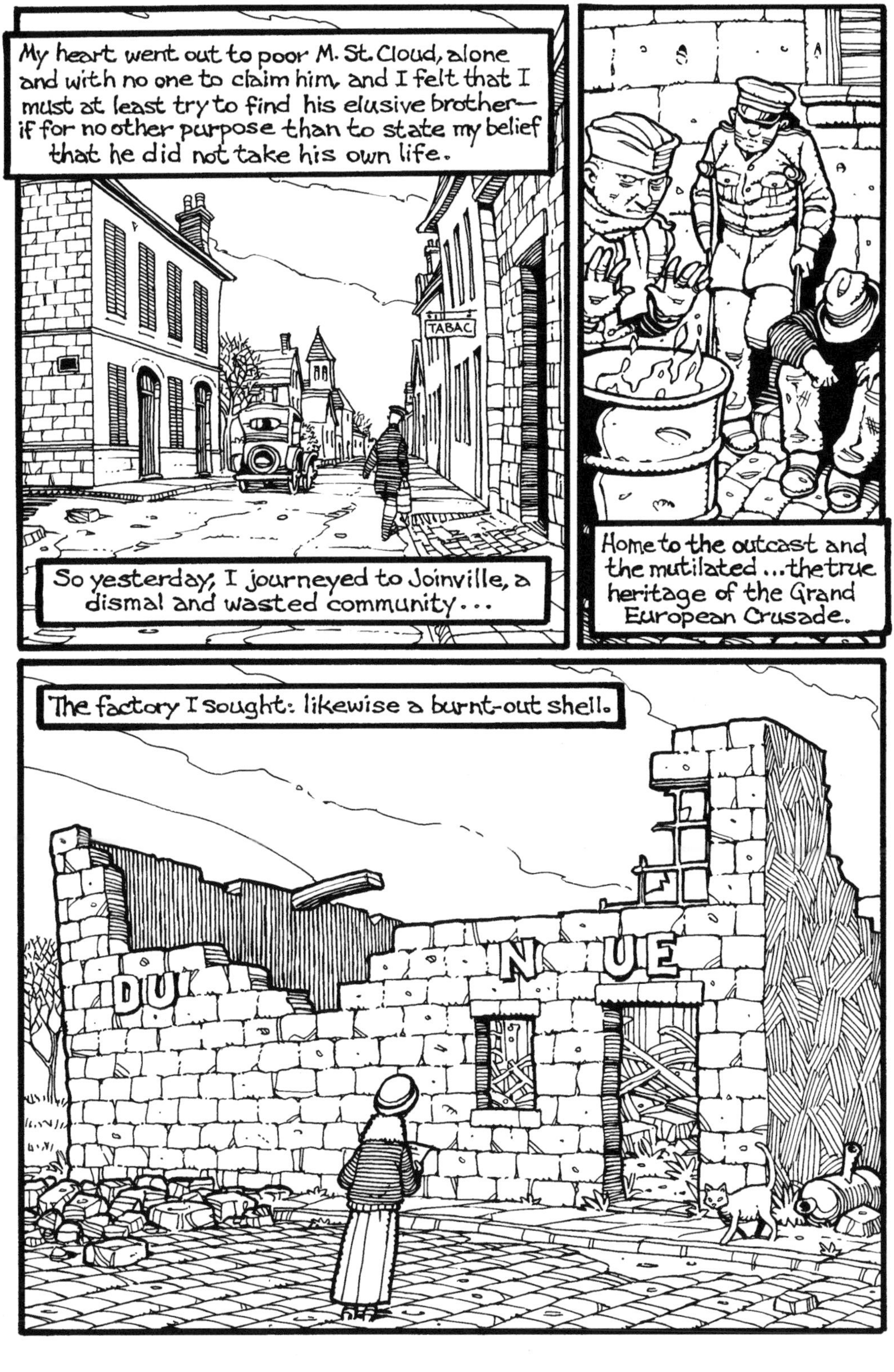
My heart went out to poor M. St. Cloud, alone and with no one to claim him, and I felt that I must at least try to find his elusive brother— if for no other purpose than to state my belief that he did not take his own life.
TABAC
So yesterday, I journeyed to Joinville, a dismal and wasted community...
Home to the outcast and the mutilated ... the true heritage of the Grand European Crusade.
The factory I sought: likewise a burnt-out shell.
DU
N
UE

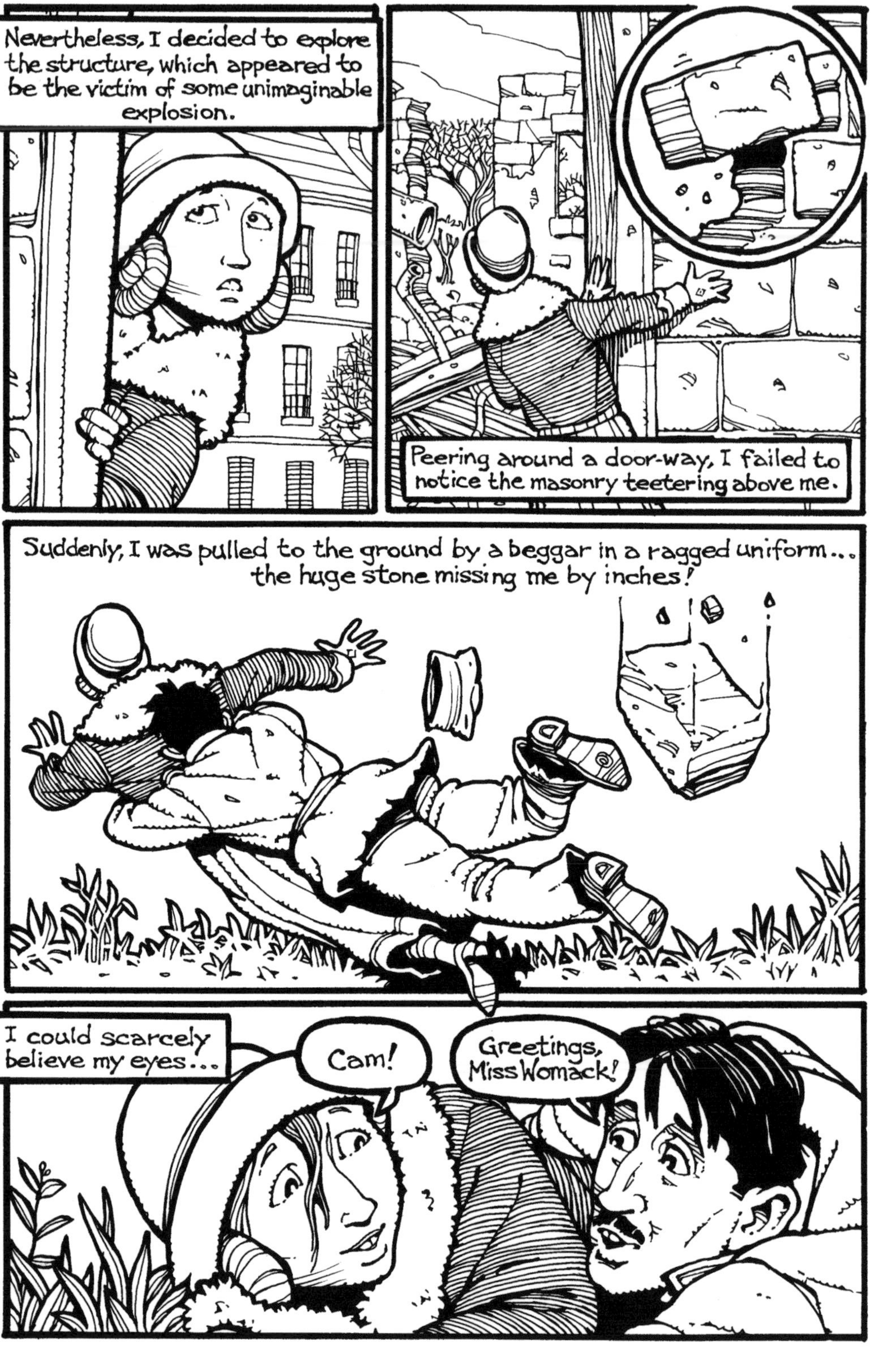
Nevertheless, I decided to explore the structure, which appeared to be the victim of some unimaginable explosion.
Peering around a door-way, I failed to notice the masonry teetering above me.
Suddenly, I was pulled to the ground by a beggar in a ragged uniform... the huge stone missing me by inches!
I could scarcely believe my eyes...
Cam!
Greetings, Miss Womack!

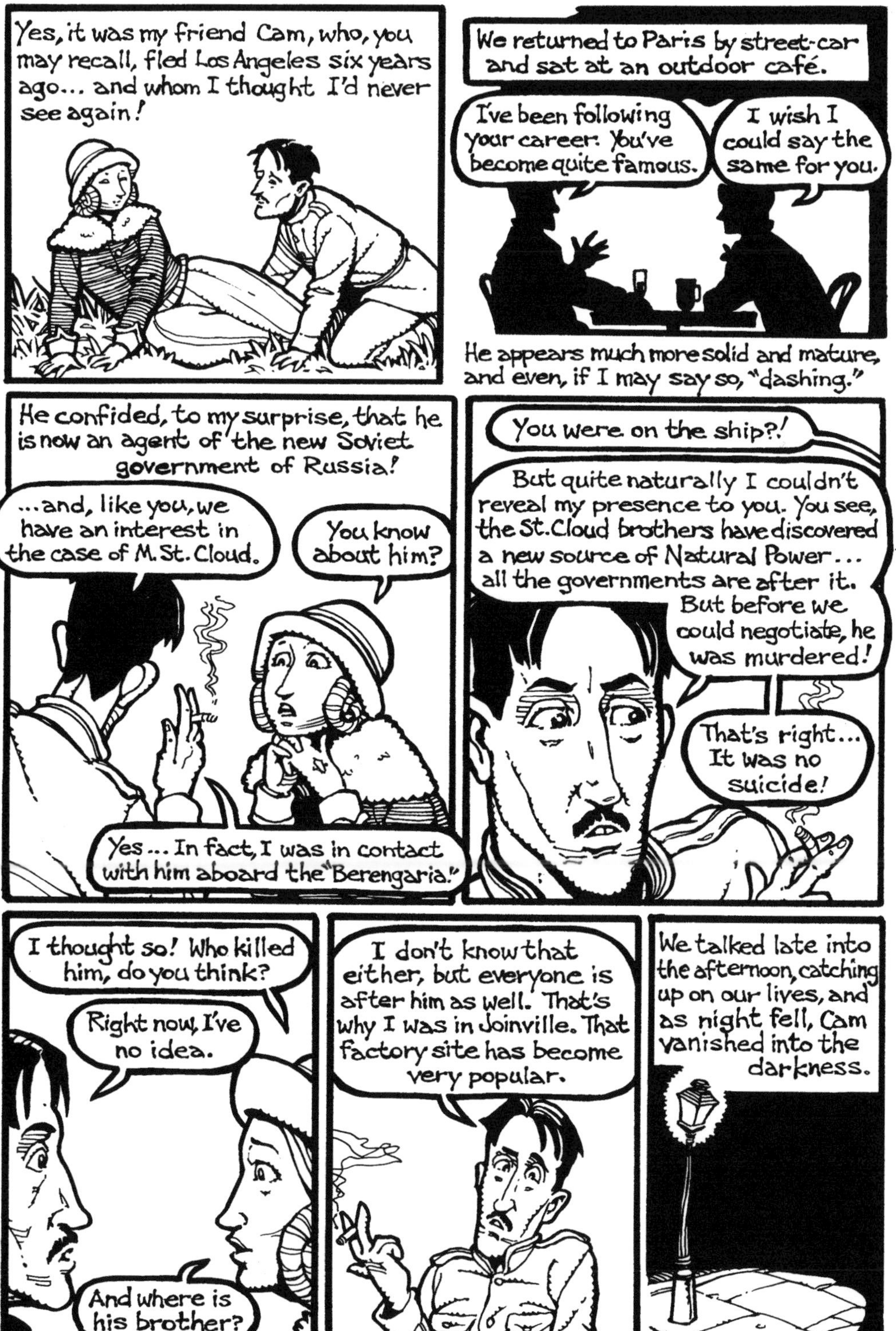
Yes, it was my friend Cam, who, you may recall, fled Los Angeles six years ago... and whom I thought I'd never see again!
We returned to Paris by street-car and sat at an outdoor café.
I've been following your career. You've become quite famous.
I wish I could say the same for you.
He appears much more solid and mature, and even, if I may say so, "dashing."
He confided, to my surprise, that he is now an agent of the new Soviet government of Russia!
...and, like you, we have an interest in the case of M. St. Cloud.
You know about him?
Yes... In fact, I was in contact with him aboard the "Berengaria."
You were on the ship?!
But quite naturally I couldn't reveal my presence to you. You see, the St. Cloud brothers have discovered a new source of Natural Power... all the governments are after it.
But before we could negotiate, he was murdered!
That's right... It was no suicide!
I thought so! Who killed him, do you think?
Right now, I've no idea.
And where is his brother?
I don't know that either, but everyone is after him as well. That's why I was in Joinville. That factory site has become very popular.
We talked late into the afternoon, catching up on our lives, and as night fell, Cam vanished into the darkness.

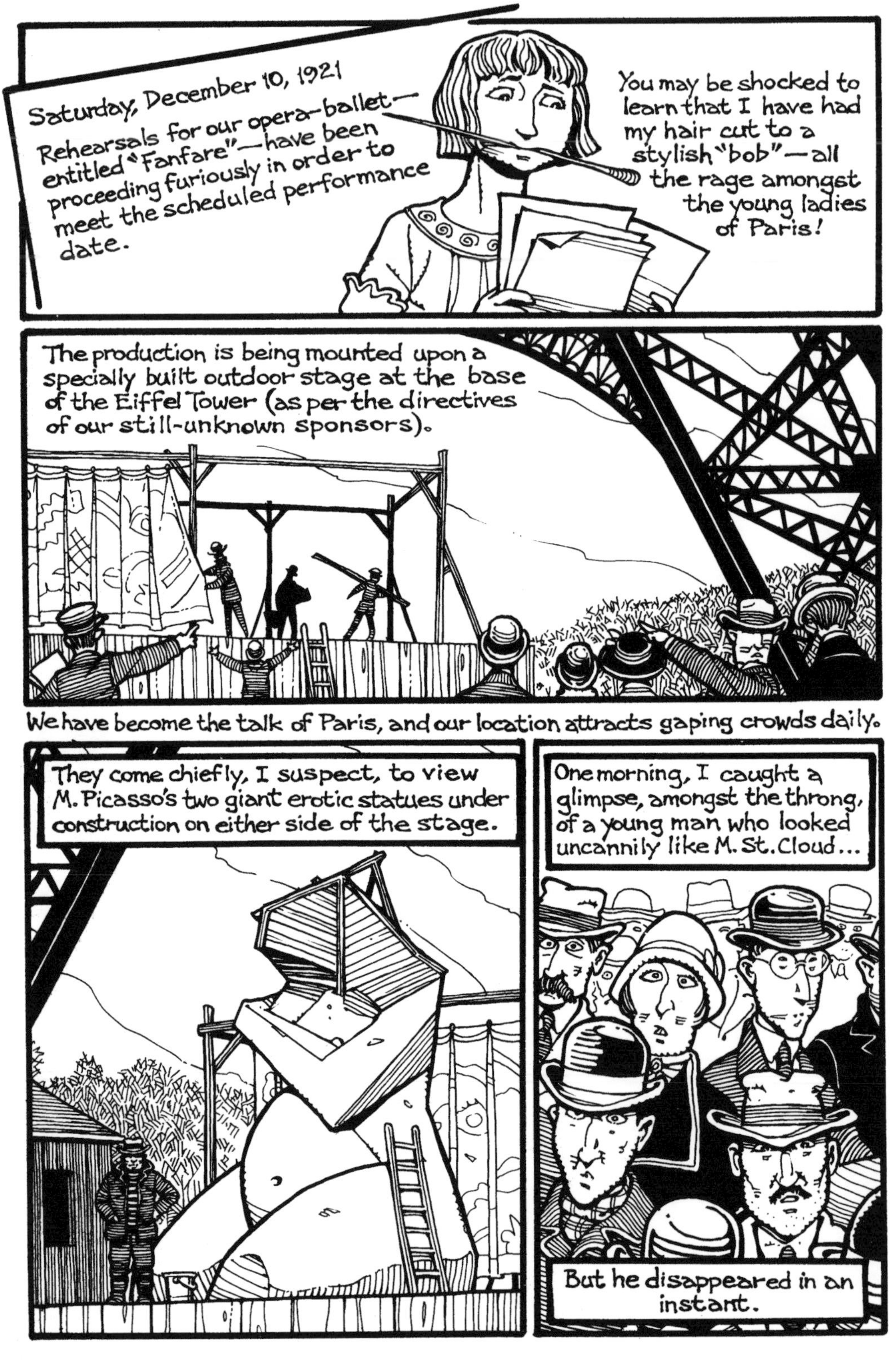
Saturday, December 10, 1921
Rehearsals for our opera-ballet— entitled "Fanfare"—have been proceeding furiously in order to meet the scheduled performance date.
You may be shocked to learn that I have had my hair cut to a stylish "bob"—all the rage amongst the young ladies of Paris!
The production is being mounted upon a specially built outdoor stage at the base of the Eiffel Tower (as per the directives of our still-unknown sponsors).
We have become the talk of Paris, and our location attracts gaping crowds daily.
They come chiefly, I suspect, to view M. Picasso's two giant erotic statues under construction on either side of the stage.
One morning, I caught a glimpse, amongst the throng, of a young man who looked uncannily like M. St. Cloud...
But he disappeared in an instant.

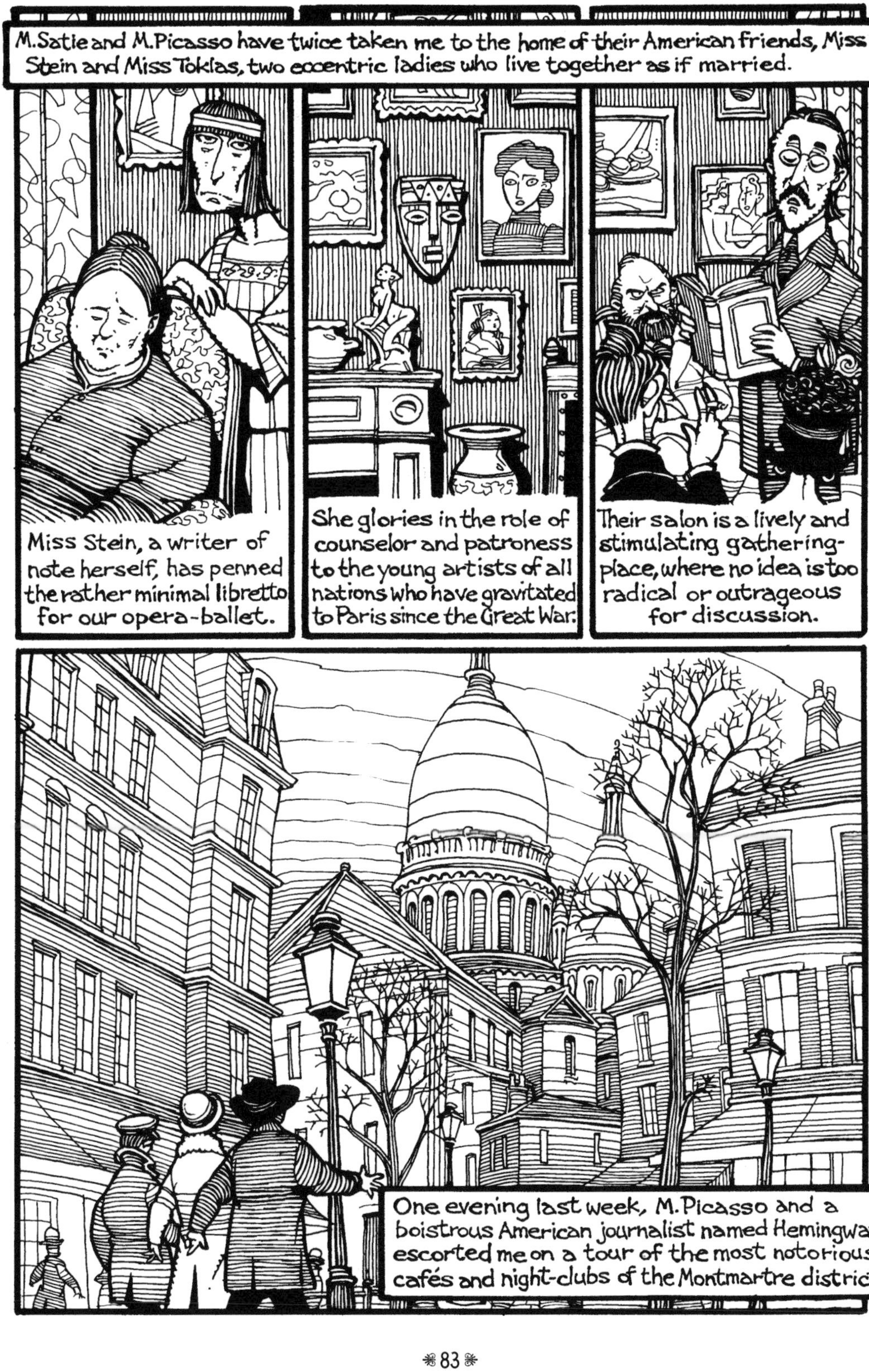
M.Satie and M.Picasso have twice taken me to the home of their American friends, Miss Stein and Miss Toklas, two eccentric ladies who live together as if married.
Miss Stein, a writer of note herself, has penned the rather minimal libretto for our opera-ballet.
She glories in the role of counselor and patroness to the young artists of all nations who have gravitated to Paris since the Great War.
Their salon is a lively and stimulating gathering-place, where no idea is too radical or outrageous for discussion.
One evening last week, M.Picasso and a boistrous American journalist named Hemingway escorted me on a tour of the most notorious cafés and night-clubs of the Montmartre district.

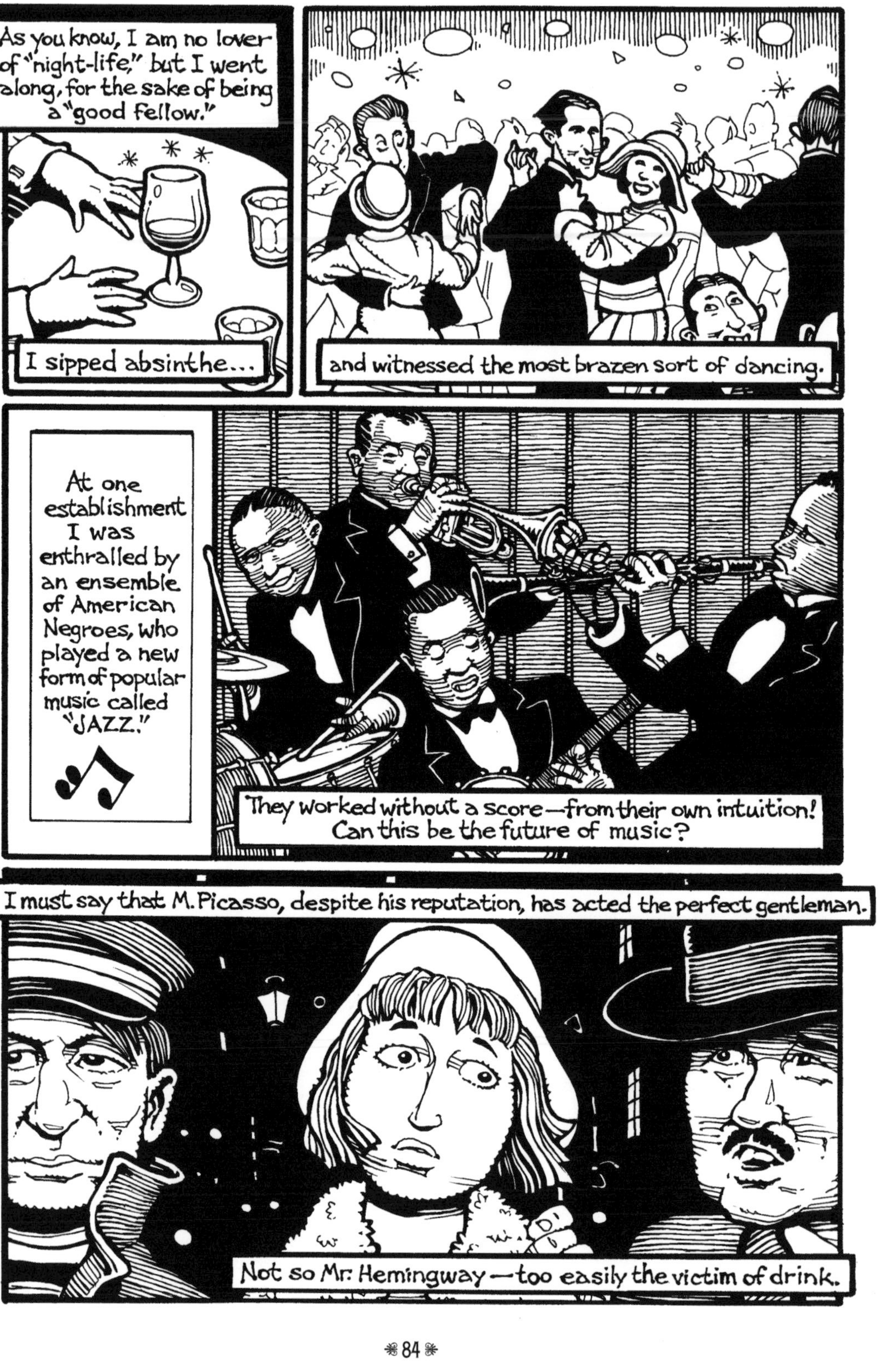

As you know, I am no lover of "night-life," but I went along, for the sake of being a "good fellow."
I sipped absinthe...
and witnessed the most brazen sort of dancing.
At one establishment I was enthralled by an ensemble of American Negroes, who played a new form of popular music called "JAZZ."
They worked without a score—from their own intuition! Can this be the future of music?
I must say that M. Picasso, despite his reputation, has acted the perfect gentleman.
Not so Mr. Hemingway—too easily the victim of drink.

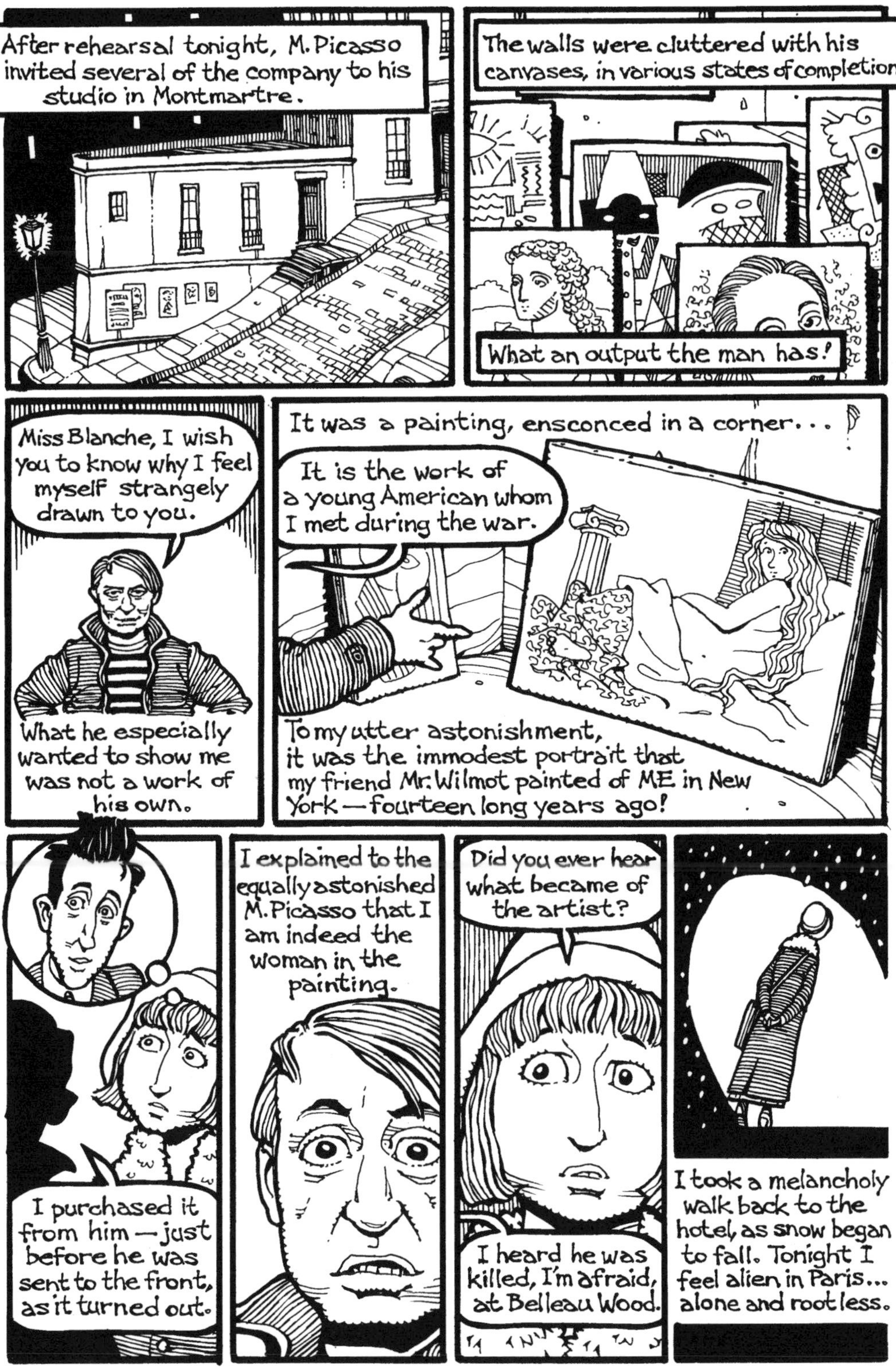
After rehearsal tonight, M. Picasso invited several of the company to his studio in Montmartre.
The walls were cluttered with his canvases, in various states of completion.
What an output the man has!
Miss Blanche, I wish you to know why I feel myself strangely drawn to you.
What he especially wanted to show me was not a work of his own.
It was a painting, ensconced in a corner...
It is the work of a young American whom I met during the war.
To my utter astonishment, it was the immodest portrait that my friend Mr. Wilmot painted of ME in New York—fourteen long years ago!
I purchased it from him—just before he was sent to the front, as it turned out.
I explained to the equally astonished M. Picasso that I am indeed the woman in the painting.
Did you ever hear what became of the artist?
I heard he was killed, I'm afraid, at Belleau Wood.
I took a melancholy walk back to the hotel, as snow began to fall. Tonight I feel alien in Paris... alone and rootless.

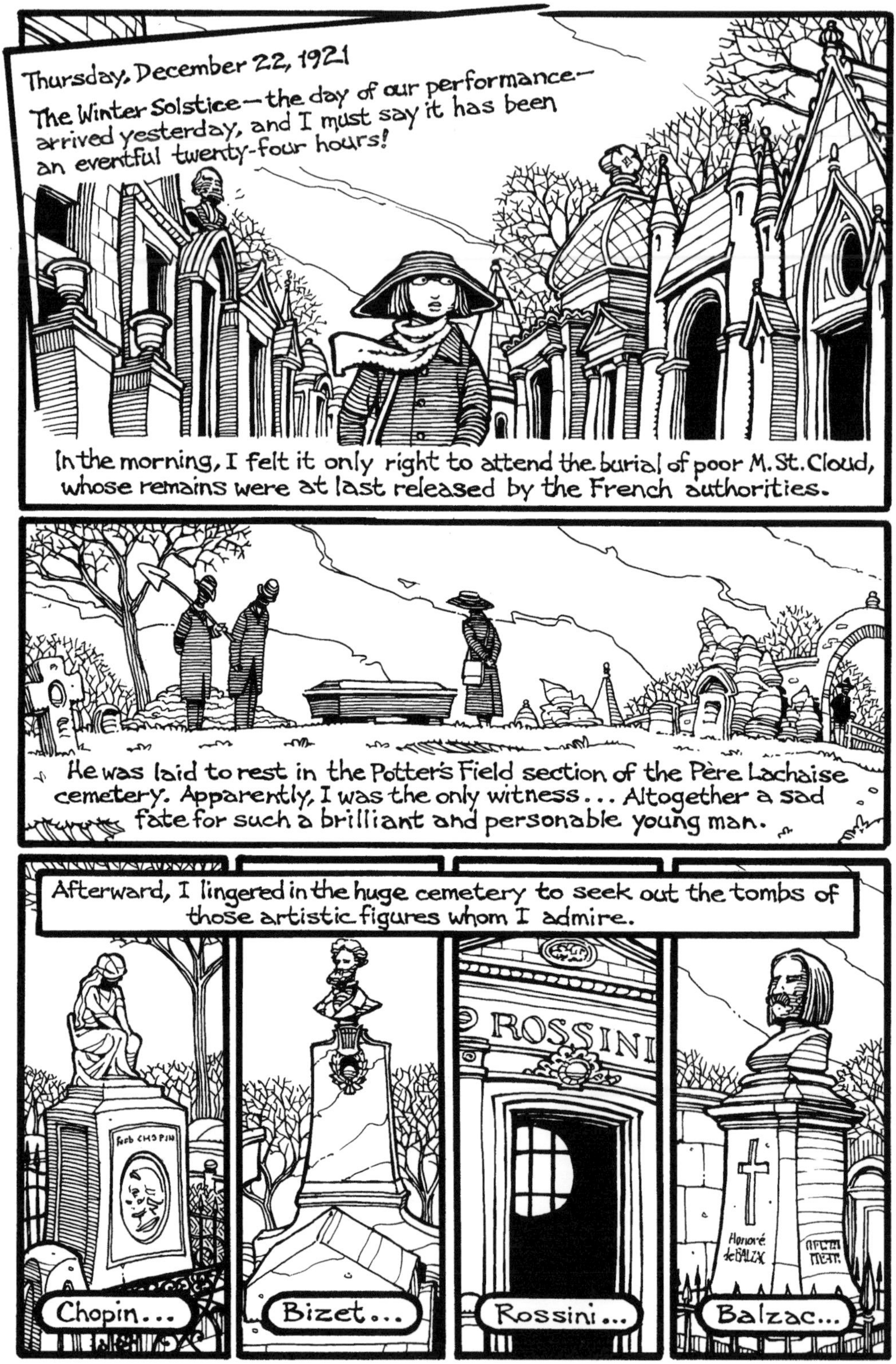
Thursday, December 22, 1921
The Winter Solstice—the day of our performance—arrived yesterday, and I must say it has been an eventful twenty-four hours!
In the morning, I felt it only right to attend the burial of poor M. St. Cloud, whose remains were at last released by the French authorities.
He was laid to rest in the Potter's Field section of the Père Lachaise cemetery. Apparently, I was the only witness... Altogether a sad fate for such a brilliant and personable young man.
Afterward, I lingered in the huge cemetery to seek out the tombs of those artistic figures whom I admire.
ROSSINI
Honoré de BALZAC
Chopin...
Bizet...
Rossini...
Balzac...

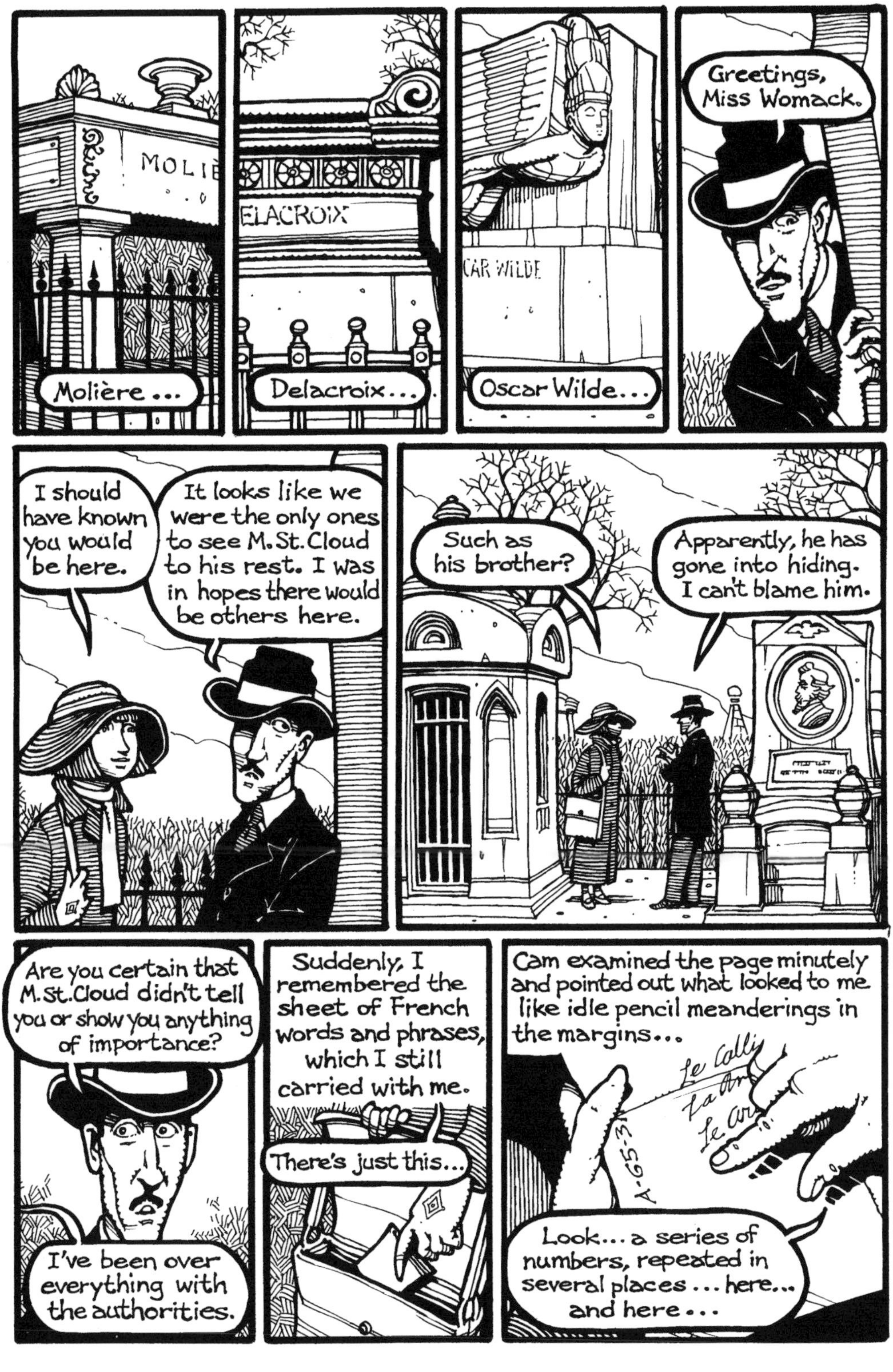
MOLIÈ
Molière...
ELACROIX
Delacroix...
CAR WILDE
Oscar Wilde...
Greetings, Miss Womack.
I should have known you would be here.
It looks like we were the only ones to see M. St. Cloud to his rest. I was in hopes there would be others here.
Such as his brother?
Apparently, he has gone into hiding. I can't blame him.
Are you certain that M. St. Cloud didn't tell you or show you anything of importance?
I've been over everything with the authorities.
Suddenly, I remembered the sheet of French words and phrases, which I still carried with me.
There's just this...
Cam examined the page minutely and pointed out what looked to me like idle pencil meanderings in the margins...
A-65-31
Look... a series of numbers, repeated in several places... here... and here...

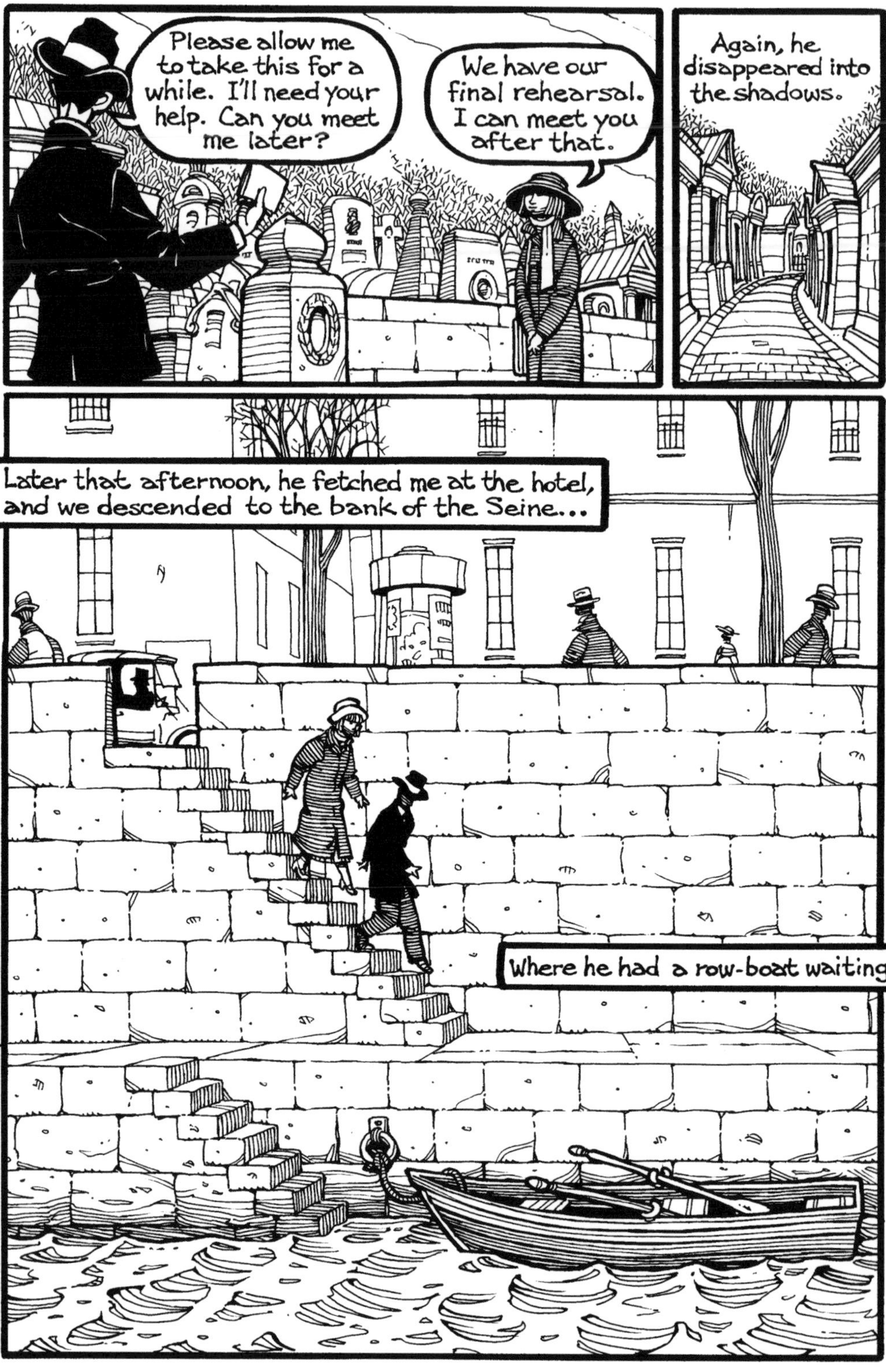
Please allow me to take this for a while. I'll need your help. Can you meet me later?
We have our final rehearsal. I can meet you after that.
Again, he disappeared into the shadows.
Later that afternoon, he fetched me at the hotel, and we descended to the bank of the Seine...
Where he had a row-boat waiting.

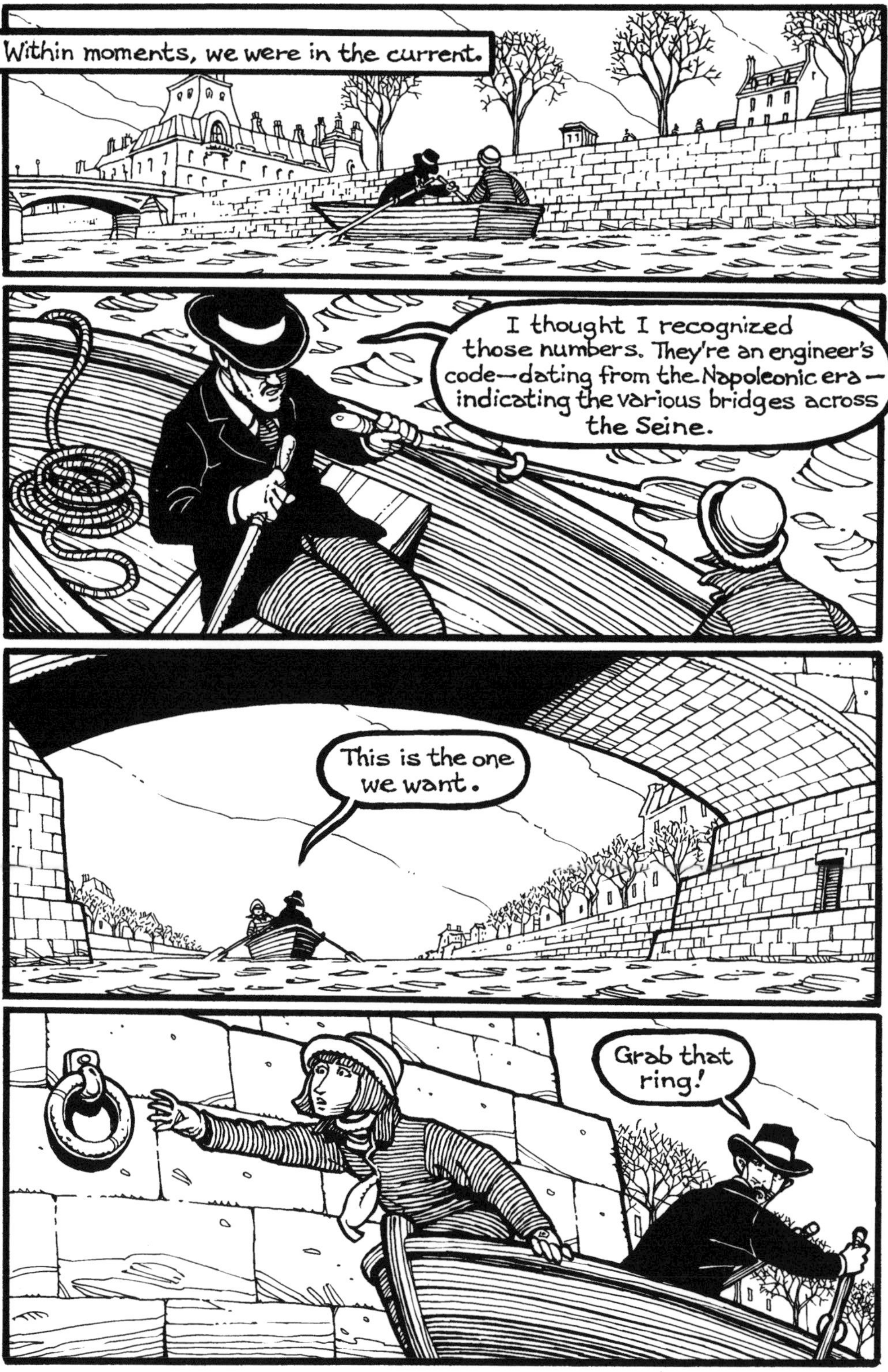
Within moments, we were in the current.
I thought I recognized those numbers. They're an engineer's code—dating from the Napoleonic era—indicating the various bridges across the Seine.
This is the one we want.
Grab that ring!

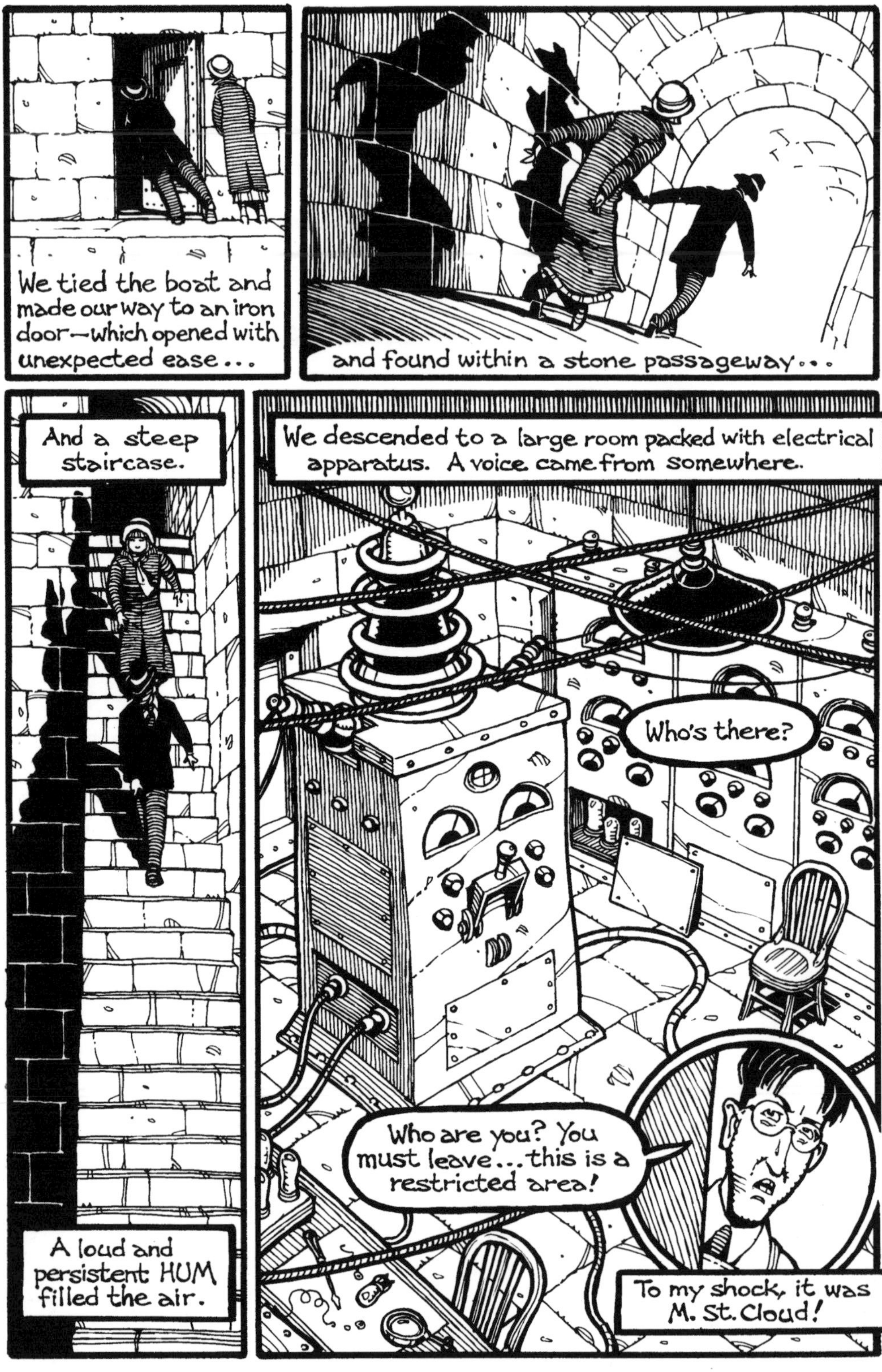
We tied the boat and made our way to an iron door—which opened with unexpected ease...
and found within a stone passageway...
And a steep staircase.
A loud and persistent HUM filled the air.
We descended to a large room packed with electrical apparatus. A voice came from somewhere.
Who's there?
Who are you? You must leave... this is a restricted area!
To my shock, it was M. St. Cloud!

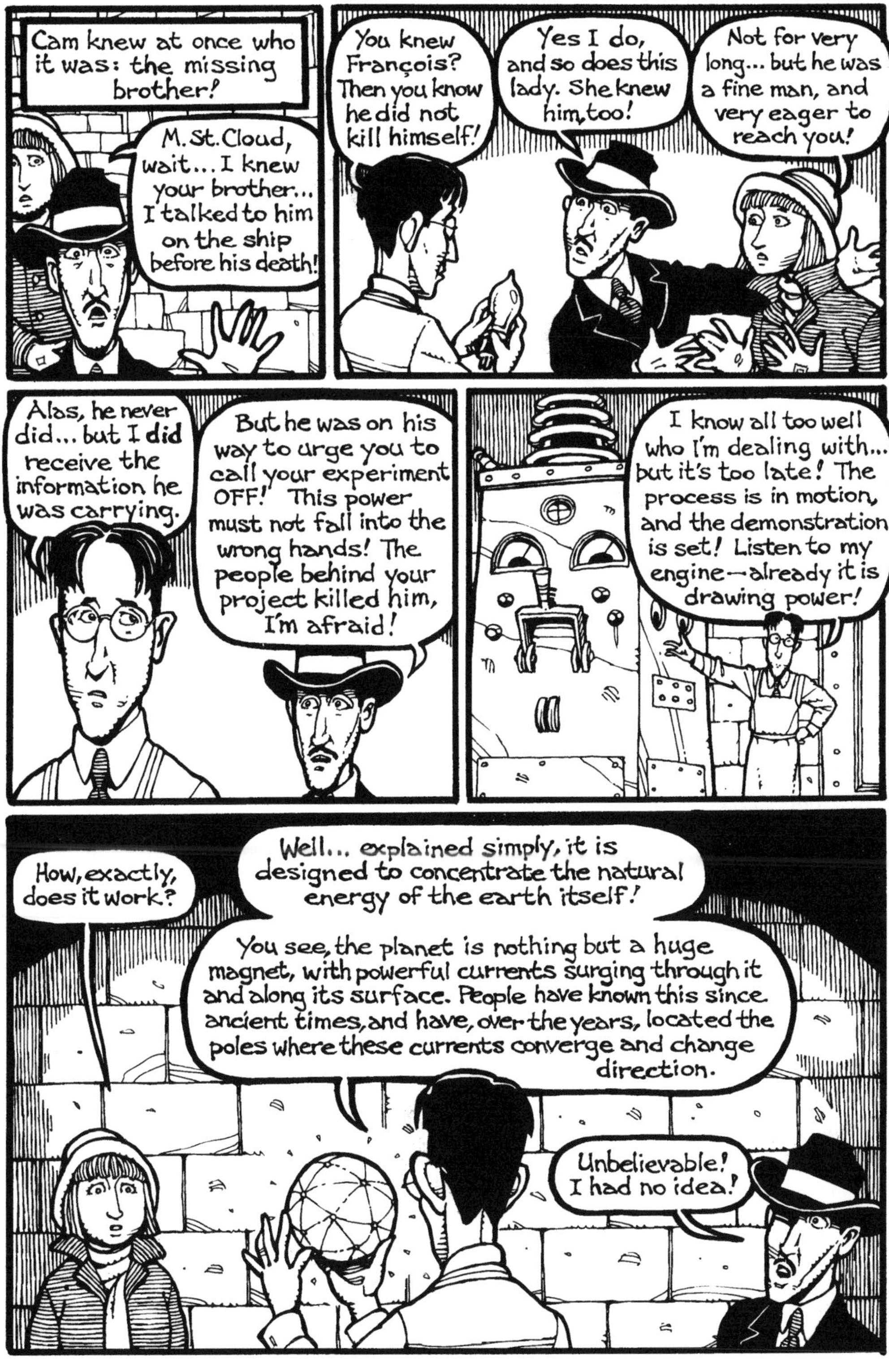

Cam knew at once who it was: the missing brother!
M. St. Cloud, wait... I knew your brother... I talked to him on the ship before his death!
You knew François? Then you know he did not kill himself!
Yes I do, and so does this lady. She knew him, too!
Not for very long... but he was a fine man, and very eager to reach you!
Alas, he never did... but I did receive the information he was carrying.
But he was on his way to urge you to call your experiment OFF! This power must not fall into the wrong hands! The people behind your project killed him, I'm afraid!
I know all too well who I'm dealing with... but it's too late! The process is in motion, and the demonstration is set! Listen to my engine—already it is drawing power!
How, exactly, does it work?
Well... explained simply, it is designed to concentrate the natural energy of the earth itself!
You see, the planet is nothing but a huge magnet, with powerful currents surging through it and along its surface. People have known this since ancient times, and have, over the years, located the poles where these currents converge and change direction.
Unbelievable! I had no idea!

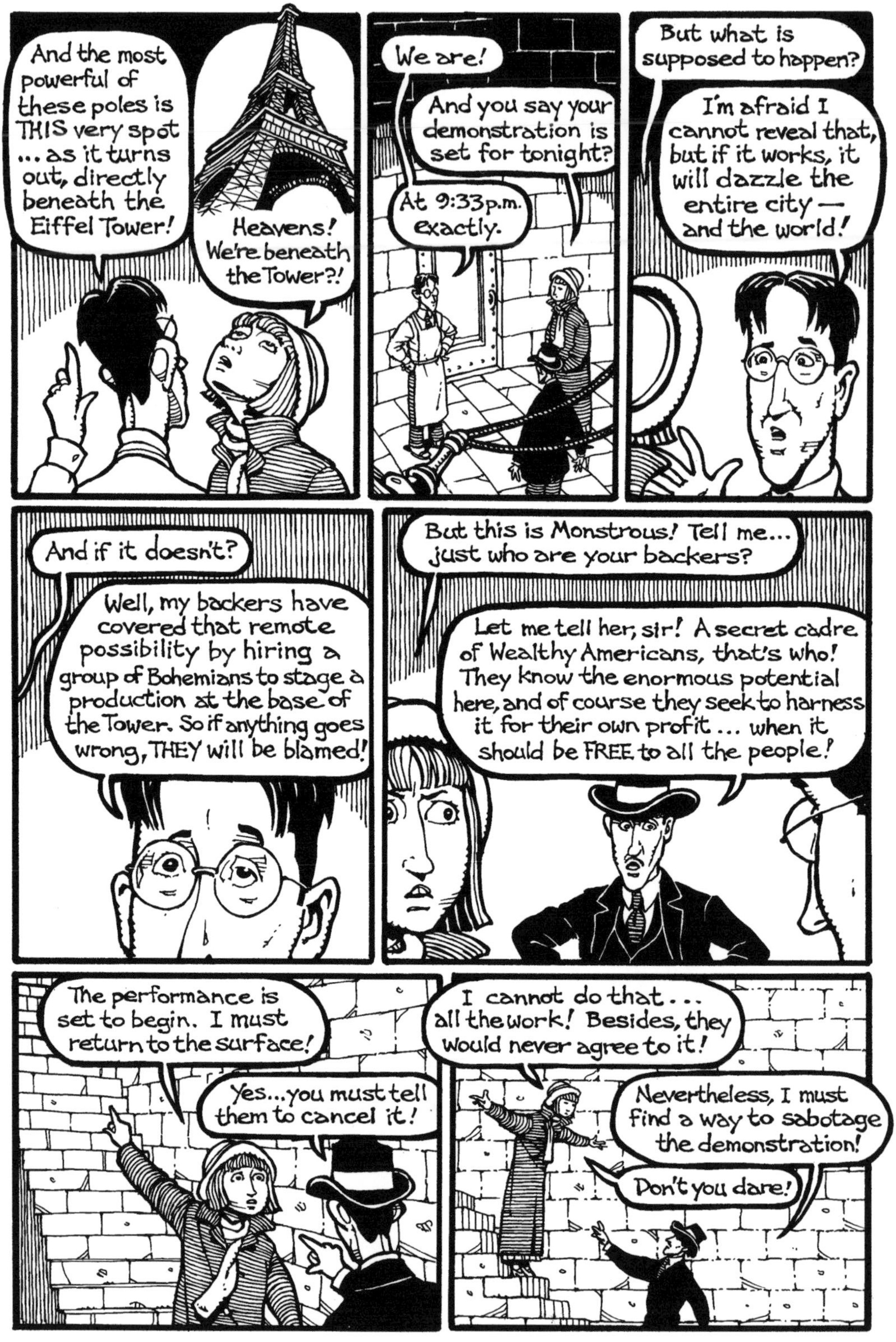
And the most powerful of these poles is THIS very spot ... as it turns out, directly beneath the Eiffel Tower!
Heavens! We're beneath the Tower?!
We are!
And you say your demonstration is set for tonight?
At 9:33p.m. exactly.
But what is supposed to happen?
I'm afraid I cannot reveal that, but if it works, it will dazzle the entire city — and the world!
And if it doesn't?
Well, my backers have covered that remote possibility by hiring a group of Bohemians to stage a production at the base of the Tower. So if anything goes wrong, THEY will be blamed!
But this is Monstrous! Tell me... just who are your backers?
Let me tell her, sir! A secret cadre of Wealthy Americans, that's who! They know the enormous potential here, and of course they seek to harness it for their own profit ... when it should be FREE to all the people!
The performance is set to begin. I must return to the surface!
Yes...you must tell them to cancel it!
I cannot do that... all the work! Besides, they would never agree to it!
Nevertheless, I must find a way to sabotage the demonstration!
Don't you dare!

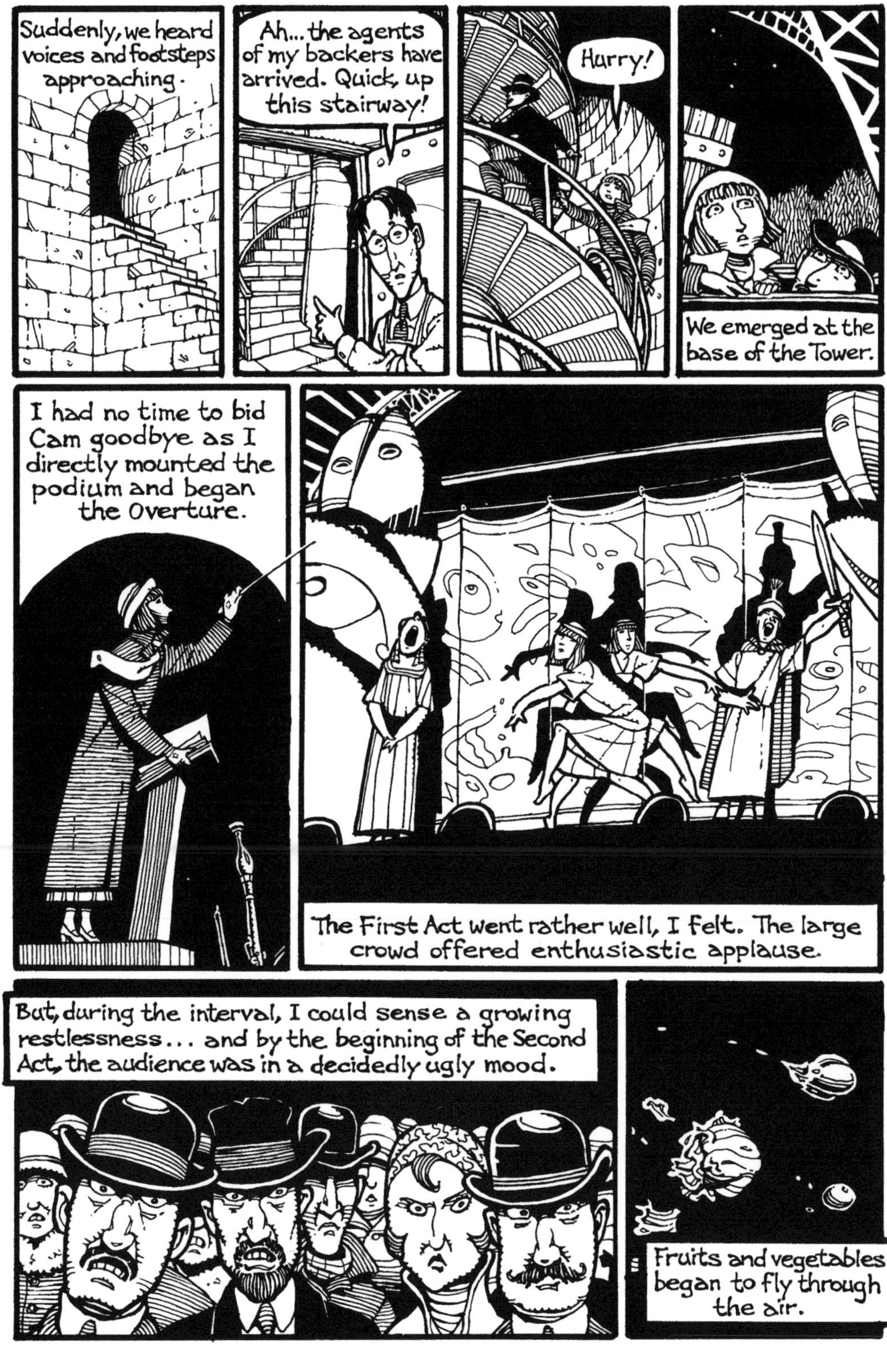
Suddenly, we heard voices and footsteps approaching.
Ah... the agents of my backers have arrived. Quick, up this stairway!
Hurry!
We emerged at the base of the Tower.
I had no time to bid Cam goodbye as I directly mounted the podium and began the Overture.
The First Act went rather well, I felt. The large crowd offered enthusiastic applause.
But, during the interval, I could sense a growing restlessness... and by the beginning of the Second Act, the audience was in a decidedly ugly mood.
Fruits and vegetables began to fly through the air.

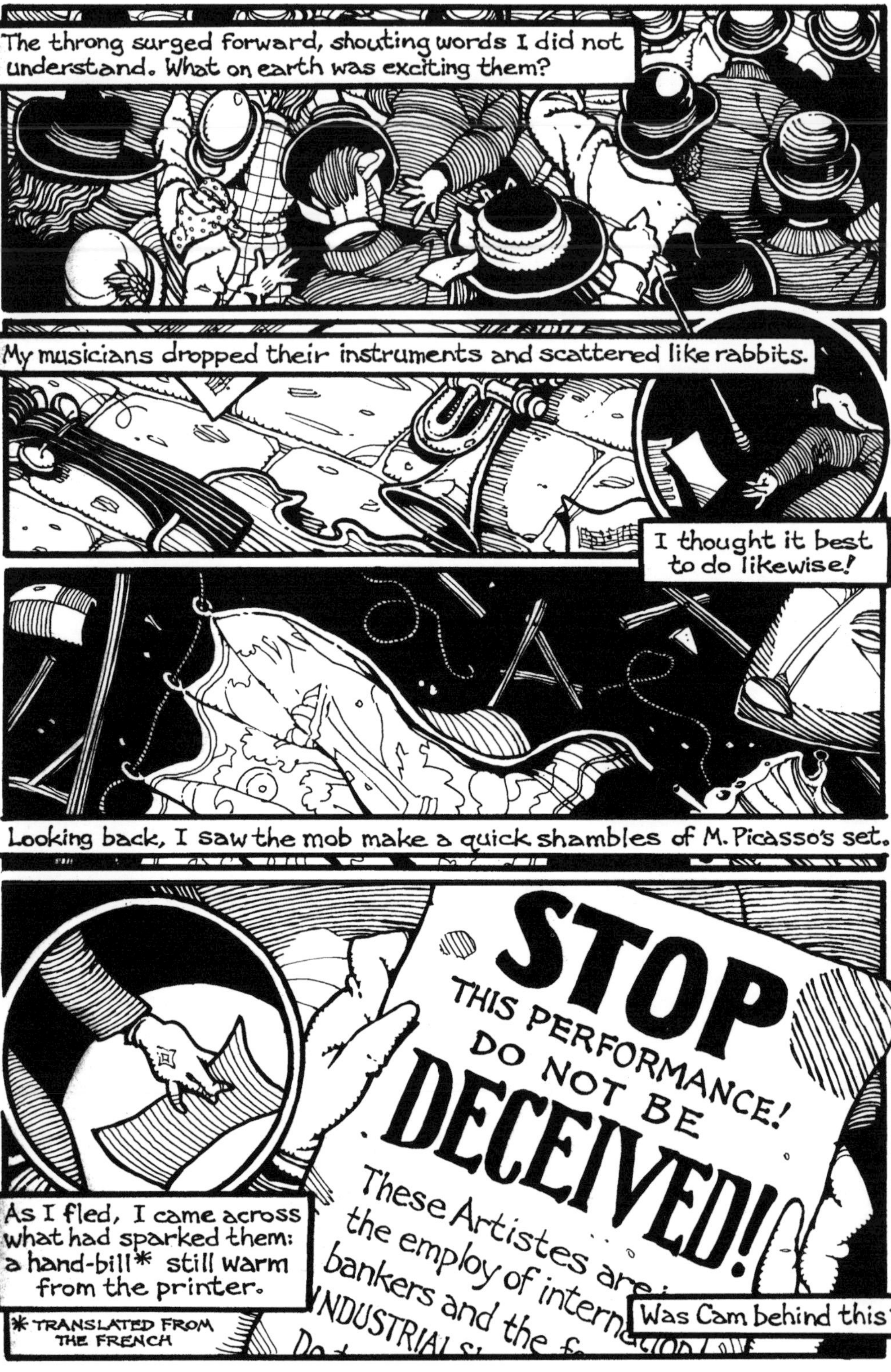

The throng surged forward, shouting words I did not understand. What on earth was exciting them?
My musicians dropped their instruments and scattered like rabbits.
I thought it best to do likewise!
Looking back, I saw the mob make a quick shambles of M. Picasso's set.
STOP
THIS PERFORMANCE!
DO NOT BE
DECEIVED!
These Artistes are
the employ of
bankers and the
As I fled, I came across what had sparked them: a hand-bill* still warm from the printer.
* TRANSLATED FROM THE FRENCH
Was Cam behind this?

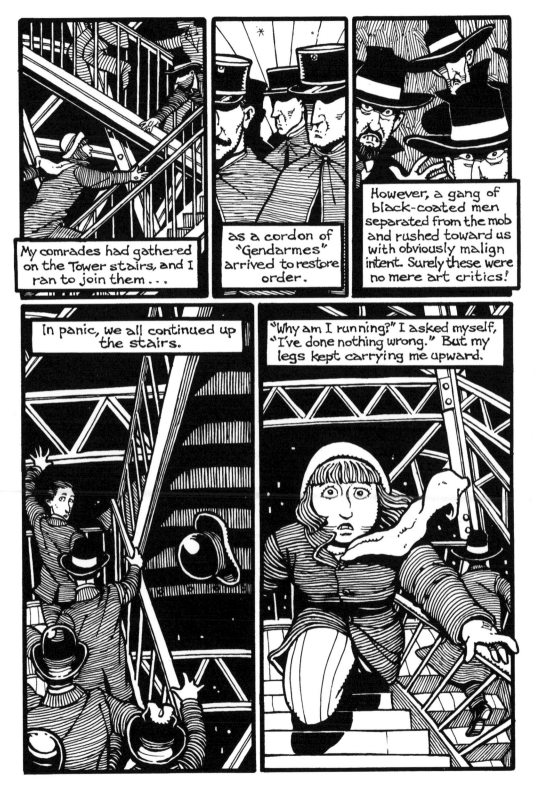

My comrades had gathered on the Tower stairs, and I ran to join them...

as a cordon of "Gendarmes" arrived to restore order.

However, a gang of black-coated men separated from the mob and rushed toward us with obviously malign intent. Surely these were no mere art critics!

In panic, we all continued up the stairs.

"Why am I running?" I asked myself, "I've done nothing wrong." But my legs kept carrying me upward.

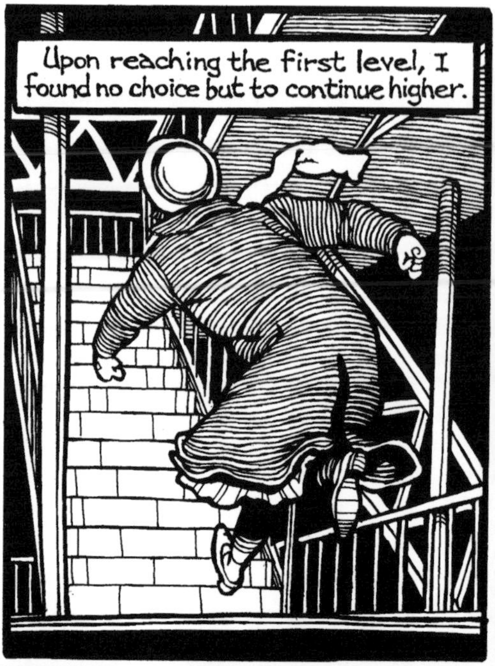
Upon reaching the first level, I found no choice but to continue higher.

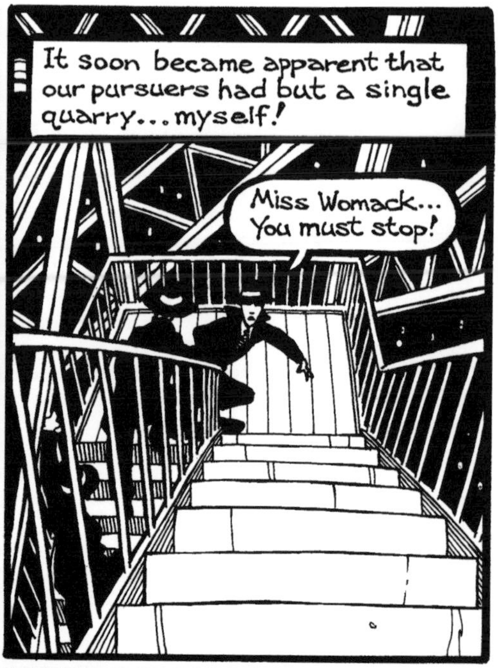
It soon became apparent that our pursuers had but a single quarry... myself!
Miss Womack... You must stop!

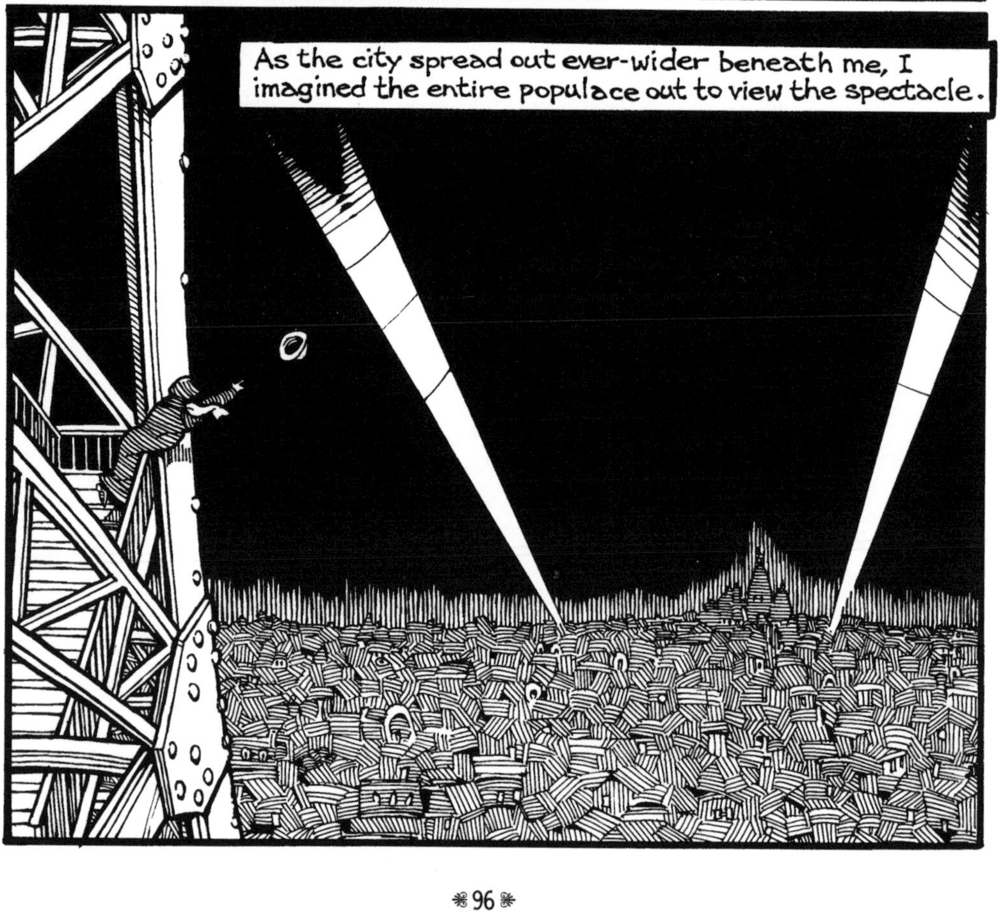
As the city spread out ever-wider beneath me, I imagined the entire populace out to view the spectacle.

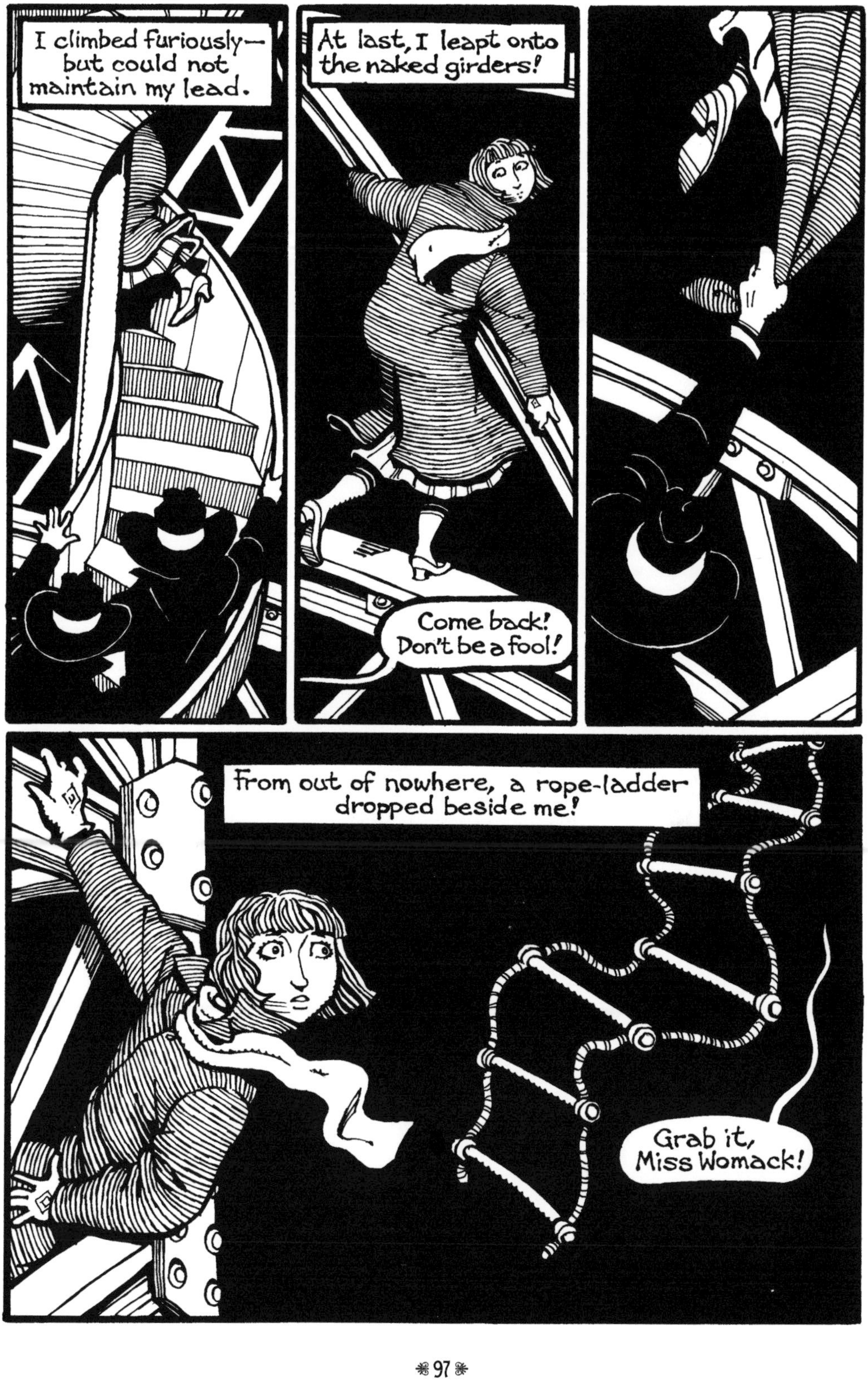
I climbed furiously—but could not maintain my lead.
At last, I leapt onto the naked girders!
Come back! Don't be a fool!
From out of nowhere, a rope-ladder dropped beside me!
Grab it, Miss Womack!

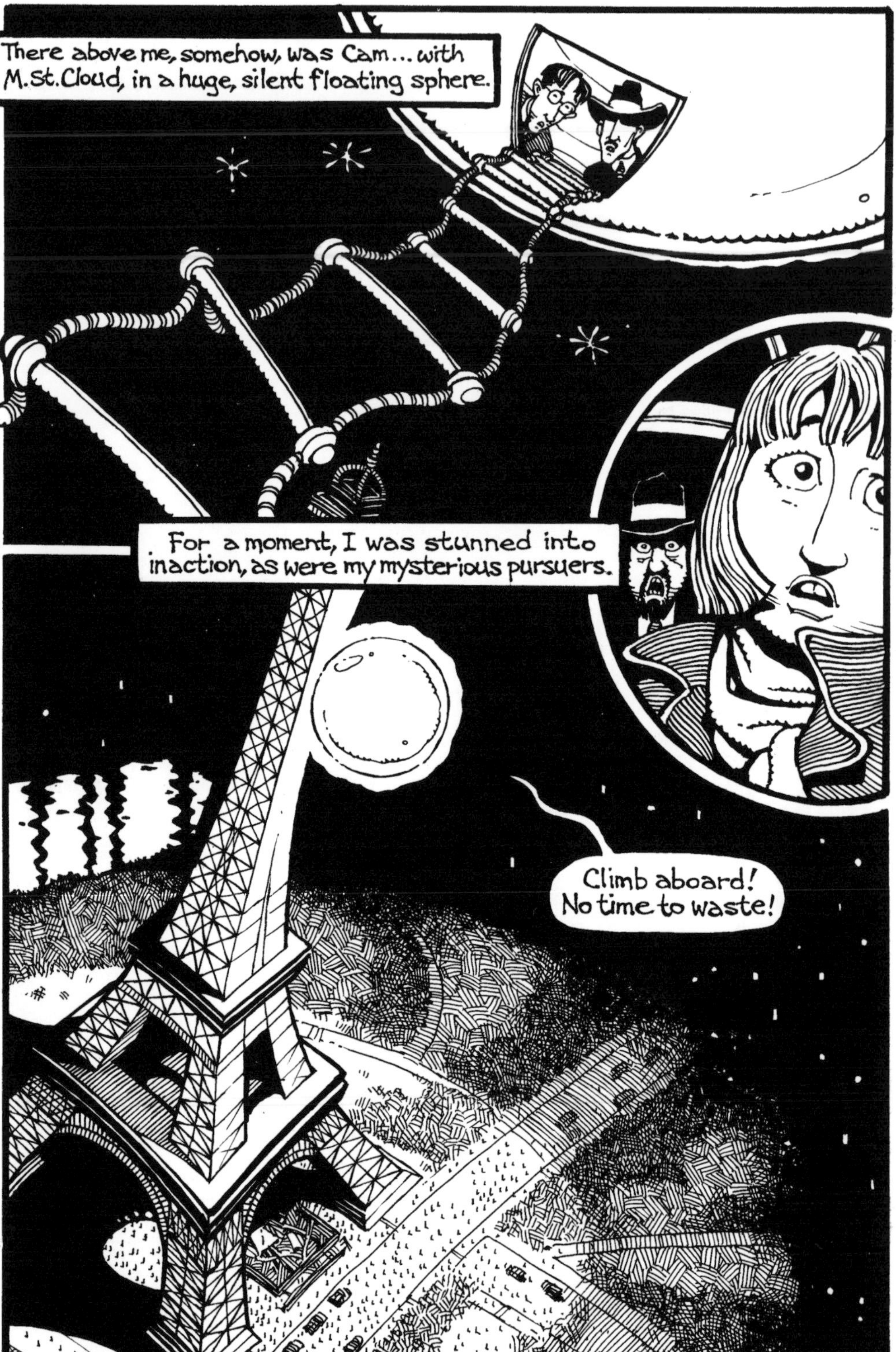
There above me, somehow, was Cam... with M. St. Cloud, in a huge, silent floating sphere.
For a moment, I was stunned into inaction, as were my mysterious pursuers.
Climb aboard! No time to waste!

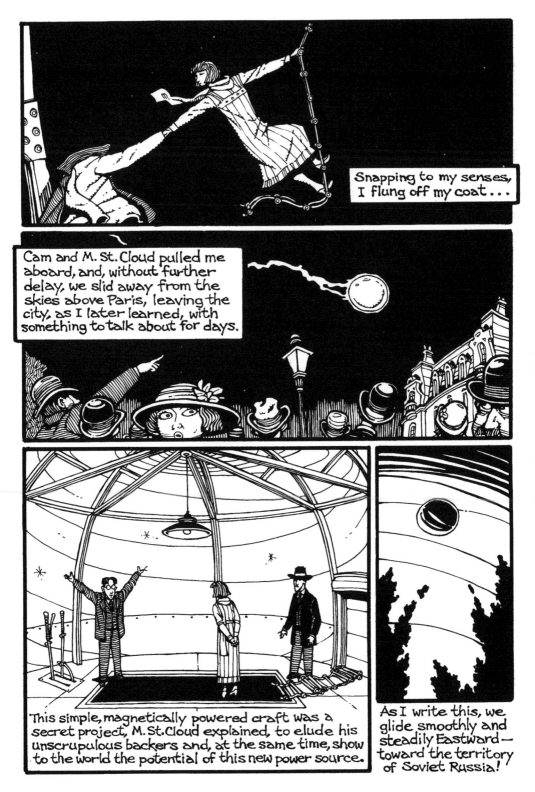

Snapping to my senses, I flung off my coat . . .

Cam and M. St. Cloud pulled me aboard, and, without further delay, we slid away from the skies above Paris, leaving the city, as I later learned, with something to talk about for days.

This simple, magnetically powered craft was a secret project, M. St. Cloud explained, to elude his unscrupulous backers and, at the same time, show to the world the potential of this new power source.

As I write this, we glide smoothly and steadily Eastward — toward the territory of Soviet Russia!

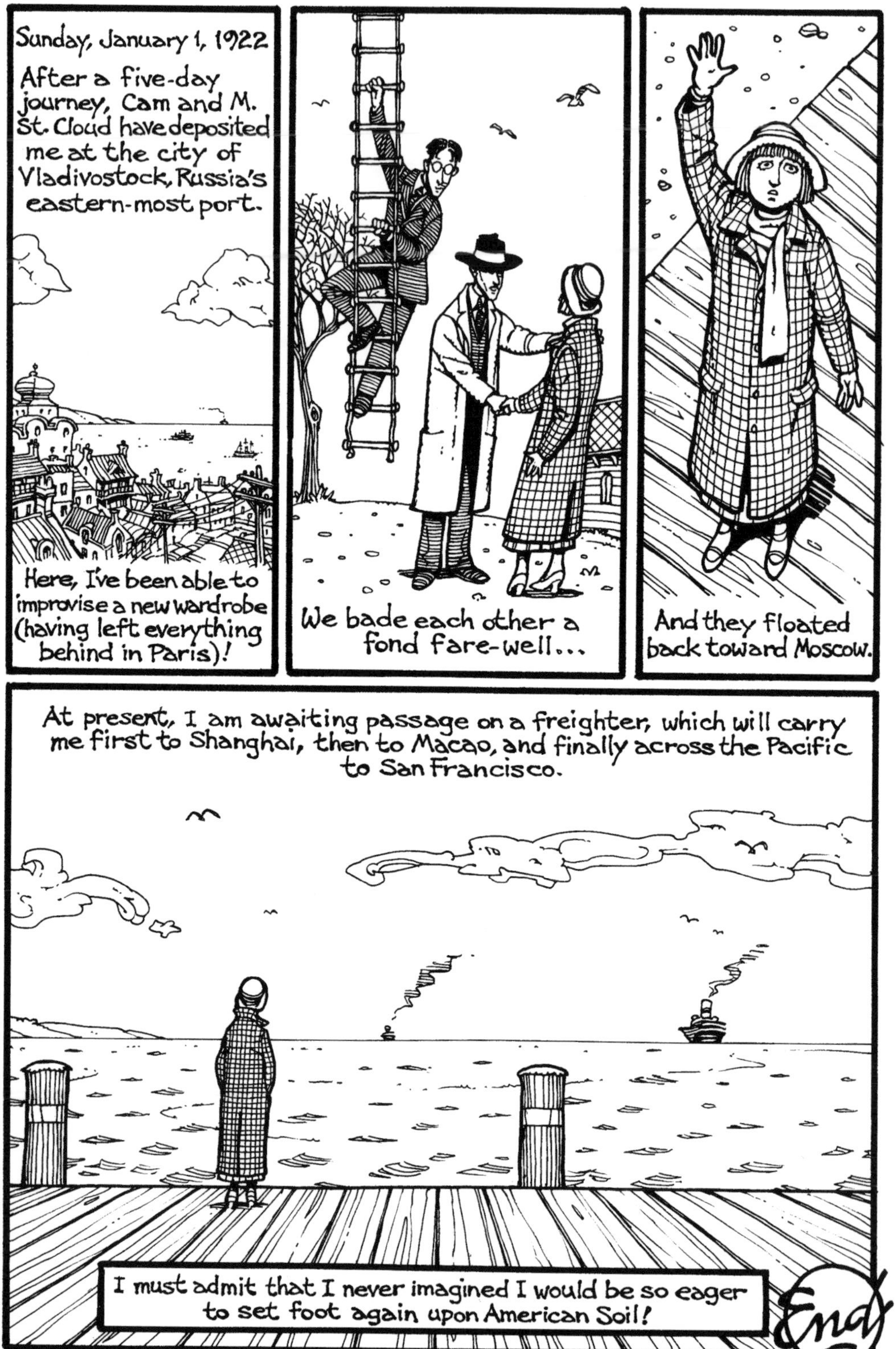
Sunday, January 1, 1922
After a five-day journey, Cam and M. St. Cloud have deposited me at the city of Vladivostock, Russia's eastern-most port.
Here, I've been able to improvise a new wardrobe (having left everything behind in Paris)!
We bade each other a fond fare-well...
And they floated back toward Moscow.
At present, I am awaiting passage on a freighter, which will carry me first to Shanghai, then to Macao, and finally across the Pacific to San Francisco.
I must admit that I never imagined I would be so eager to set foot again upon American Soil!
End

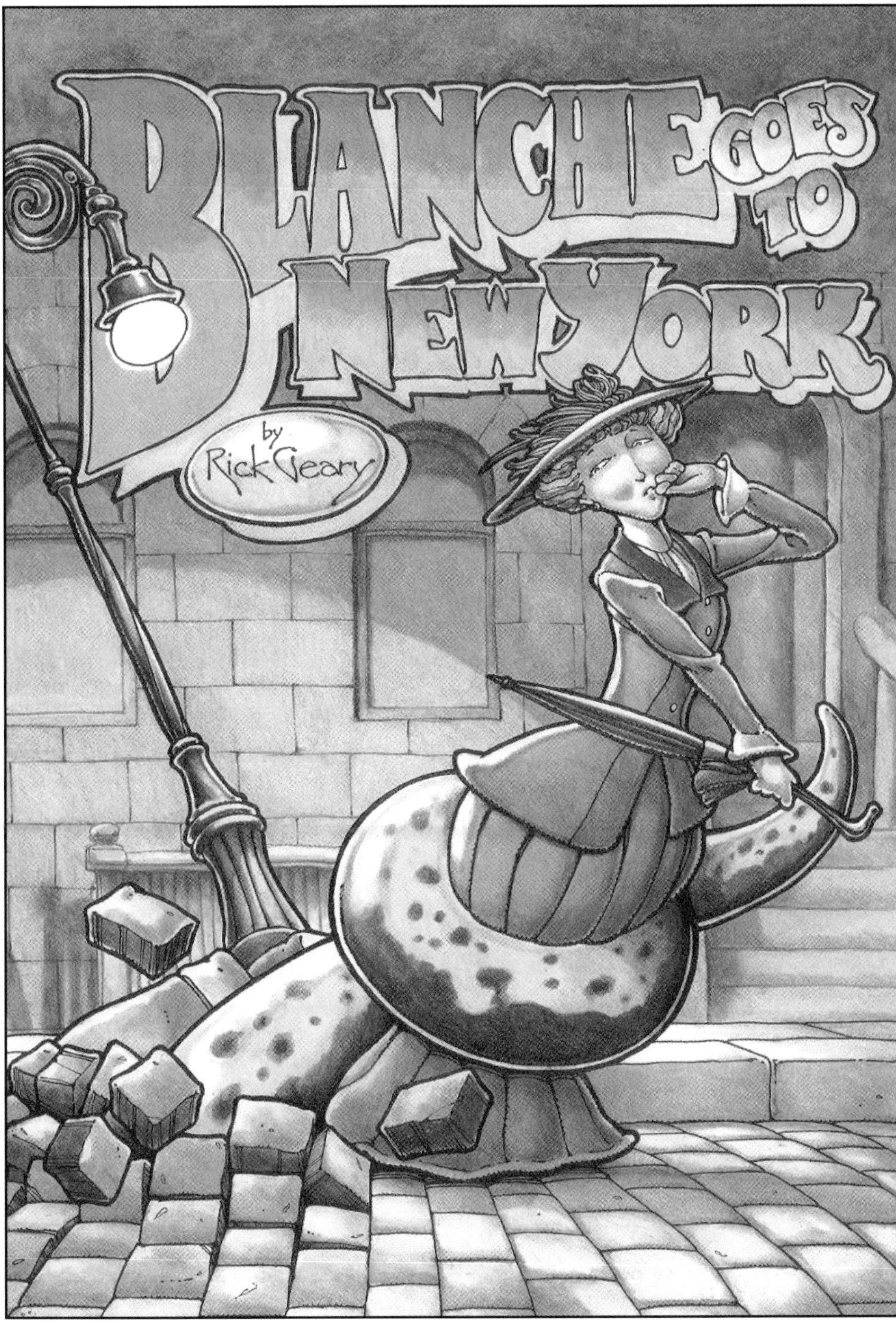
BLANCHE GOES TO NEW YORK
by
Rick Geary

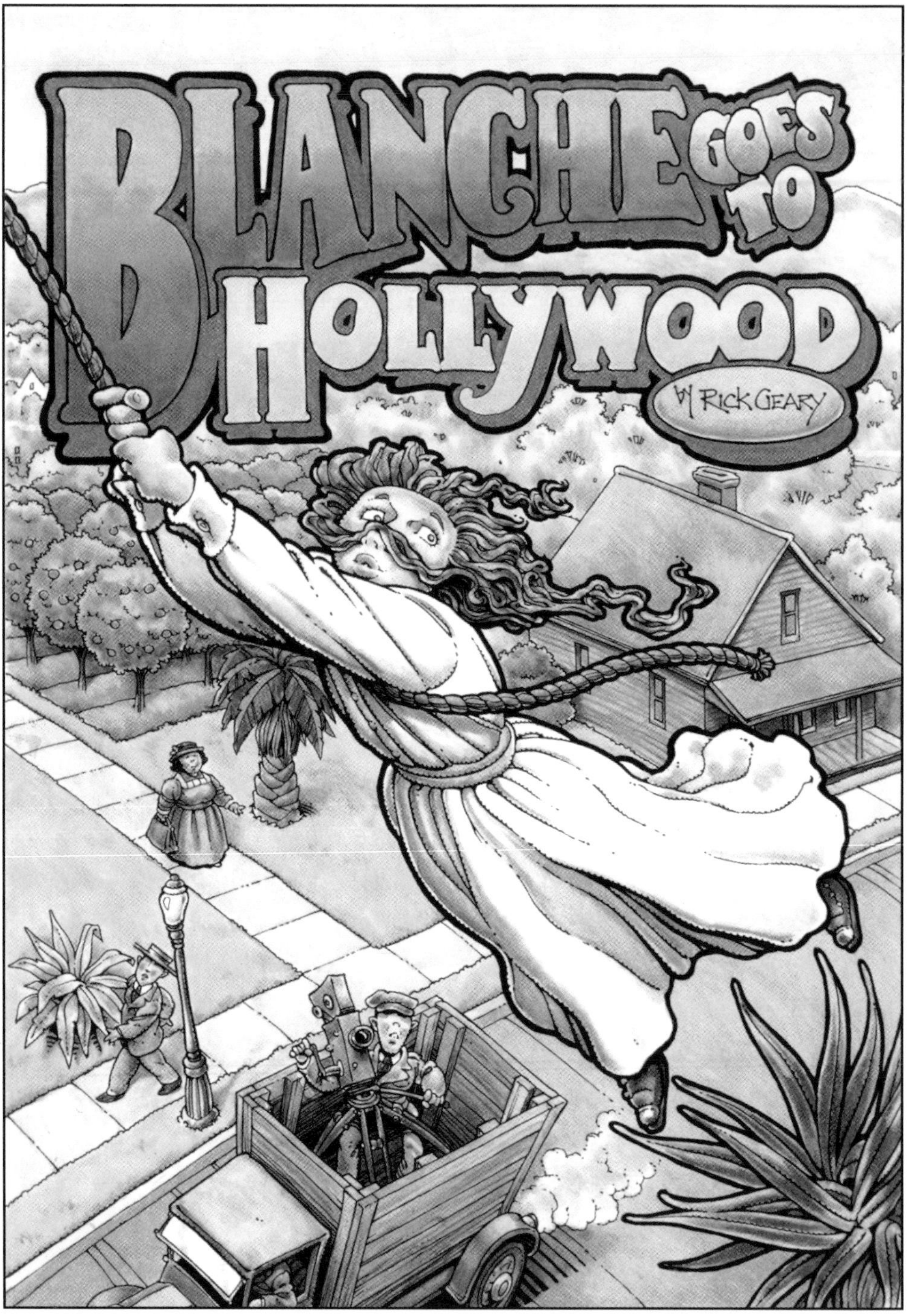
BLANCHE GOES TO HOLLYWOOD
BY RICK GEARY

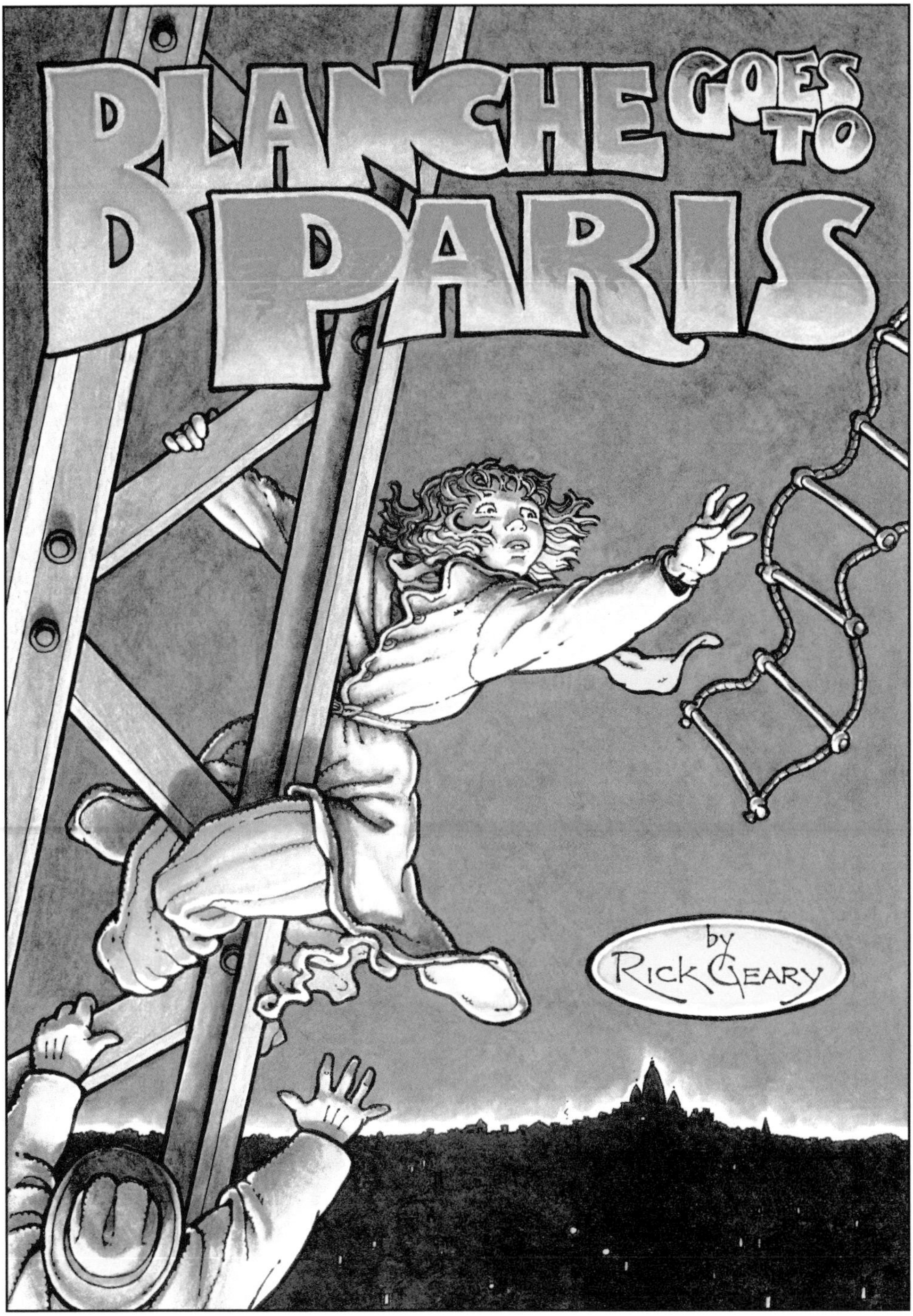
BLANCHE GOES TO PARIS
by
RICK GEARY

Editor
Diana Schutz

Book Design
Heidi Whitcomb

Digital Production
& Cover Color
# Dan Jackson

Publisher
Mike Richardson

⇒▻⊷•⊶◅⇐

⇒▻⊷•⊶◅⇐

This volume collects *Blanche Goes to New York* and *Blanche Goes
to Hollywood*, both originally published by Dark Horse Comics,
along with *Blanche Goes to Paris*, first published by Headless
Shakespeare Press, Seattle.

Published by Dark Horse Books
A division of Dark Horse Comics, Inc.
10956 SE Main Street
Milwaukie, Oregon 97222
darkhorse.com

First edition: April 2009
ISBN 978-1-59582-258-1

1 3 5 7 9 10 8 6 4 2

Printed in China